Business Library

Business Library

Aditya Rajput

RANDOM

RANDOM PUBLICATIONS

NEW DELHI (INDIA)

Business Library

ISBN 978-93-5111-555-7

Published in 2015 in India by

RANDOM PUBLICATIONS

4376-A/4B, Gali Murari Lal, Ansari Road
New Delhi-110 002
Phone : +9111-43580356, 011-23289044, 011-43142548
e-mail: sales@randompublications.com,
info@randompublications.com, randomexports@gmail.com

Reprinted 2026

Type Setting by : Friends Media, Delhi-110089

Preface

There are a variety of library types and sizes. State laws governing how a library is established, levies taxes, issues and pays for debt, qualifies for state-funded revenue and performs other business functions vary depending on the type and size of a library.

While a private business enterprise can be viewed as a single economic entity with one group of assets, liabilities and equity accounts that are normally reflected in a single set of financial statements, a library may have several funds, each of which has its own assets, liabilities and fund equities. A library may be a combination of several distinctly different operations, each of which functions, and must be reported on, independently from any other fund. The coupling of these different options, social and business, designates the communication methods and the policies that libraries choose on occasion. The synthesis and the identity of the unity that we call 'library users' is a continuing changed variable, as it strands upon the dynamic of human mobility, potential individual needs, and behavioural rules of societies. Users can turn into non-users, actually without caution, but not without any cause.

As far as methods of carrying out stock verification are concerned the parent organisation may involve or may not involve external persons in the team of stock verification and may decide to exclude certain types of material in the library.

The rest of the methodology of verification depends on the provisions already made in the design and organisation of library records. There are a number of methods followed for stock verification. The most crude method is to numerically count the number of documents and it practically does not serve any purpose except to know the number of documents lost.

The emergence of the new information economy comprised of computer networks that link users to one another or to larger organisations is creating a class of singular information users. To aid users in participating in the information economy, libraries designed a virtual presence to deliver information services, usually in the form of a 'digital library.' Digital libraries can offer a more varied informational experience to the community of online users.

Libraries, with their traditional strengths of information collection, description, organisation, and dissemination, can provide a more holistic learning experience for these new user communities.

It is hoped that this book shall find its place with anyone who is interested to know and learn more about the basics of business library.

I would like to thank my team for standing beside me throughout my career and writing this book. My special thanks go to "Random Publications" who have published the book.

– Aditya Rajput

Contents

1

Introduction to the Library

INTRODUCTION AND PURPOSE

Recently, librarians have struggled to understand their relationship to a new breed of Web services that, like libraries, connect users with the information they need.

While a few outside observers have proclaimed the death of libraries as a result of this new competition, it is clear that libraries continue to offer unique and valuable services to their communities.

These services, known as Web 2.0, do have effects on library services. They offer new service models, methods, and technologies that can be adapted to improve library services. Furthermore, because of widespread use of these services, there are cultural changes affecting library users' information seeking behaviours, communication styles, and expectations.

The term Library 2.0 has been introduced into the professional language of librarianship as a way to discuss these changes.

What Library 2.0 is and what it means are still under constant discussion in the biblioblogosphere. This chapter is designed to be part of that ongoing discussion.

Most early discussions of Library 2.0 revolved around public library services. Now that the term has gained traction, it is being discussed in the academic sphere as well.

This chapter works to establish a theoretical foundation of Library 2.0 in academic libraries, or Academic Library 2.0.

WHAT IS LIBRARY 2.0

LOOKING BACK TO THE ROOTS

The term Library 2.0 was introduced by Michael Casey in September 2005. To this day, Casey continues to be one of the most outspoken advocates of the Library 2.0 concept. Additionally, the British ILS vendor Talis took an early interest in promoting the term.

The term was exposed to a wider audience when Michael Stephens discussed Library 2.0 on the ALA's Techsource Blog. Other major voices in the discussion of Library 2.0 include Jenny Levine, John Blyberg and countless other librarian and library student bloggers. After over a year of discussion, it appears that the term has received a stable place in the professional discourse. However, there still is a good deal of disagreement over both the meaning and value of the term. In the only peerreviewed article published on the topic, 'Library 2.0 Theory: Web 2.0 and Its Implications for Libraries', Jack Maness explains:

- "A more exact definition and theory for Library 2.0 is necessary to focus discussion and experimentation within the community, and will be valuable in the implementation of new web based services in the next several years."

There is still no agreed upon focussed definition. At this point, the definition and relevance of Library 2.0 will be discussed and a preliminary definition proposed. For readers unfamiliar with Web 2.0 concepts the next stage will provide the appropriate background. The term 'Library 2.0' has evoked controversy. The critiques typically fall into two categories. Each of these will be addressed in context and an answer to each of the criticisms will be proposed. This exercise will uncover weaknesses in some of the current definitions of Library 2.0.

The two categories of criticism are:

1. The term 'Library 2.0' is confrontational in that it declares, or implies, all prior library services obsolete and in need of replacement; and
2. The term 'Library 2.0' is meaningless in that it provides nothing new to the professional discourse. It essentially means nothing more than progressive librarianship.

THE 'CONFRONTATION' CRITICISM OF LIBRARY 2.0

Many librarians believe the term is confrontational because they have taken the 2.0 as a declaration that there was an obsolete Library 1.0 that needs to be replaced. First, it suggests of a misunderstanding of how the '2.0' has different origins, and thus different meanings in the two terms, Web 2.0 and Library 2.0. As will be discussed in the next stage, the term Web 2.0 was created to describe the differences between second and first generation web applications. This language makes it apparent that Web 2.0 is an evolution of Web 1.0. In fact, by using version numbers to describe this occurrence, it is made clear that Web 2.0 is an updated version, not an entirely new 'application'.

Web 2.0 defines itself as one subset of the Web that is evolving from an earlier Web subset. However while Library 2.0 can, and should, be extended beyond web services, its origin lies in the term Web 2.0 and related changes in web services. Consequently, the use of 2.0 in the case of Library 2.0 should not be taken to represent an entirely new generation of library services, but instead to represent a subset of new library services that are occurring because of the changes brought on by Web 2.0 services. Thus the '2.0' in Library 2.0 signifies the term's relationship to Web 2.0, while the '2.0' in Web 2.0 signifies its differences from Web 1.0. Another way to understand this distinction is through an analogy. If Library 1.0 is to Web 1.0 as Library 2.0 is to Web 2.0, then Library 1.0 would describe how libraries adapted to the Web prior to Web 2.0 services. Consequently, Library 1.0 would itself describe only a subset of library services as opposed to all pre-Library 2.0 services.

A second reason that some librarians have taken a reactionary stance against the term Library 2.0 is because it has been described and defined as disruptive by many of its proponents. This rhetoric appears to have occurred largely as a way to force laggards into realising the importance of how both Web 1.0 and Web 2.0 are changing the way many library services are and should be provided. Unfortunately, this way of describing Library 2.0 has often obscured the value of the term to those who in principle agree with what it represents. To step back and look at this rhetoric more carefully, as disruptive as it may be, Library 2.0 services are clearly built upon and beside existing library services and values.

If this were not the case, the term library would be dropped altogether. It is at this point that the second reason for distrust of the term comes to light.

THE 'MEANING' CRITICISM OF LIBRARY 2.0

Other critics argue that, apart from the buzz, Library 2.0 has no meaning beyond the already well established user centered approach that has long been applied by progressive librarians.

Much of this comes from the imprecise language with which Library 2.0 has been described. There are two ways that imprecise language has obscured the value of the term Library 2.0. The first occurs when necessary attributes of Library 2.0 services are referred to as the definition.

For example, Michael Casey and Laura Savastinuk offer the following definitions in their article on in Library Journal:

- The heart of Library 2.0 is user centered change. It is a model for library service that encourages constant and purposeful change, inviting user participation in the creation of both the physical and the virtual services they want, supported by consistently evaluating services.
- What makes a service Library 2.0? Any service, physical or virtual, that successfully reaches users, is evaluated frequently, and makes use of customer input is a Library 2.0 service. Even older, traditional services can be Library 2.0 if criteria are met. Similarly, being new is not enough to make a service Library 2.0.

While the rest of the article focuses primarily on technological changes brought on by Web 2.0, taken at face value, this definition appears to promote the same user centered approach to services that has been practiced by progressive librarians for years. While there are some librarians resistant to change and insulated from the outside world, there have always been innovators pushing the limits of library services.

Consequently, there must be more to Library 2.0 than what is presented in this definition. The part of the definition that states 'inviting user participation in the creation of both the physical and virtual services" has its roots in Web 2.0 concepts, but that is not clear by this definition. It is important to note this definition is taken out of context and that the authors work to explain the background that brought them to this conclusion. However, without including the thought process between the background and the definition, what is new about Library 2.0 is lost. Were these aspects of Library 2.0 stressed, the concept's value as a unique service model might become clear. Only once this unique aspect of Library 2.0 is solidly understood, do the derivative principles make sense. The second way that imprecise language has confused this discussion is by conflating Web 1.0's effects on libraries with Web 2.0's effects. One of the primary reasons this seems to occur is the different origin of version numbers in the terms Web 2.0 and Library 2.0. If Library 2.0 is to be a useful concept for adapting library services to changes brought on by Web 2.0, then it must somehow be distinguished from changes brought on by the web in general. One example of this confusion is the following definition proposed by Ken Chad and Paul Miller in the Talis whitepaper, 'Do Libraries Matter?

The Rise of Library 2.0":

- Library 2.0 is a concept of a very different library service that operates according to the expectations of today's library users. In this vision, the library makes information available wherever and whenever the user requires it.

However, Web 1.0 presented this need and many library services have been designed to meet it. OPACs, online article databases, and 24/7 Virtual Reference services already provide such access. While many of these services are not yet compatible with handheld devices, adding this ability would be meeting a need brought on by the web in general and not Web 2.0. Making an OPAC accessible from a mobile phone wouldn't change the nature of the service. Instead it is simply updating it to remain compatible with current technology. One can learn more about the backlash against broader definitions of Library 2.0 by reading Walt Crawford's piece 'Library 2.0 and 'Library 2.0'.

A DEFINITION PROPOSED

- Library 2.0 describes a subset of library services designed to meet user needs caused by the direct and peripheral effects of Web 2.0.

This definition explains that Web 2.0 precipitates changing user needs and that Library 2.0 services meet these needs. This definition includes all implementations of Web 2.0 methodologies and technologies by libraries.

However, by defining library services in terms of user needs, it leaves open the possibility that some Library 2.0 services may not implement Web 2.0 methodologies or technologies. However, the above clarifies that Library 2.0 only describes services responding to the user needs brought on by the effects of Web 2.0 services.

This limits the definition to exclude library services meeting needs brought on by Web 1.0 or other non-Web 2.0 technological advancements. Furthermore, this defines Library 2.0 as different from Web 2.0. Library services which directly apply Web 2.0 methods in the Library 2.0 setting are still a unique subset of Web 2.0.

This subset is special because Web 2.0 focuses largely on information based services, which makes it of particular interest to the library profession. More importantly, Web 2.0 is primarily a commercial term that is framed with a profit motive in mind.

However, when Web 2.0 methodologies and technologies are applied to libraries, the conversation is reframed around providing quality library services. Additionally, Library 2.0 includes services which are not themselves Web 2.0, but instead responses to effects of Web 2.0.

In these ways, the definition both narrows Library 2.0 to a subset of Web 2.0 and also widens it to a include non-Web 2.0 services.

Because this definition proposes a causal relationship between Web 2.0 and Library 2.0, it is important to step back and examine Web 2.0 before proceeding to develop a theory of Library 2.0.

LIBRARY RULES

Working Hours

1 The library shall remain open for service during the working hours observed by the National Academy of Higher Education/University Grants Commission.

2 The" library hours may be changed from time to time according to the service of the National Academy of Higher Education/University Grants Commission.

Loan Privileges

3. The following categories of persons will be allowed to make use of the library resources:
   - Employees of the University Grants Commission/National Academy of Higher Education.

- In-service and Pre-Service training participants.
- Teachers/resources persons etc. deputed by UGC/NAHE for teaching.
- Members of the Board of Governors of UGC/NAHE.
- Other persons allowed in writing by Director General/Librarian.
- University/University Department Librarians.

4. Persons desirous of using the library must apply for membership on a form obtainable from t he library.
   - A borrower's card will be issued to each member on presentation of which reading material will be issued (except rule 3.6 for which the Librarian will maintain a proper record). The same procedure will be followed when the books are returned. This card will not be transferable and should be surrendered at the time of obtaining a clearance certificate.
   - A borrowers card will be valid up to the date mentioned on it. A borrower should get the card renewed before it expires, if he so desires.
   - Members should not mark or write on their borrower cards in any way Defaulters may be dealt with as per rule 30.
5. A Member, who loses his card shall at once inform the Librarian. A duplicate card will be. issued. Any member sub- lending reading material from the library on his card to any other person shall do so at his own responsibility.

Loan Period

6. The following categories of members shall observe the loan schedule mentioned against each.

1. Members of the Board of Governors	4 books for 15 days
2. Employees of UGC/ NAHE`	1 book for 15 days
i. Officials	2 book for 15 days
ii. Officers	2 book for 15 days
3. In service/pre-service trainees (during their training period - at the NAHE/UGC)	2 books for 7 days
4. Teachers/resource persons	5 books for the period of their stay
5. Other persons allowed in writing by Director General/Librarian	3 books for 15 days
6. University/ University Department Librarian.	2 books for 1 month

Relaxation of loan schedule will be at the discretion of the Librarian:

7. Books borrowed once may be issued provided these are not required by other members. Books will not be reissued more than twice. Books will have to be presented for re-issue. However, in case of need the Librarian may relax the condition.

8. Reading material of the following nature shall not be issued but can be consulted in.the library (except in special cases *e.g.* classroom use of a teacher for a short period/photocopying purposes)
   - Reference material (*i.e.* Encyclopaedias, dictionaries, atlases and the material marked 'R')
   - Theses, reports, pamphlets, syllabi, acts etc.
   - Microfilms, slides, cassettes, tape recorders and other allied material.
   - All unprocessed material.
   - Current periodicals.
   - Other material assigned by the Librarian.

Damage and Loss of Books

9. Book(s) lost, dam ed, or mutilated in any way by a member shall have to be replaced or paid for. The cost of such book(s) shall be double the prevailing cost plus an additional 25 per cent departmental charges. The price of rare book(s) shall be decided by the Librarian.
10. If books and other materials borrowed from the library are not returned notices will be issued. In case the books are not returned even after the second notice, Rule 9 will be applied.
11. The amount realised from a member as cost of lost or damaged book(s) or material(s) or for not returning the books after due notices shall be credited to NAHE Library's head 'Books and Journals'.
12. Book.,(s) or other material lost or found to be lost on stock-taking shall be reported to the competent authority for write-off.
13. If a member leaves his organization without returning books borrowed from this library, the price of the book(s) will be adjusted against his dues with the organization. (In case there is no outstanding balance in his name, the price will be paid by his guarantor).

Weeding

14. On receipt of a written request from the Librarian, the Director General shall depute one or two members other than the library staff for weeding out outdated worn-out and/ or seriously damaged or mutilated books and other materials. He/ She/ they shall submit their recommendations in writing to the competent authority for approval.

Write-off Losses

15. The Librarian shall report all books/ non- print material damaged, and/or worn-out through fair wear and tear to the competent authority for write off action.
16. Losses to the extent of 3 per cent per annum of the available stock

in an open access library shall be written off by the competent authority.

17. Losses to the extent of 2 per cent per annum of the available collection of a close access or partially open access library shall be written off by the competent authority.
18. Losses written off by the competent authority shall be struck off from the stock and the records of the library, including public catalogues, and transferred to the with-drawl register indicating the authority under which the losses were written off.
19. The permanent irrecoverable loans of mutilated, damaged and worn-out books found to be beyond repairs during the physical verification of the library shall also be reported to the competent authority for write-off.

Mail Loan

20. The library shall offer postal loan service to the Librarian(s) of the out station Universities provided Rule 4.2 is followed. University Librarian/ Department Librarian will be responsible for Safe return.
21. In view of the insecurity of mail, inconveniences of the postal-loan service and other discrepancies of non-receipt of materials expected to arise by this/these facility (ies) loss of book(s) and other materials shall be safeguarded by adopting the Registered Parcel procedure of dispatch to avoid loss in transit.
22. In case there is a loss in transit, it shall be recorded by the Librarian and reported to the competent authority for write-off action.

Inter-Library Loans

23. With a view to extending and/or utilizing book and non-book resources of other institutions of higher education in the country, the Librarian shall enter into, and maintain any mutually agreed upon interlibrary loan system with Academic, Research, Special, Public and Government Departmental Libraries.

General Rules

24. Members shall not mutilate, or damage by writing or marking on pages, any book or publication, nor shall they trace or perform mechanical reproduction of any material belonging to the library without formal permission of the Librarian. Violation of this rule shall require replacement of the damaged volume or payment of its price as specified under rule 9.
25. If one volume of a set/series is damaged and it is not available separately, the whole set shall have to be replaced or paid for by the member as specified under rule 9.

26. Following Rules 24 and 25 paying the cost the member may, if he/ she so desires, retain the damaged book(s) or volumes for which the price has been recovered from him/her.
27. Members are advised to inspect books or other material at the time of issue. They must direct the attention of the staff at the Charging Desk to defects, if any.
28. The Library Reading Room shall remain open during stock-taking but the borrowing privileges will remain suspended for the same period. All books on loan 'with the members must irrespective of the date-due, be returned to. the library before the date of stock-taking. Two week advance notice will be given.
29. All members must without fail intimate, the librarian of any change of address.
30. The Librarian is authorized to withdraw library facilities from any member who is found misusing the library material or facilities.
31. Members of the library shall deposit their personal belongings at the counter near the entrance.
32. In case any personal reading material has to be taken in-side the library, permission must be sought from the Librarian. All reading material issued to them shall be shown to the attendant at the exit before leaving.
33. Eating, sleeping, smoking and audible conversation within the library premises is prohibited.
34. Members shall make their own arrangement for carrying book(s) etc. from and to the library.

INTRODUCTION TO WEB 2.0

Before proposing a theory of Library 2.0, it is important to gain a solid understanding of Web 2.0 and its related principles.

Unfortunately, similar to Library 2.0, there have been many competing definitions of Web 2.0. To see why this confusion occurs, one need look no further than the origins of the term.

In "What is Web 2.0: Design Patterns and Business Models for the Next Generation of Software", Tim O'Reilly explains that Web 2.0 was originally formulated as a way of understanding how the most successful Internet companies differed from their peers.

A list of the concepts, methods, and technologies which set these companies apart was then drawn up. The resulting list was defined as Web 2.0. Consequently, the original definition of Web 2.0 was itself a list.

Furthermore, while many of the items on the list are related to one another, there is no single theory uniting them. Figure shows the meme map O'Reilly created to display these various concepts.

For purposes of consistency, O'Reilly's terminology will be used. This stage will describe the key concepts and methods of Web 2.0 and then briefly describe some of the underlying technologies. Common examples from the web will be incorporated throughout the discussion.

Once these key concepts have been articulated, it will be possible to determine the different types of effects that Web 2.0 has on libraries. The first two concepts to be discussed are leveraged by all Web 2.0 services.

Because of this, these two principles are foundational to many of the concepts to be discussed later in this stage. These concepts are the Read/Write Web and the Web as Platform.

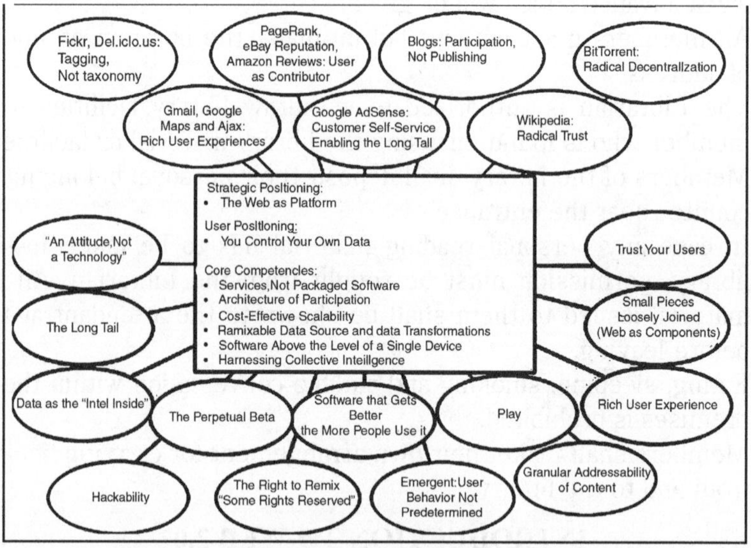

Fig. Web 2.0 Memr Map

THE READ/WRITE WEB

One of the primary characteristics of Web 2.0 services is that they take advantage of the Read/Write Web. The Read/Write Web is the term given to describe the main differences between New Media and Old Media.

Old Media, including Web 1.0 sites, were defined by a one way broadcast. Traditional types of media such as newspapers, radio, and television, were distributed through media designed for a unidirectional information flow. However, the web was designed to support multidirectional information flows. Furthermore, traditional media are static, while the Internet can be dynamic.

Once a page is printed on paper, it cannot be edited, but once a page is printed on the web, it can be edited ad infinitum. Because the Web is dynamic in this way and also designed for information to flow in all directions, it is possible to design tools which allow consumers of the web to alter and add to the pages they visit. This would include altering existing works or creating original works hosted on distant servers. As Web 2.0 services leverage the Read/Write Web in various ways, this concept and its related tools will be discussed throughout this section.

To get an idea of how the read/write tools enable users' unprecedented communication abilities, examples of two types of Web 2.0 services which epitomise the read/write web will be introduced. Blogs are an excellent example of web services which incorporate read/write characteristics to foster conversation instead of broadcast.

There are five features of blogs that have proven most interesting in this respect. First, as content management systems, blogs are easy to create and update. Furthermore, most are run on free blog software and many, like Blogger and Livejournal, are hosted on the servers of that software provider. Combined, these attributes encourage many new users to begin blogs.

In fact, approximately 100,000 new blogs are created each day. Second is the syndication aspect. Blogs consist of posts in reverse chronological order. Most blog software comes with a built in back end of RSS, which allow readers to subscribe to the blog with an RSS reader and receive new posts much as they would receive an e-mail. This allows users to keep up to date with new content as it is created. Worth noting is that RSS feeds are now integrated into many web sites. Third are permalinks, or post pages.

A permalink is an individual page where each post is stored by itself. Because each post has its own URL, it has made it possible for other bloggers to link to individual posts from their posts, which in turn creates conversation. Fourth are trackbacks, or backlinks.

A trackback connects a post on one blog back to a cited post on another blog. This places a copy of the citing post on the permalink page of the original post. Fifth and last is the comment feature.

This allows readers to comment on a post. Like a trackback, comments appear below the original post on the permalink page. Different readers and the original author can then add commentary on the original post, or responses to earlier comments. Like RSS feeds, comments are being included on many other services as well. Collectively, these features enable conversation to occur between all combinations of authors and readers.

This leads to a discussion of a second type of web service that epitomises the connection between read/write tools and communication. Social networking services, such as MySpace and Facebook have shown incredible popularity over the past few years. These sites are based on the premise that each user gets their own personal space where they can create a personal profile and connect with all of their friends in the community. In this way, users can connect to their friends' friends and communicate with large groups of friends at once.

Like blogs, these sites make it very easy for users to create content and build in incentives to encourage frequent updates and interactions with other users. For example, MySpace not only includes blogging features, but also encourages the sharing of photos, music, and videos. Like blogging, these services are successful because they enable and encourage communication between end users. Now that the concept of the Read/Write Web has been established, the second concept underlying all Web 2.0 services will be discussed.

THE WEB AS PLATFORM

By their very nature, companies described as Web 2.0 conduct their core business on the Web. At one time, software developers were limited to developing robust applications for the desktop.

However, new web technologies and business models have made it possible to develop applications that run in a web browser. This ability has been deemed using the 'Web as Platform' and is different from traditional applications in a number of ways.

Two of the main differences are what O'Reilly describes as the "End of the Software Release Cycle" and "Software Above the Level of a Single Device". "End of the Software Release Cycle" is more commonly, though less precisely, referred to as 'perpetual beta." The idea behind this is that web services need to be constantly updated, a concept that includes experimenting with new features in a live environment to see how customers react.

This cycle of feedback and response is possible on the web because software can be updated on the host servers as opposed to on individual computers, thus making new releases appear seamless to the end user. "Software above the level of a single device" refers to web applications that can run on any hardware and operating system platform that supports standards based web browsers. Consequently, it is possible to develop web services which can operate both on a desktop computer and a cellular phone.

One last quality of the Web as Platform is that it allows for applications to leverage the web as a communication network. O'Reilly explains that Web 2.0 services are designed to "make the most of the intrinsic advantages of that platform." This is often accomplished through using tools of the Read/Write Web. The concept of 'The Long Tail' highlights one way the read/write capabilities of Web 2.0 services explicitly build on the strength of the web.

THE LONG TAIL

The Long Tail is a term introduced by Chris Anderson to describe how the web makes it possible to provide services to small niche groups. To explain how it works, an example related to libraries will be introduced. Anderson uses a similar example in his article that coined the term. Originally, it was difficult to publish a book related to a very specific interest because its audience would be too limited to justify the publisher's investment.

While university presses make it possible to produce books related to specific interests in academia, they are still relatively limited in scope. However, the web lowers the barriers for distributing a book related to a specific interest because it can empower writers to connect directly with international audiences interested in extremely narrow topics. To see why this is so, three reasons will now be discussed. First, read/write capabilities of the web allow amateurs to publish and distribute their materials directly to the web for a minimal cost.

This eliminates the need for a publisher, bookseller, or other sort of middleman and drastically lowers the barriers for entry into the marketplace. Before these capabilities were introduced, content producers were still largely dependent on middle-men to distribute their media on the web.

It is important to note that the read/write web makes this possible for all types of traditional media, not just books. Second, the web virtually eliminates barriers of space. It accomplishes this because the web is a virtually unlimited storefront.

While a physical bookstore or library has real physical limitations to the inventory it can hold, a virtual bookstore or library can hold a theoretically ever-expanding inventory because of the affordability of digital storage space and the ability of a visitor to explore any part of this space. Furthermore, geographic barriers are eliminated. No matter where in the physical world one logs on, the unrestricted web is the same.

This allows writers to reach global audiences in a more efficient manner than possible with traditional media. Third, the web helps connect people with others who have the same narrow interests.

Search technologies can help users find content for which they are looking. However, Web 2.0 tools also automate ways to connect specific content with appropriate audiences. One way this is accomplished is through harnessing the collective intelligence of their users. In fact search itself is powered in this way.

HARNESSING COLLECTIVE INTELLIGENCE

O'Reilly offers numerous examples of Web 2.0 companies harnessing collective intelligence. One exceptional example of the power of collective intelligence is Google's PageRank algorithm. Instead of evaluating the relevance of web sites based solely on their content, PageRank examines how many links point to a page, and from what sites those links come. In essence, PageRank asks the entire web what is and is not important based on how sites link to one another.

Most of the other best examples of this phenomenon revolve around how Web 2.0 companies harness the collective intelligence of their users to gain an advantage over competition. Wikipedia is possibly the most extreme example of this. Because each user is encouraged to contribute, an increase in users yields an increase in contributions. This in turn creates better articles which attract new users. As a consequence, Wikipedia is constantly improved by its users, and as it gains new users and improves in quality, there is less reason to participate in a competing project. By encouraging users to annotate book records with reviews early on, Amazon began to accumulate valuable data that their competitors did not have.

Once Amazon attracted a critical mass of reviewers, there was little reason for existing or new reviewers to switch to another site. This example of harnessing the collective intelligence of one's users also demonstrates how very small markets can be served through encouraging customers to provide services to other customers.

In this example, many books that would otherwise have little or no annotation now include valuable reviews by specialist reviewers.

The example of Amazon will be discussed more fully when Library 2.0 is addressed. Worth noting is that these same methods and the underlying technologies help consumers communicate to one another about products they buy and services they use. This has many cultural ramifications and is altering how some companies do business.

The Cluetrain Manifesto put this phenomenon to words in 1999. Utilising the collective intelligence of users describes one method Web 2.0 services employ to continually improve based on user contributions.

However, a service such as a social networking site does not necessarily need to harness collective intelligence to improve. For example, in a social networking service, each user adds value to the network regardless of whether it harnesses the collective intelligence of its users.

NETWORK EFFECTS

Network Effects are another way for Web 2.0 services to leverage the unique characteristics of the web to their advantage. In fact, Network Effects explain why additional contributors increase collective intelligence in these examples. Social Software researcher Fred Stutzman explains Network Effects as they relate to social software in the following:

- Stated quite simply, social technologies benefit from an economy that awards value to the service as more people join the service. This, of course, is the network effect; a network gains value as more people join the network.

The easiest way to explain this concept is through examples. eBay is probably the most straightforward. eBay is an online auction house open to everyone. Each new buyer or seller on eBay increases the strength of the network by either increasing the inventory or adding another possible bidder. The network effect becomes obvious once a critical mass of users joins because if someone wants to sell something, they have to go to the marketplace with the buyers. If eBay has millions of users and a yard sale would attract 100 customers, then eBay is clearly a more likely place to sell one's goods. To gain a deeper understanding of this concept and how it applies to Web 2.0 service read "Metcalfe's Law Recurses Down the Long Tail of Social Networking", or Stutzman's evolving theory of the 'Network Effect Multiplier' which applies Network Effect theory to social networks and Web 2.0 services. However, the leveraging of Network Effects and collective intelligence only work because Web 2.0 services amass datasets through the process of collecting user contributions.

CORE DATASETS FROM USER CONTRIBUTIONS

As has already been discussed, the key method that Web 2.0 companies use to collect unique data sets is through user contributions. These contributions are then organised into databases and analysed to extract the collective intelligence hidden in the data. To this point, only explicit contributions from users have been discussed.

However, Web 2.0 companies also excel in collecting and analysing customer actions. Amazon.com, for example, does not simply collect users' explicit contributions, but also generates suggestions based on both a user's own and other customers' past behaviours. Amazon tracks users and attempts to offer suggestions based on items viewed by customers.

So if someone were to buy a piece of software, Amazon might suggest purchasing a book on using that software. Furthermore, the suggested book might be one that other users bought along with the software.

More than likely, a book that is also highly rated by customers would come to the top of the list. An actual transaction such as this typically takes many more variables into account and entices the customer with additional intelligent offers based on the collective knowledge of all Amazon users.

To review, users are encouraged to contribute data by giving users the ability to interact and engage with the site and one another. Users' explicit contributions and implicit actions are then collected, organised, and analysed to extract collective knowledge that can be applied to the direct improvement of the site.

LIGHTWEIGHT PROGRAMMING MODELS

The move towards database driven web services has been accompanied by new software development models that, in some cases, lead to greater flexibility.

For example, O'Reilly explains that Web 2.0 often uses 'lightweight programming models'.

This partly includes simple ways to loosely share and process datasets between partners. This enables mashups and remixes of data. The most common example of this idea is Google Maps. People are able to create mashups by combining the Google Maps data and application with other geographic datasets and applications.

This is made possible by the provision of APIs. An API allows third parties, either through licensing or open, to create new ways to view or utilise datasets.

These and other 'lightweight programming models' allow independent developers to programme their own additions or mashups, which in turn can be shared with other users. In this way APIs can allow users to function as developers.

They are contributing to the read/write web through writing code instead of writing text. This also allows maximum leveraging of datasets. Now that the key concepts and methods of Web 2.0 have been introduced, it is possible to begin analysing how library services are effected by Web 2.0. The next stage will examine these characteristics of Web 2.0 to see in what ways they affect library services.

LIBRARY 2.0 THEORY AND METHODOLOGY

A definition of Library 2.0 solidly rooted in its origins in Web 2.0.

The proposed definition of Library 2.0 was:

- Library 2.0 describes a subset of library services designed to meet user needs caused by the direct and peripheral effects of Web 2.0.

It was determined that Web 2.0 originated as a list of characteristics of successful web properties.

Combining this definition of Library 2.0 with the core concepts of Web 2.0, an expanded definition is now proposed:

- Library 2.0 describes a subset of library services designed to meet user needs caused by the direct and peripheral effects of Web 2.0 services leveraging concepts of the Read/Write Web, the Web as Platform, The Long Tail, harnessing collective intelligence, network effects, core datasets from user contributions, and lightweight programming models.

This definition of Library 2.0 is broad enough to account for all effects of Web 2.0 on the library world. One way Web 2.0 concepts and methods might affect libraries would be through direct application of these concepts and methods to library services. An example of this would be to allow user tagging in the OPAC.

A second way Web 2.0 services might have an effect on library services is by direct use of Web 2.0 services to provide library services. This would include setting up an account with a commercial photo sharing site, such as Flickr, to share library photos with patrons. A third way Web 2.0 might affect libraries is through cultural or behavioural changes brought on by Web 2.0 services. An example of this would be promoting library events to young adults through a MySpace account. Lastly, Web 2.0 services might affect the environment in which libraries function. This would include changing information literacy courses to account for changes in the information landscape, such as Wikipedia muddling issues of authority. Worth noting is that library services designed to meet user needs brought on by Web 2.0 might not themselves implement Web 2.0 principles. While many of the above examples might appear obvious, there are also many examples which take more contemplation.

Consequently, it would be helpful to have a theoretical framework to help derive actual services to deal with these effects. One way to determine the effects of Web 2.0 on libraries is to take each of the seven principles of Web 2.0 and ask how it might cause each of the possible types of effects explained above.

This would mean asking four sets of questions. Furthermore, many of these effects occur together, making it necessary to ask multiple sets of questions. The following sets are not meant to be all inclusive, but only a starting point. An example of each set will be provided using the examples articulated above.

SERVICE-BASED ON WEB 2.0 CONCEPTS

The first set of questions concerns implementing a library service-based on a Web 2.0 concept. How might concept *X* be implemented to improve service *Y* or create service *Z*? What other concepts of Web 2.0 would such an implementation employ? Do any other services exist which use this concept in the same way? Are our users familiar with other services that use this concept? What user population could be served by this? What are the drawbacks of incorporating a service powered by this concept? To gain an understanding of how this concept might be applied, a hypothetical application follows.

How might the concept of harnessing collective intelligence be implemented to improve cataloging? Are there any other services using tagging to allow users to categorise items? Do our users use any services that incorporate tagging? What user population would be served by incorporating tagging in the catalog? Would the positive outcomes outweigh the negatives?

USING A WEB 2.0 SERVICE FOR PROVIDING LIBRARY SERVICES

The second set of questions concerns implementing a library service through use of an existing Web 2.0 service. What concept or concepts of Web 2.0 power this service? What services does it provide? This service utilises concept(s) *X* and provides feature(s) *Y*; how might using this service improve services for our users? Could this service be used to improve or supplement service *Y*? Would use of this service provide our users with something beyond what the library already offers?

Does it provide our users with something additional to the existing value of the service? Are our users using this service or similar services? What population would this service target? What drawbacks might arise from using this third party service? Would our use of this service utilise the Web 2.0

concepts inherent in the service? If so, the first set of questions should be also be applied. A hypothetical application of this questioning will now be presented. Flickr utilises all seven concepts of Web 2.0 services. Flickr enables users to contribute, organise, share, and discuss photos. Might Flickr be useful for posting photos of library sponsored events? This would allow users to discuss and share photos in ways that were previously unavailable. If enough of our patrons use it, there might be a network effect; what effects might that have? Should we teach our users how to use Flickr instead? Are our users familiar with Flickr or similar services which enable commenting and tags? Which of our users are likely to use this service? What are potential drawbacks to hosting our photos on Flickr's servers and site instead of our own?

SERVICES IN RESPONSE TO CULTURAL EFFECTS OF WEB 2.0

While the first two sets of questions concern the direct effects of Web 2.0, the third and fourth sets of questions concern harder to identify peripheral effects. Set three concerns cultural changes including behavioural and habitual. In the *Internet and Everyday Life*, a number of early studies are presented which show how Internet use becomes closely connected to offline life.

Because many Web 2.0 tools are social or collaborative in nature, their effects often extend deeply into users' lives, affecting how people work, communicate, and socialise. Given this background, a core set of questions concerning these effects can be proposed.

How are our users using services that employ *X* concept(s)? How are these services affecting our users' lives outside of the library? How do these services affect the information seeking behaviours and communication habits of our users? What other types of changes in user behaviours and expectations are occurring because of their use of services employing *X* concept(s)? How can we alter service *Y* or create service *Z* to meet this need? A possible application of this follows. Teens are avid users of MySpace. How are they using it? Is it an extension of their offline social life? Is it their primary form of electronic communication? Is it used for planning face to face meetings? How much of their online time is spent at this site compared to the library web site? This site has built in features to invite friends to events. Maybe more teens would get the notifications about our events if they were posted in MySpace? Teens appear to be very honest and open on their profiles. Maybe we could solicit more and better feedback by setting up a profile for the library? Are other populations we serve using MySpace?

SERVICES IN RESPONSE TO ENVIRONMENTAL EFFECTS OF WEB 2.0

The fourth and final set of questions deals with peripheral effects on the environment in which libraries function. The primary way Web 2.0 services affect the library environment is through changing the information landscape. Because these services are data driven, they introduce entirely new types of information resources, information seeking behaviours, and user expectations.

The following set of core questions is a good starting point for dealing with these effects. How are services using concept *X* changing aspect *Y* of the environment in which libraries operate? How do Web 2.0 implementations of concept *X* alter the types of information to which users are exposed? How are information resources developed through concept *X* different from traditional resources? How does concept *X* effect the ways users interact with information resources? What are the positive and negative aspects of these new resources? What skills do users need to interact responsibly with these resources? What services would assist users to benefit from these new resources? An example application of this method of questioning follows.

Wikipedia employs the principle of collective intelligence towards the writing of an encyclopaedia, a reference tool. Each article can be written by any number of unidentified authors. This method eliminates the traditional methods for determining authority. Wikipedia users are not only able to read articles, but also edit them.

The idea powering Wikipedia is that a critical mass of users will pool their intelligence and edit out the improper information. It is difficult to tell which articles are correct and which are filled with honest mistakes or partisan agendas. However, many articles are adequate starting points for research and offer citations to other resources on the web. Furthermore, the number of contributors makes it possible to publish articles on obscure and specific topics that would not be covered by a traditional encyclopaedia.

Also, this new type of editorial process is quick and can provide articles on current events more quickly than traditional resources. Users need to understand how Wikipedia is different from traditional reference works. They need to understand how it works, so they can assess accuracy. They also need to learn how to contribute appropriately. This would include a solid understanding of plagiarism and how their contribution might affect their identity. Maybe a course in how wikis work would be helpful?

ACADEMIC LIBRARY 2.0

UNDERGRADUATE STUDENTS AND WEB 2.0

To begin, a number of questions related to undergraduates will be posed according to the proposed methodology. How are undergraduates using Web 2.0 services? What concepts are employed by those services? How does use of these services affect the information seeking behaviours, communication styles, and habits of undergraduates? It could be argued that academic libraries are in a unique position to apply Web 2.0 concepts. Multiple studies by the Pew Internet and American Life Project have shown this age demographic to be most likely to participate in creating web content. It is frequently assumed that this is because they are 'net natives,' as many of them grew up with the Internet. A report from the Pew Internet and American Life Project was titled "Teen Content Creators and Consumers: More than half of online teens have created content for the Internet; and most teen downloaders think that getting free music files is easy to do".

This title alone points out both the quantity of teens who have created content and the number able to find free music. Finding free music normally involves using peer-to-peer software, which itself is a Web 2.0 concept. Among other findings, the report shows that teens are more likely to create and read blogs than are older demographics.

In addition to these findings, an earlier report titled, 'Content Creation Online' determined that broadband users are more likely to create content as well. Therefore, in context of a typical residential college campus, an already active population is being given always—on broadband access, which further entices participation in Web 2.0 services. Assuming that teens of today will be university students of tomorrow, the typical student for the foreseeable future will be comfortable with Web 2.0 tools.

Do teens continue to be power users of Web 2.0 tools when they enter college? Most college curricula now require students to participate online. Even if students are not required to create web sites for class, most are required to use course management software such as Blackboard or WebCT. While the dominant course management systems do not fully utilise the concepts of Web 2.0, they do incorporate read/write tools such as discussion forums and workspaces for online collaboration.

Many colleges are now beginning to offer alternative solutions for online courses such as wikis. Even more interesting, and more important, is the way freshmen at a residential school are introduced to new technologies. When entering college, freshmen appear to accept the current technology as the way it always was. This is important both for looking at how undergraduates currently use new Web 2.0 services, and because of the ease of integrating new services into college lifestyle.

Two examples will be used to illustrate this point. First is Instant Messaging. Unfortunately, no hard data is available to illustrate this point, but the author is able to speak from personal experience as a freshman in 1998.

AOL Instant Messenger was first released in May 1997. To most Internet users, this was their first introduction to instant messaging. As an entering freshman in August 1998, AIM was overwhelmingly accepted by most students at this author's residential college as the primary form of communication. Because no one had been to college before, it was taken for granted that always on broadband access and reliance on Instant Messaging were simply part of college life. A more compelling and recent example of this phenomenon comes from Fred Stutzman's current studies of freshman Facebook usage at the University of North Carolina at Chapel Hill.

Over the past few years, Stutzman has used a web crawler to track freshmen usage of Facebook from the summer before entering school through their first academic year. While the data he has gathered is truly fascinating. In the first year of his study, he found that by the first day of class, 85 per cent of freshman had a Facebook account.He also found a strong and direct correlation between when accounts were created and orientation sessions held over the summer. Essentially, students were introduced to Facebook by their orientation leaders and consequently accepted it as part of college life.

Stutzman also found that, by semester's end, 94 per cent of freshman had accounts. A lot of the accompanying data shows that students were also very active users of Facebook. Furthermore, Stutzman is developing a compelling theory of 'Situational Relevance' to explain this data.

It is his argument that students use Facebook because it helps them become oriented to their new environment. Entering a new environment, where they do not know anyone and need to build a new social network, students embrace Facebook as a tool for learning about other students and navigating college life.

In addition to nearly being universally adopted by undergraduates, Facebook is an excellent example of a Web 2.0 service. Facebook is a highly successful social networking service designed for college students.

Apart from demonstrating freshman adoption habits, Facebook provides specific clues as to how academic libraries might implement Web 2.0 services. Facebook implements most of the features and concepts relevant to Web 2.0. As a social networking service, network effects occur.

With almost 100 per cent of students using Facebook at many universities, the network effect is very strong.

Furthermore, Facebook is powered by user contributions. Users not only create personal profiles, but are also encourage to upload and tag photos, to comment on one another's profiles and photos, to create groups, and to manage event invitations. New features are regularly added.

Some of the newer features include a blogging service and a tool for sharing digital media. Given this integration of tools, users of Facebook are exposed to most of the typical types of Web 2.0 applications and thus most types of Web 2.0 concepts.

Now that it has been determined that academic libraries serve a unique audience that both quickly adopts and frequently uses Web 2.0 services, it is possible to pursue further lines of questioning. If students are already using services such as Facebook and Blackboard, how do these products fit into their lives? How does use of these services guide libraries in the process of developing new services or using existing Web 2.0 services?One approach to answering this question is to examine how these technologies already fit into student life and then determine the library's role in this picture. Furthermore, because these services relate to students' offline lives, they too must be examined.

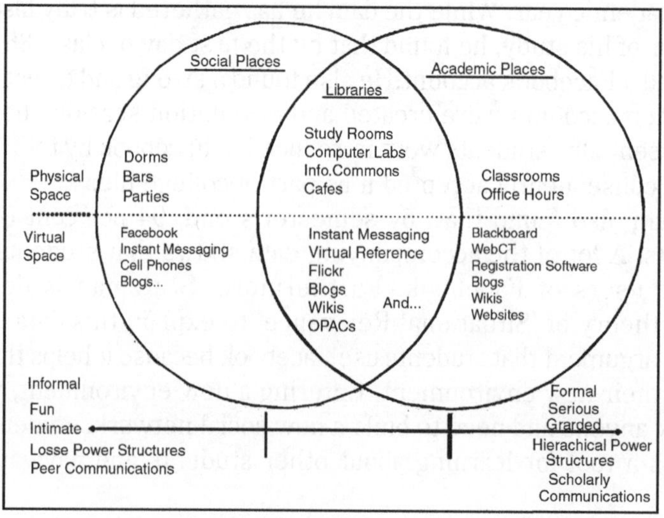

Fig. Academic Library 2.0 Concept Model, Basic.

Figure introduces one conceptual framework that applies this method. This model analyses the library's position as a physical place in student life and then draws parallels with the library's place online.

The model is based on the idea that most of student life is divided between the social and the academic and that physical libraries have traditionally provided a unique location that mixes the two. The bottom of the model displays the various spectra between social and academic places with libraries falling near the middle. One end is the strictly academic formal classroom. Here the professor is an authority to the student.

At the opposite end is a party, a purely social occasion. It could be argued that libraries have traditionally provided a place where students could collaborate on school work without the pressure of being watched by an authority figure, thus allowing them to socialise while they work. Of course, this space also provided students with whatever research materials and reference assistance they might need.

Towards this end, librarians have traditionally tried to maintain strict patron confidentiality so as to keep the library a safe haven from authority. Furthermore, many academic libraries now provide popular materials collections to provide residential students with materials for pleasure reading, thus further blending the line between social and academic space. Recent trends in academic libraries have moved closer to blending this line by adding coffee shops, WiFi access, and Information Commons.

If one accepts that the physical library provides students with this blended environment, then one might ask, "How might the library provide a similar virtual space?" To find an answer to this question, this model creates a parallel spectrum describing a student's virtual life.

At the academic end of the spectrum, lies course management software such as Blackboard. Similar to the classroom, this space is controlled by the professor and has the same authority structure. On the social end of the spectrum, is Facebook. Students traditionally think of this as a safe social place devoid of authority figures. This is demonstrated by the fact that students have recently been punished for information they post to Facebook. Stutzman's research demonstrates this feeling of safety. Given this spectrum, what virtual place might the library provide for students? One possibility would be virtual group study rooms.

Such a place might provide the read/write tools to enable students to collaborate remotely and asynchronously on course projects. This space might also provide resources and links to live reference help to assist students in their work. This place would be different from Blackboard because professors would not be able to review students' discussions.

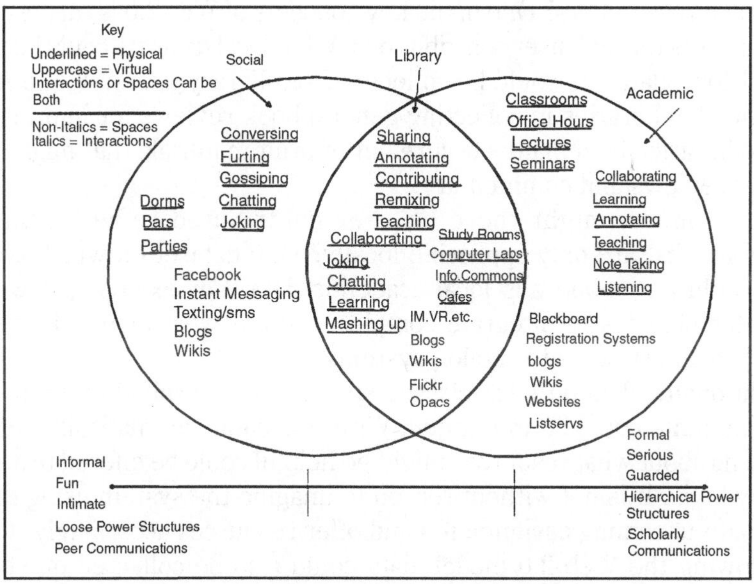

Fig. Academic Library 2.0 Concept Model, Detailed.

The boundary between physical and virtual has vanished. Furthermore, this model includes interaction types as well as places. Instead of focussing on exact tasks such as shaking hands (physical) or commenting (virtual), this model looks at interactions from a broader prospective.

However, the basic goal is to facilitate thoughts about how to design virtual and physical places according to the types of interpersonal interactions our patrons will be having in those environments. Worth noticing is that all of the interactions mentioned occur in both the physical and virtual places. Furthermore, there soon will be more places inhabiting both physical and virtual.

This would include the example of online group study rooms. Now that the place of Web 2.0 in students' lives has been introduced, it is possible to pursue more specific enquiries into how Web 2.0 concepts and services can be applied in academic libraries.

HARNESSING COLLECTIVE INTELLIGENCE TO SERVE LOCAL NEEDS

Not only are undergraduates power users of Web 2.0 services, but academic libraries still hold nearly a virtual monopoly over providing their required academic information needs. Furthermore, professors and graduate students remain similarly dependent on libraries to provide research materials. Even though some tools like Google Scholar and Google Books offer alternative routes to library materials, academic libraries provide collections and services customised to the unique needs of their institution.

How then might Web 2.0 concepts and services be employed to serve local students and researchers? One of the key concepts of Web 2.0 is that of creating unique datasets through user contributions. What local datasets could be mashed up? What local datasets could be collected from library users? While Amazon is way ahead of libraries in collecting general book reviews for in print books, academic libraries hold many obscure out of print materials that might benefit from user reviews and commentary.

Furthermore, might there be user contributed reviews, tags, and commentary that are only applicable locally? One dataset on which academic libraries hold a monopoly is local academic data. For example, it would be possible for libraries to integrate complete lists of what materials are being used for which classes into catalog systems.

Additionally, data on what classes students are enrolled in, their syllabi, and assignments could be integrated. With this data, automatically generated suggestions about what resources might be helpful could be offered to a student once they login. It is not without reason to imagine the system using this data to anticipate upcoming assignments and offer resources accordingly.

Following the Web 2.0 model, data could also be collected on students' behaviours in the catalogs. As courses are repeated, the system might learn what resources work for certain assignments and offer a suggestion such as, "In the past other students studying this topic have looked at these resources." Even better, if students provide ratings and reviews on resources, the system might be able to suggest, "Other students have found this item useful when researching this assignment." All of this data is unique to an individual institution making this data uniquely available to academic libraries.

Along these lines, students could tag items with course numbers, assignment titles, or professors' names. Of course all this would be built on top of existing data unique to that library. These suggestions need not be limited to Catalog records, but could grow to include databases, e-journals, and even individual articles if vendors could be convinced to allow each institution to annotate items with local information. One major issue that is brought up when discussing this type of service is privacy. Any usage or sharing of patron data would need to be optin allowing patron granular level controls of how their data is used.

This would need to be accompanied by appropriate information literacy instruction in privacy, identity, and intellectual property. However, this instruction is particularly important to assist students with their interactions with these services outside of the library.

EFFECTS OF THE READ/WRITE WEB ON THE ACADEMIC ENVIRONMENT

The preceding discussions demonstrate how many implementations of Web 2.0 concepts and services are dependent on providing users with read/write capabilities. A few of the cultural ramifications of this will now be discussed. One way to examine this is by looking at the effects of the Read/Write Web on scholarly publishing. Traditionally, excluding study spaces, academic libraries expected patrons to use the knowledge they gained from the library to assist with writing projects that occurred outside of the library under established editorial methods.

Eventually, this knowledge would trickle back in through traditional media sources such as journals and books. One way to look at the read/write web in relation to publishing is that it has accelerated this process.

Now it is possible for readers to feed their knowledge back into the system in real-time. While academic libraries have always been places of reading, Academic Library 2.0 is a place of both reading and writing. However the process always recognised patrons would write their ideas down and that they would eventually re-enter libraries as part of the scholarly and historical record. Furthermore, librarians have always trusted that the majority of their users strive to distinguish that which is good and true.

This is the foundation of the principles of democracy, academic scholarship, and intellectual freedom. However, Academic Library 2.0 demands a more explicit trust in the majority. Librarians must continue to trust that most readers are curious, intelligent and compassionate. The only difference is that the evidence of these attributes will be created and stored on our servers immediately and without editorial control. An example can be used to explain why this trust must be more explicit in Library 2.0. It has always been easier to put hate group propaganda in the stacks than it has been to host hate groups in meeting rooms because the first can be obviously lost among the true and good arguments around it. In fact, it is only noticed when someone searches for it.

In the meeting room or on a library hosted blog, that hate speech is much more obvious and thus harder to ignore. This explicit trust necessary for Library 2.0 is rooted in the principles of academic scholarship and intellectual freedom. These ethics encourage librarians to have faith that if any such bigotry is posted to a political discussion hosted on a library blog, it will quickly be drowned out by the voices of more responsible patrons. Moreover, those patrons will cite other sources on the web and in our collections.

They might even make a compelling enough argument that the minds of a few lurkers are changed. This same principle underlies Wikipedia and, if user contributions are to be accepted into library systems, this principle must be accepted by librarians.

This is what intellectual freedom is all about. This is what libraries have always been about. Web 2.0 has simply accelerated the process. In this way Library 2.0 speaks to some of the best of traditional library values, and, in so doing, keeps the library at the forefront of defending intellectual freedom.

ACADEMIC LIBRARY 2.0

Now that some of the primary cultural, environmental, and methodological ramifications of Web 2.0 on academic libraries have been introduced, a synthesised view of what Academic Library 2.0 would look like will be proposed.

What would such a system look like when fully implemented? Patrons would have a single logon to a central account where they could manage all of their interactions with research materials. On day one, a student's course information would be loaded into the system, along with the syllabi for all of his or her classes.

The syllabi would provide links to both required and suggested materials in the OPAC, databases, school bookstore, and Amazon.com. Each class would have links to items tagged by students and faculty with that course number.

There would also be links of items tagged by students with the professor's name. Furthermore, each assignment that was used in past semesters would have links to supplementary materials both students and faculty had tagged as useful for that assignment. While researching, students and faculty would be able to annotate whole records or articles, as well as individual pieces of records. They would be able to comment, discuss, tag and review items. This would be done across the OPAC, databases, and the open web.

Their central account would provide them with access to all of their notes, as well as a tag cloud. When browsing, other people's annotations could be turned on and off at will. Students and faculty would have granular privacy controls that would allow them to keep all of their information private, share it with just friends, just students, just the campus community, or the public.

Additionally, students and faculty would be able to use a pseudonym when sharing. Of course, some usage guidelines would be in place to prevent such egregious abuses as slandering another member of the community. Students and faculty would be able to establish private working groups where they could share, discuss, and annotate items both asynchronously and synchronously through discussion boards, chat software, co-browsing, blogs, wikis, or project management software.

Of course, librarians could be summoned into personal or group workspaces to assist with the research process. All of this data would be exportable in a standardised format and be the intellectual property of the contributors. This would allow transfer of information between this and other systems as well as allowing students and faculty to take their information with them when they leave the University or to delete old items from public view.

An API would also be available to allow students and faculty to develop mashups of library system datasets and other datasets.

People would be able to establish a friend network similar to social networking software like Facebook. Ideally this would be standardised across campuses allowing collaboration among students and faculty at different institutions.

Possibly, this could be automatically generated through pulling data from the Facebook API or a similar existing network. A built in RSS reader would enable students to pull in data from various sources such as a friend's favourites or new recommended materials.

This would present students with a snapshot of what is occurring in their areas of study. Collected data would be analysed to determine trends and patterns and the system would be adjusted accordingly.

Among other things, this would include consistent updates to the interface, search algorithms, and recommendation systems. This data could also be used to detect trends in research habits and develop appropriate collection development strategies.

This would be especially effective if data were pooled at a national level. Information literacy classes would instruct students and faculty in the use of these and other Web 2.0 services. Instruction would also teach students about responsible content creation.

This would include teaching them about intellectual property so that they could maintain appropriate control over their contributions to various services and so that they can remix others' data legally.

It would also include instruction on issues of privacy and how what students create online can be connected to their identity and affect their life in the physical world. Instruction would explain how to evaluate and contribute to non-traditional resources such as Wikipedia.

As increased familiarity and usage of these tools begins to have a greater effect on habits of face to face communication, the boundary between physical space and virtual space will become blurred. Some physical spaces will have a more modular structure to mirror the online work environment. Spaces will be designed for collaboration by providing tools such as tablet PCs, smart boards, and their descendants.

All web services will be compatible across devices, including cell phones and handheld devices. Notifications and communications will be received through RSS, texting (SMS), or any other means the patron desires.

NATIONAL LIBRARY OF INDIA

The National Library of India at Belvedere, Kolkata, is the largest library in India by volume and India's library of public record. It is under the Department of Culture, Ministry of Tourism and Culture, Government of India. The library is designated to collect, disseminate and preserve the printed material produced in India. The library is situated on the scenic 30 acre Belvedere Estate, in Kolkata. The Library is the largest in India, with a collection in excess of 2.2 million books.

AIMS

- Acquisition and conservation of all significant national production of printed material, excluding ephemera.
- Collection of printed material concerning the country, no matter where it is published, and as a corollary, the acquisition of photographic records of such material that is not available with in the country
- Acquisition and conservation of foreign material required by the country.
- Rendering of bibliographical and documents services of current and retrospective material, both general and specialised.
- Acting as a referral centre purveying full and accurate knowledge.

HISTORY

The Calcutta Public Library

The history of the National Library began with the formation of Calcutta Public Library in 1836. That was a non-governmental institution and was run on a proprietary basis. People contributing ₹300 in subscription became the proprietors. Prince Dwarkanath Tagore was the first proprietor of that Library. ₹300 at that time was a significant amount, so poor students and others were allowed free use the library for some period of time.Lord Metcalfe, the Governor General at that time, transferred 4,675 volumes from the library of the College of Fort William, Calcutta to the Calcutta Public Library. This and donations of books from individuals formed the nucleus of the library. Both Indian and foreign books, especially British, were purchased for the library. Donations were regularly made by individuals as well as by the government.

The Calcutta Public Library had a unique position as the first public library in this part of the world. Such a well-organized and efficiently run library was rare even in Europe during the first half of the 19th century. Because of the efforts of the Calcutta Public Library, the present National Library has many extremely rare books and journals in its collection.

The Imperial Library

Built after the model of the Town Hall at Ypres. A fine example of the Public Buildings in Calcutta.The Imperial Library was formed in 1891 by combining a number of Secretariat libraries in Calcutta.

Of those, the most important and interesting was the library of the Home Department, which contained many books formerly belonging to the library of East India College, Fort William and the library of the East India Board in London. But the use of the library was restricted to the superior officers of the Government.

Amalgamation of the Calcutta Public Library and Imperial Library

In 1903, Lord Curzon, the Governor-General of India, conceived the idea of opening a library for the use of the public. He noticed both the libraries—Imperial Library and Calcutta Public Library were under-utilized because of limited access and lack of amenities. He decided to amalgamate the rich collection of both of these libraries. The new amalgamated library, called Imperial Library, was formally opened to the public on January 30, 1903 at Metcalfe Hall, Kolkata.

Metcalfe Hall had earlier been the residence of the Governor-Generals Wellington, Cornwallis and Warren Hastings:

- "It is intended that it should be a library of reference, a working place for students and a repository of material for the future historians of India, in which, so far as possible, every work written about India, at any time, can be seen and read."—*The Gazette of India*

Declaring the Imperial Library as the National Library

After Independence the Government of India changed the name of the Imperial Library to the National Library, with the enactment of the Imperial Library Act, 1948, and the collection was shifted from the Esplanade to the present Belvedere Estate. On February 1, 1953, the National Library was opened to the public, inaugurated by Maulana Abul Kalam Azad. B. S. Kesavan was appointed the first Librarian of the National Library.

Discovery of Hidden Chamber

In 2010, the Ministry of Culture, the owner of the library, decided to get the library building restored by the *Archaeological Survey of India* (ASI). While taking stock of the library building, the conservation engineers discovered a previously unknown room. The ground-floor room, about 1000 sq. ft. in size, seems to have no opening of any kind. The ASI archaeologists tried to search the first floor area for a trap door, but found nothing.

Since the building is of historical and cultural importance, ASI decided to bore a hole through the wall instead of breaking it. There was speculations about the room being a punishment room used by Warren Hastings and other British officials, or a place to store treasure. After six months of study, it was determined to be not a room at all, but merely "a block stuffed with mud, perhaps constructed by the British architects to strengthen the base of the building."

COLLECTION

Indian Languages Collection

The National Library receives books and periodicals in almost all Indian languages. These are received under the *Delivery of Books and Newspapers Act 1954*. Language divisions acquire, process and provide reading materials in all major Indian languages. Hindi, Kashmiri, Punjabi, Sindhi, Telugu and Urdu language divisions maintain their own stacks. Other language books are stacked in the Stack division.

Language divisions are also responsible for answering reference queries. The library has separate Indian language divisions for Assamese, Bengali, Gujarati, Hindi, Kannada, Kashmiri, Malayalam, Marathi, Oriya, Punjabi, Sanskrit, Sindhi, Tamil, Telugu and Urdu. Sanskrit language division also collects and processes Pali and Prakrit books. English books published in India are collected under D.B. Act.

Assamese Language Collection

In 1963, a separate division was established in the National Library to collect and process Assamese books. At present the division has 12,000 books. This collection has some works published between 1840 and 1900. Some of the important publications are Asamiya Larar Mitra by Anandaram Dhekiyal Phukan, Larabodh Byakaran by Dharmeswar Goswami, Prakrit Bhugol by Lambodara Datta and several volumes of Sri Sankardev's Kirattan, Gunamala, Srimad Bhagavad, Bargit, Rukmini Haran Nat, and Ankiyanat. Volumes of the periodical Arunodoi are also available in the collection.

Bengali Language Collection

The library has 85,000 books in its Bengali collection. The collection contains very rare and valuable books as well as periodicals published from the last quarter of the 18th century. Early Bengali plays and novels are well represented. The collection has many rare items such as the manuscripts of Sarat Chandra Chattopadhaya, Bibuti Bhushan Bandao padhaya, Jibanananda Das and Bisnu De.

154 letters of Netaji *Subhas Chandra Bose* written to his nephew Sri *Asok Nath Bose* and letters to *Sarat Chandra Bose* are also available in the collection. The collection has the complete set of Rabindranath Tagore's works, except a few of his early works. This includes 190 first editions of Tagore's works.

Some of the rare and important works in this collection are: A Grammar of the Bengal Language by Nathaniel Brassey Halhed, which is the earliest printed book in Bengali, Henry Forster's A Vocabulary in Two parts, English and Bangalee, William Carrey's Dialogues, Intended to Facilitate the Acquiring of the Bengali Language, Ram Ram Basu's Raja Pratapaditya Charitra, Mrityunjay Vidyalankar's Batris Simhansan, Ramayana translated by Krittibas and published in five volumes, Mahabharat translated by Kashi Ram Das, Chandicharan Munshi's Tota Itihas, Jayanarayan Ghosal's Sri Karunani-dhanavilasa, William Carey's Dictionary of the Bengali Language, 2 volumes.

There are 400 titles of Bengali periodicals including many rare 19th century periodicals such as Digdarshan first Bengali monthly and the first issue of Samachar Darpan—the first Bengali weekly.

Gujarati Language Collection

The library has 37,000 Gujarati books. 1100 of them are titles published prior to 1900. This collection also has 30 albums of paintings by Kanu Desai published between 1936 and 1956. Ancient Jaina miniature paintings are well reproduced in Sri Jaina Chitravali, Sri Jaina Chitra Patavali and other valuable books edited by Sarabhai Nawab.

The authentic editions of the poetic works of medieval Gujarati poets such as Narsinh Meheta, Mirabai, Premanand and Symal Bhat are also part of the holdings. The rare titles include Robert Drummond's Illustrations of Grammatical Parts Guzerattee, Maratta and English Languages, translations of Aesop's Fables by Bapushastri Pandya Raykaval, Edalji Patel's Suratani Tavarikh and Jnana Chakra—a Gujarati encyclopaedia in 9 volumes.

Hindi Language Division

Hindi is one of the official languages of India. The collection building of Hindi books has been continuing since the time of the Imperial Library, and a separate division was established in 1960. At present 80,000 Hindi books are in the library collection.

The collection has rare works published during the last decades of the 18th Century. Many of the publications published by Lulloo Lal, the first printer, publisher and writer of Kolkata, are represented in this collection. The following rare books published by Lulloo Lal are in the library: Braja Bhasha Grammar, Lataife Hindi, Rajaniti, and Prem Sagur. In addition, the library has The Oriental Linguist with an Extensive Vocabulary English and Hindoostanee and Hindoostanee and English by John B. Gilchrist, Hindi-Roman Orthoepigraphical Ultimatum by John B. Gilchrist, Rajneeti by Narayana Pandit, Sudamacaritra by Haldhara Dasa, Raga Kalpadruma, Baital Pachisi by Duncan Forbes, Dictionary of Hindee and English by J. T. Thompson, Yavan Bhasa ka Vyakaran by Hooper William, Siva Simha Saroja by Siva Simha Senagar, Hindi Pradipa edited by Balkrishna Bhatt, Brief Account of the Solar System in Hindi, and a microfilm copy of Bal Bodhini—a monthly journal for women edited by Bharatendu Harischandra. There are also about 1200 rare first issues of important journals.

Kannada Language Collection

A separate Kannada division was set up in 1963 in the National Library. In 1960, the library purchased the personal collection of H. Channakeshava Ayyangar. It consists of 1300 books published between the last two decades of the 19th century and the first three decades of the 20th century. An important contribution towards building the collection was the efforts of *G. P. Rajaratnam*, a noted Kannada author. Immediately after the enactment of the D.B. Act, Rajaratnam toured the erstwhile Mysore State to create awareness among the publishers about the Act. He collected about 1500 books without any expense to the library. The Kannada collection in the library is particularly useful for the study of the cultural history of Karnataka. At present there are 32,000 Kannada books in the library.

Kashmiri Language Collection

The Kashmiri division was formed in 1983. Currently the library has 500 Kashmiri books. Some of the important items in this collection are Muhammad Yusuf Teng's Shirin Qalm, Wiyur edited by Ghulam Muhammad Rafiq, Ghulam Nabi Khyal's Akah Nandun, Nurnama and compiled by Muhammad Amin Kaim, Fazil and Kashmiri's Krishna Lila.

Malayalam Language Collection

The Malayalam division was established as a separate division in 1963, with around 5000 books. Now the collection has 34,500 books. The earliest printed book, Centum Adagia Malabarica, a Latin translation of Malayalam proverbs, dates back to 1791. The Latin translations are printed alongside the Malayalam originals.Rare and old books include Robert Drummond's Grammar of the Malabar Language, Dr Gundart's Malayalam-English Dictionary Vartamanapustakam by Parammachkal Govarnnodoracchan, Appu Nedungadi's Kundalata and Chantu Menan's Indulekha.

Apart from these, many works representing earlier periods are part of this collection. A few of these are Ramacaritam, works of Niranam, Cerussery's Krishnagatha, Vatakkan Pattukal, Ezuttachan's Adhyatama Ramayana, Ramaprattu Variyar's Kucelavrtam, and Kuncan Nampyar's Tullol.

Marathi Language Collection

The Marathi division was established in 1963 with a collection of 8900 volumes. The division now has 37,000 books in its collection. In 1954 the National Library purchased the library of the Bengal Nagpur Railway Indian Institute, Kharagpur, which had a good number of Marathi books. Sir Jadunath Sarkar collection also has about 350 Marathi books, mostly on the history of the Marathas. The division has many rare and old Marathi publications.

These include William Carey's A Grammar of the Mahratta Language and Dictionary of the Maharatta Language, Simhasana Battisi, Raghuji Bhonsalyaci Vanshavali, Vans Kennedy's A Dictionary of Maratta Language, Nava Karar, A Short Account of Railways by K. Bhatwadekar, Charles Hutton's Bijaganit, Tukaram's Abhangachi Gatha edited by Vishnu Parashuram Pandit and Shankar Pandurang Pandit, Itihasaprisiddha Purushanche va Striyanche Povade edited by H. A. Acworth.

Oriya Language Collection

A separate Oriya division was established in 1973. The Imperial Library had only 133 books; later the collection was increased to 425 books. Currently, the division has 19,500 books. The oldest publication available in the Oriya collection dates back to 1831. It is Rev.

Amos Sutton's Introductory Grammar of Oriya Language. Some of the other rarities in the collection are Jayadeva's Gitagovinda, translated by Dharanidhara, Amos Sutton's An Oriya Dictionary, 3 volumes, Dharmapustakara Adibhaya, and Purnacandra Odiabhasa Kosh, a lexicon of the Oriya language compiled by Gopalachandra Praharaj.

Punjabi Language Collection

A separate division for the acquisition and processing of Punjabi language books was established in 1974. Most of the works in this collection are of recent origin. There are a few old and rare Punjabi books, such as William Carey's A Grammar of Punjabee Language, Samuel Starkey's A Dictionary of English Punjabee, Geographical Description of the Panjab, Bhai Santosh Singh's Guru Paratap Suraj Granthavali and Gurudas Bhai's Vars.

Sanskrit, Pali and Prakrit Languages Collection

Sanskrit has a rich literature in many fields of knowledge. A separate division in the library collects and processes Sanskrit books. At present the division has over 20,000 Sanskrit books, printed in the Devanagari script. Almost all Indian language divisions possess Sanskrit works printed in their respective language scripts.

The library also has a rich collection of Sanskrit works edited or translated with original scripts, in English and many other foreign languages. The collection attracts scholars from India and abroad. Apart from Sanskrit, books in Pail and Prakrit languages are also collected and processed by this_division. At present the library has about 500 books in Pali and a comparable collection of books in Prakrit.

Sindhi Language Collection

Since 1957, the library has been building a collection of Sindhi books. At present the library has 2100 Sindhi books. Shah Abdul Latif's Shah Jo Rasalo and Shah Jo Sher are the rare items in this collection.

Tamil Language Collection

The Tamil division was formed in 1963. The division currently has 57,000 books. Apart from this, the library has 1000 Tamil books and 300 Tamil manuscripts in the Vaiyapuri Pillai collection. There are many rare and old works among the Tamil titles.

Early printed Tamil books in the library include the Tamil Bible, John Philip Fabricius's A Malabar and English Dictionary, a Tamil translation of John Bunyan's Piligrim's Progress, and Caldwell's Comparative Grammar of DravidianLlanguages. The collection also includes standard editions of five great Sangam Classics.

Telugu Language Collection

The Telugu division was started in the National Library in 1963. The collection has a good number of old Telugu books published since the earlier decades of the 19th century. Some of the rarities in Telugu available in this collection are William Carey's Grammar of Telugu Language, C.P. Brown's A Vocabulary of Gentoo and English, Vakyavali, Catalogue of Telugu books in the British Library, London compiled by L. D. Barnett.

Urdu Language Collection

Like Arabic and Persian, the Urdu collection was substantial since the days of Imperial Library. Special collections such as the Buhar Library, Hidayat Husain collection, Zakariya collection and Imambara collection have some Urdu books and manuscripts.

In 1968 a separate Urdu division was set up formed in the library. At present it has more than 20,000 books. Some of the oldest are Uklakhi Hindee or Indian Ethics, and Mir Muhamad Taki's Kulliuat-e-Mir.

English Language Collection

The National Library has an invaluable collection of books in the English language, because of the systematic development by Calcutta Public Library and the Imperial Library. Way back in 1848, an attempt was made to acquire journals issued by the foreign learned institutions.

Serious works were purchased in larger numbers than light literature. The same policy has been pursued in recent times. Although the library has English books and other reading materials in almost all subjects, the collection is especially rich in the humanities, British and Indian history and literature

Foreign Languages Collections

One of the aims of the National Library is to collect all the books published on India, anywhere in the world and in any language. At the same time it collects reading materials on other subjects in different languages for the use of the country. The Imperial Library had a good number of Arabic and Persian works and a few other foreign language books.

In 1985 the European Languages Division was reorganized and five separate divisions were formed. These are East Asian Languages Division, Germanic Languages Division, Romance Languages Division, Slavonic Languages Division,West Asian and African Languages Division. The foreign language works are mainly acquired through purchase, gift and exchange. The divisions mentioned are responsible for collection development, collection organisation and information dissemination to the readers in the respective languages. They also maintain their own stacks and provide reading facilities.

East Asian Languages Collection

A separate division collects, processes and preserves Chinese and other East Asian languages. At present the collection has 15,000 Chinese books and one thousand each in Japanese, Korean, Tibetan, Nepali and Thai languages.

Germanic Languages Collection

The Germanic Languages division was formed in the library in the year 1985. The division has books in German, Dutch, Norwegian and Swedish. But the largest number of books is in German. The division has book exchange agreements with seven Germanic language-speaking countries. Berliner Zeitung, a newspaper published from former East Germany is available in this collection.

Romance Languages Collection

Romance Languages division came into existence in 1985, along with other foreign languages divisions. Although the collection includes books and other materials in languages belonging to the Romance group, the largest number of books is in French, about 5000. About 2000 Romanian and a handful of books in Italian and Spanish are also available.

Slavonic Languages Collection

The collection has books in Slavonic languages, spoken in Russia, Poland,

Bulgaria, the Czech Republic, Slovakia, former Yugoslavia and other countries and peoples of the region. It deals with reading materials in 28 languages. But the largest collection is in the Russian language. At present the division has 65,000 books.

West Asian and African Languages Collection

The Buhar Library may be considered the nucleus of West Asian and African languages collection. The division has a handful of books in other West Asian languages such as Hebrew and Amharic. The largest number of books is in Persian and Arabic, approximately 12,000 in Arabic and 12,000 in Persian. The collection includes the lexicons compiled and prepared by Indians authors of the past and edited by the 'native' scholars of the College of Fort William and European orientalists of the said college.

The division also holds a large numbers of historical works published under the Bibliotheca Indica series of the Asiatic Society of Bengal in the 19th century. A large number of Arabic and Persian books and manuscripts can also be found in Sir Abdur Rahim Collection, Hidayat Husain Collection, Zakaria Collection and Imambara Collection. Sir Jadunath Sarkar Collection also has 200 Persian manuscripts. These manuscripts relate mainly to the later Mughal period and the early years of British rule.

Rare Books

The National Library has an impressive number of rare books and other reading materials. In 1973, a separate Rare Books division was established. At present the books published prior to 1860 are considered rare books, along with limited and first editions, books distinguished by their design, illustration or history, and a few other criteria. Along with rare books, manuscripts and microfilms of the library are also stacked in this division. The division also provides reading facilities to the users who wish to consult these items. At present the division has 4700 monographs, 3000 manuscripts and 1500 microfilms

Manuscripts

National Library has about 3600 rare and historically important manuscripts in different languages. These manuscripts are preserved separately along with other important and rare books in the Rare Books division.

Science and Technology Collection

Following the recommendations of the Reviewing Committee, the Science and Technology division was set up in 1972. The basic function of this division is to collect and disseminate the core material in science and technology. At present the division holds about 17,000 books and monographs and 800 current print periodicals. The division provides reading facilities and has an open access stack system.

Indian Official Documents

All the publications of Government of India, State Governments, Union Territories, Government Undertakings, Autonomous Bodies are collected, processed and preserved separately. A separate division for this purpose was established in 1972. The library owns a rich collection of Indian official documents from the days of the East India Company to the present.

The collection also includes the documents published by the Government of Great Britain relating to India. A good collection of Myanmarese documents and few documents of Aden, Sri Lanka, Persian Gulf Political Residency are also part of this collection. At present, the division holds around 4,90,000 documents.

Foreign Official Documents

The National Library is one of the repository libraries for United Nations Organisation and its agencies. Thus all the publications of UNO and its agencies are received by the library free of cost. These documents are processed and stacked separately. The library also receives publications of the governments of the United States of America, Great Britain, Canada, the Commonwealth nations, and the publications of the European Economic Committee.

Almost all the volumes of the sessional sets of British Parliamentary papers since the beginning of the 19th century are available. Apart from the depositary copies, the library acquires selected foreign publications through purchase. At present the library has around 400,000 foreign official documents.

Newspapers and Periodicals

All the newspapers and periodicals in Indian languages are received and processed in their respective language divisions. But English newspapers and periodicals, both the Indian and foreign, are acquired and processed separately. A separate Serials division is responsible for acquiring and processing of English newspapers and periodicals.

The library has a rich collection of late 19th and early 20th century newspapers and periodicals, but almost all of them are incomplete sets. There are catalogues for periodicals, newspapers and gazettes available in the library up to 1953.

Maps and Prints

The library has an extensive collection of maps from the 17th century onwards. Indian topographical sheets of earlier days and maps of natural resources, population, transport and communication systems, agricultural production, soil, vegetation and the geology of India form the major part of the collection. At present the library has 85,000 printed maps, 54 cartographic manuscripts, and 280 atlases

Microforms

The library has around 500 rolls of Microfilms and 1000 Microfiches. These are preserved in the Rare Books division. The Census of India is one of the most important and rare document available in the form of Microfiches...

CONSERVATION ACTIVITIES

One of the basic functions of the National Library is to conserve the printed heritage for future generations.

For this purpose the library has separate divisions for physical, chemical, reprographic and digital conservation:

- *Physical Conservation*: Books damaged by human error or by natural causes are mended, repaired and bound in the Binding division. Journals are bound by volume.
- *Chemical Conservation*: The Laboratory division of the library, established in 1968, is taking care of the chemical treatment of books. Advanced procedures of chemical treatment are adopted to restore brittle and damaged books. The library is in the process of developing non-chemical treatment system for the preservation of printed materials. An indigenously developed fumigation chamber is being used to destroy the eggs and larvae of insects and termites. Encapsulation is another method of preservation that has been developed by the library.
- *Reprographic Preservation*: Most of the 19th century newspapers, Arabic, Persian and Sanskrit manuscripts have already been microfilmed. 5000 rolls of microfilms are already produced so far by the Reprography division.
- *Digitisation*: The scanning and archiving of rare and brittle books and other documents on compact disc has started. English books and documents published before 1900 and Indian publications preceding 1920 are considered for digitisation. 9140 selected books in Indian and English languages have already been scanned and stored—a total of over 3.2 million pages.

2

Library Marketing and Management

LIBRARY SKILLS AND MANAGERIAL CHALLENGES

Our skills and background as librarians can both help and hinder our managerial exfforts. If we think consciously about these linkages, we can learn to become more effective in any managerial position.

Positive connections include:

- *The ability to collect and analyse information:* Throughout your managerial career, you will need to utilize these skills in activities ranging from creating a budget, to strategic planning, to writing a marketing plan.
- *The urge to share information:* Any organization benefits from the free flow of information; close-mouthed managers foster inefficiency, rumors, and resentment.
- *The ability to organize knowledge:* Again, this will be useful in activities as large as strategic planning and as seemingly small as keeping updated and organized personnel files.
- *The tendency to build networks:* No manager can "go it alone," and librarians' propensity to share information, stories, experiences, and acquired knowledge with one another will stand you in good stead here.
- *The belief in the principle of equity of access and treatment:* As useful when it comes to staff as when dealing with library customers.

On the other hand, tendencies you need to be careful of as a library manager include:

- *The notion that "the patron is always right:"* When you extend your wish to make life comfortable for your patrons to bending over backward to make life easy for your staff, you run the risk of not pushing your people to their fullest.
- *The wish to avoid conflict:* Studies and personality tests consistently show that librarians tend to tip the introverted and conflict-avoiding side of the scale. This is a generalisation, but watch for these

tendencies in yourself and be willing and able to step in to manage conflicts among your employees and with your patrons.

- *Emphasis of the philosophical over the practical:* Library school tends to foster a black-and-white worldview of philosophical idealism; managers eventually need to learn to compromise.

Additional linkages will be emphasized in the appropriate chapters, but always be open to understanding the ways in which your background as a librarian affects your work as a manager. Make a conscious effort to manage as a librarian. Overall, remember that you are a *library* manager, and that the ways in which you manage your people and institution need to be true to the principles and practices of librarianship. Ultimately, working effectively as a library manager demands developing a new way of thinking and behaving, while remembering your roots as a librarian or building a background in librarianship.

MAKING THAT TRANSITION

As you adjust to your management role, the first transition from managed to manager can be the hardest. As a non-management employee, you may have been provided with an orientation, directions, and fairly explicit instructions on your day-to-day duties when settling into a new position.

As a manager, you may be thrown into a new job with little direction or instruction on how to proceed; management positions are often largely what you make of them. Although you will have a broad outline of your administrator's, board's, or institution's expectations, part of your job will actually be to define your own specific responsibilities and role within your department, library, or section.

Even after the first transition or two gives you an idea of what to expect, the transition into any managerial position can be tricky throughout your career. Transitional periods are inevitably stressful for both you and your new staff, as everyone involved is dealing with a fairly major change and needs to renegotiate relationships and work patterns. But while your staff members' daily work will most likely remain relatively constant, providing them with an underlying stability to draw upon while weathering the changes your arrival brings, you will face the additional task of redefining yourself as a supervisor, a department head, or an administrator. The first few months in a managerial position can be critical in establishing your credibility, settling comfortably into your new role, and setting out your management style and strategies.

This transitional period, while difficult, also presents the opportunity to begin as you mean to continue, to build relationships and alliances with your staff, supervisors, and colleagues, and to lay out your vision for your department, section, or organization. It is always harder to switch gears later than to chart your course from the outset. Take time, however, to get to know your staff, their personalities, their strengths, and their weaknesses before launching into a major change initiative. In some ways it can be especially difficult to take over a position from a previous manager who seems to have run the zoo in a less than optimal manner. Library staff will have developed an understandable mistrust of those in a management role.

Much of your time at the outset may be spent undoing the damage your predecessor left behind, rather than in moving forward with your own initiatives and ideas. As one manager survey respondent notes: "Be aware that your staff may not trust you or your motives at first." This can be frustrating, so work on maintaining your own energy and enthusiasm. New library managers often come in brimming with ideas, but need to have the willingness first to learn the library's organizational culture and to lay the groundwork of trust needed for their initiatives' success. Also think about the ways in which succeeding an ineffective manager can actually work in your favour.

Any moves you make may lead to improvements—and there will be a general predisposition towards change. If you were promoted from within, having suffered with the rest, you will also have insight into what not to do when you move into a management role. Another manager survey respondent even explains her theory of management as: "Having seen library management done badly, I try to think: what would my old boss have done–and do the opposite."

One staff survey respondent suggests: "Never forget what it's like to have a bad boss, and don't turn into one yourself." If you have experienced a history of incompetent or ineffective managers, though, it may take you some time to overcome your own distrust of management and realise that you are now one of "them". Librarians who are promoted into a managerial position from within will find that their former coworkers will have particular preconceptions and expectations for their behaviour as a manager, based on past conversations and behaviour as an employee. Your former colleagues may no longer be quite sure how to interact with you. Oregon State University Librarian for Systems Applications says that: "the biggest surprise for me was that people I had worked with for more than five years viewed me as a different person simply because I had become a manager."

They would sometimes agree to concepts that I presented, even though in reality they had very different views on the issue. I found this disconcerting because I wanted and expected them to express their honest opinions. As any manager, your relationships and interactions with non-managerial staff members will inevitably change. Katharine Salzmann, Archivist/Curator of Manuscripts, Southern Illinois University at Carbondale, explains:

"I don't know if it was exactly a surprise, but the biggest adjustment I had to make was simply realizing that I was a 'boss.' I wasn't fully prepared for the role and how people's expectations of me would change, or how my working relationships with individuals would change."

This is not to say that you cannot have good, friendly working relationships with your staff members, but your relationships as manager and managed will tend to take on a different flavour than that of your relationships with your professional peers. You need to consider how important it is to you to be liked, as opposed to being respected as a manager. If you have tended to find most of your friends through work, you may need now to extend that circle outside your institution's walls. If, on the other hand, you come from the outside to assume a management position in a given library, your first step before defining any new goals will be to familiarize yourself with the institution's existing mission and organizational culture, as well as with the people who will be working for you. You will need to settle into your new environment and to give people a chance to settle into the inherent change your arrival brings.

You will of course have your own theories, ideas, and priorities–as well as responsibility for those imposed from above and outside. If you appear to be swooping in with a completely new agenda, however, you will undoubtedly meet with fierce resistance from existing staff. People need a compelling reason to move out of their comfortable routines, and need to feel as if they are a part of any change. Make it a point to learn from and work with your staff from the very beginning.

Realise also that the fact that your administration made the decision to hire from the outside rather than promote from within may mean that it is consciously looking for new perspectives and fresh ideas. Capitalize on this desire for change by enlisting administrative, institutional, and/or board support for your initiatives from the outset. Your goals have a greater chance of success if they receive consistent support throughout the management hierarchy of your organization. Successful management is undoubtedly more complicated than just "doing the opposite" of what your previous less-than-competent boss used to do.

A good first step, though, as you begin defining your role as a manager, is to think back to all of your experiences as someone who has been managed, inside or outside of a library environment. Identify both the role models you do, and those you do not, wish to emulate. Debbie Hackleman notes that "in some cases I learned by observing others–both what worked well and what I would choose to do differently.

Observing negative examples is often quite useful." Of course, it is always easier to identify negative experiences and to dwell on what not to do. This is a useful beginning, and you should always keep your previous managers'–and your own– missteps firmly in mind. Dwelling on the negative, however, fails to provide us with a solid foundation for deciding what *to* do, for making the decisions that help propel both our careers and institutions forward, and for establishing our own management style. The next task, therefore, involves deciding where to go and how to begin. Before implementing any changes, you will need to identify the goals for your institution, section, or department, within the larger goals of the organization, larger institution, or system.

You need to provide yourself and your staff with a larger context for your work, in order to successfully define both what you do and why you do it. Lastly, realise that, in any management situation, you will also be compared to your predecessors. Whether comments tend to run along the lines of: "That's not how Ms. X used to do it," or: "We're so glad not to have to waste our time pleasing Mr. Y anymore," it will take staff some time to settle in and become accustomed to your way of managing things.

Remember, you are not the first person to ever face this transition— and, if you should ever leave your position, your staff will be equally as glad to explain to your successor just what she is doing differently. Do not get hung up on people's tendencies to bring up the past; libraries are long-lived institutions, and each library's history includes a long line of managers and management styles. Focus on carving out your own place and creating your own part of your institution's history.

WHAT A LIBRARY MANAGER DOES

The ways in which library managers spend their time of course vary among institutions and different levels of management—and in a sense, this is what this entire book is about! But there are some similarities among the roles and responsibilities of most managers. The basic job of any manager is to direct her resources and people towards accomplishing the defined goals of the institution.

Higher-up managers may be responsible for defining these larger goals; section or department managers may set goals for their part of the whole in terms of the larger mission of the library; and libraries, as service institutions, need overall to define and to prioritize these goals in terms of the needs of their patrons or customers. As a library division manager at the Josephine County Library System, Oregon, explains: "Fight for the patrons, and every decision that is made should be made because it will make it easier for the patron." Any traditional managerial activity fits into this broad definition. You supervise and evaluate library staff in order to ensure that they work effectively to provide the services your patrons need and expect.

You keep the technology and facilities in your institution humming along so that customers have a comfortable, safe, and useful place to work, as well as the tools to meet their informational needs. You help create a culture of customer service, realizing that your approach and that of your employees goes a long way towards creating an atmosphere in which you can effectively serve your community.

The way in which you manage people largely defines their attitudes towards their work, which in turn defines how smoothly the organization runs. You hold the authority to make decisions within your institution, and are responsible for making those decisions in the way that will best accomplish institutional goals. You are responsible for ranking the importance of various activities in terms of these goals, for prioritizing goals themselves, and for allocating resources to best accomplish library goals.

WOMEN IN MANAGEMENT

Although librarianship is still a female-dominated profession, many observers have noted that men hold a disproportionate number of administrative positions, that they tend to receive higher compensation than women in the field, and that subfields of the profession with a higher concentration of male workers tend to be higher-paid. These discrepancies are beginning to change in some subsets of the profession; female *Association of Research Libraries* (ARL) directors, for example, now make slightly more than their male counterparts, although there are fewer of them overall. This change in the salary structure of the top positions at large research institutions, however, fails to extend to other management positions and library environments. Female library managers can network with others to work to conquer these and other challenges. ALA's Library Administration and Management Association, for example, has a women administrator's discussion group.

ALA also has a *Committee on the Status of Women in Librarianship* (COSWL), which has among its goals that of helping women advance into managerial positions, and maintains a Feminist Task Force. Although still under represented, especially in "top" jobs, relative to their presence in the profession, women make up an ever-increasing proportion of those in library management positions. This in turn results in an ever-increasing number of other female managers with whom you can network. You can also network with female managers in other professions; there are a number of organizations for professional women that will help you. Women are also more likely to face interruption of their careers for family reasons.

The lower pay in librarianship relative to that in many other professions means that female librarians may be more likely to take time for child care, elder care, and other personal responsibilities than will their more highly paid non-library partners. Work to create the same flexibility and opportunity for your staff as you would appreciate from your institution. Be open to job sharing, flexible schedules, and telecommuting options, when the type of position and an individual's personality and work ethic make these ideas a reasonable possibility. A number of library responsibilities can be effectively carried out off-site, including functions such as collection development and Web design.

Libraries that fail to support flexible work options risk losing some of their best employees. Further, be supportive of pay equity efforts; do not dismiss them now that your own salary has increased with the assumption of your managerial duties. Some argue that women have a distinct managerial style, that their ways of interacting with people inevitably differ from the "male" style of management and communication. Depending on who you read, you will find arguments that female styles of management are either a better or a less effective way of managing. Remember that you will need to develop your own style—as appropriate to your organizational culture, your staff, your own personality, and your library's goals.

NON–LIBRARIANS AS LIBRARY MANAGERS

Non-MLS holders face particular challenges as library managers. Those new to the library environment may find that, although their existing managerial skills are transferable, it still takes time to understand and fit into the library world. Paraprofessional mid-level managers may encounter a prejudice for the MLS among degreed administrators and other department heads. Non-MLS library managers must develop a deep understanding of the functions of their institution, especially of the particular section or project for which they are responsible.

As one manager survey respondent stresses:

"I think it is essential for a library manager to know the basics of the functions he or she is managing. For example, I wasn't familiar with the specific tool my cataloger used at my last job, but at least I knew cataloging, so I could help her when needed and know when she was or wasn't doing her job."

You need to understand the work your staff is doing in order to properly evaluate whether they are doing this work well and efficiently. The process of developing this insight may be as simple as taking the time to observe and ask questions, or it may take some reading or coursework, depending on your situation and background. While MLS librarians value the degree, they also generally value experience and expertise. The best way to impart that value and to elicit their respect is by example.

PARAPROFESSIONAL MANAGERS

Paraprofessional managers occupy a unique place in a library's hierarchy. Although you may fill a managerial position that appears in an equivalent level on an organization chart as your MLS peers, you may have a more difficult time promoting your ideas to those administrators that have an unconscious preference for the degree—and you may receive a lower salary.

This observation is not intended to rekindle the ongoing debate over the value of the MLS, but rather to make you aware of some of the issues you might face as a paraprofessional manager in many library environments. If your organization will help cover the costs of a degree and you can see a clear career path for yourself, you can consider going back to school and earning your MLS. The fantastic combination of a library degree and your previous library and management experience should equate to higher salaries and more options in your future, if you intend to stay in the library field. Many librarian managers got their start in paraprofessional positions and then earned the degree after working in the field for a number of years, enabling them to move up and to advance their careers in library management. In any case, realise that library school, while it may prepare people to be librarians, rarely prepares them for a career in management. Your MLS counterparts have no particular advantage *as managers.* The library skills and outlook that help create a good library manager, further, are by no means unique to degree holders.

VOLUNTEER MANAGERS

You may be entering a library management position in a small and/or remote library as a volunteer manager, on a full or parttime basis, without specific library experience—and without compensation! Much of the information in this book will also be applicable in a volunteer situation, but you will need to adapt any advice, as appropriate, to smaller libraries and to your unique circumstances. As a volunteer manager, you also may be responsible for all library activities, from organizing a collection, to checking out materials, to managing others.

Non-MLS library managers thrown into or assuming one of these library management positions should investigate Dave Sutton's *So You're Going to Run a Library: A Library Management Primer*, which is a useful guide for any manager new to libraries, especially in small institutions. If you are a volunteer manager, congratulations on feeling so strongly about the value of libraries that you are willing to donate your time and effort to keeping one going in your community or in your institution.

One of your first steps should be to try to find a more experienced library manager to serve as your mentor and to help answer your inevitable questions about both librarianship and management. Again, here, a willingness to learn and to grow in your position will serve you well. Part of being a good volunteer manager may also include inspiring others to volunteer, as well as constructively directing and praising their energies.

NON–LIBRARIANS (NEW TO LIBRARIES)

If you enter library management from another profession, you may be taken aback by the amount of controversy the appointment of a non-librarian to a library administrative–especially a director–position in a larger institution can cause. This can be especially difficult if you begin calling yourself or are hired as a "librarian." As a non-MLS administrator, realise that you have walked into an ongoing argument about the importance of the MLS degree.

Some of the professionals who have spent the time, money, and effort to earn a master's in library and information science feel strongly about the value of the degree, pointing out that non-M.D.s who work in doctor's offices are never called doctors; public school employees without degrees and certification are not considered qualified to work as teachers. Institutions that call non-degree holders "librarians" and award them with administrative posts, in this view, merely contribute to an erosion of the value of the MLS degree.

This feeling is exacerbated by a general public perception that all library workers are "librarians" and questions such as: "You have to have a master's degree for this?!" as well as an ongoing internecine argument about the value of the degree and about the quality and rigour of some graduate programmes. Your assumption of an administrative position can stir up all of these feelings and arguments, but realizing that the tension stems from a number of factors can help you take criticism less personally and prepare yourself to field people's concerns.

If there seems to be an argument or an undercurrent of feeling among staff that you are less entitled to your position due to your lack of an MLS, you may begin to feel defensive about your ability to do the job.

This is a situation in which you will do best by expressing your willingness to learn from your staff. As Mary Pergander, Head Librarian, Lake Bluff Public Library, Illinois, notes of her pre-MLS management experiences: "I did not know as much about libraries as my staff did. I trusted them to teach me, they trusted me to lead them. It worked out fine." Although you may understand the basic similarities among the duties involved in administrative positions in different environments, only time will demonstrate your ability to serve effectively as a *library* administrator. Acknowledging the strengths and knowledge base of your employees, while also demonstrating the unique perspective and skills you bring to your position, is the best combination to begin winning over your staff.

Any good manager learns from her staff in any environment; you will need to do so more overtly, and will need to rely on your professional staff in areas where your knowledge is lacking. Make a point of learning about the issues that affect today's libraries. Keep up to date, for example, by reading Weblogs and library news sites each morning. Start with major resources such as *American Libraries* and *Library Journal*, each of which posts breaking library related news stories online.

Then, branch out further to include a couple of resources in your library's area of specialty. Librarians value information and the informed. Your interest in issues important to the field will help you assimilate into the library culture. As one respondent to the staff survey states: "My current manager does not have an MLS, nor does he have much knowledge of libraries. While I do appreciate his dedication to his work and his willingness to take action, I wish he would take more opportunities to understand and observe our work." Also be sure to join relevant local and national associations and to network with other managers, library workers, and librarians.

MANAGING YOURSELF

Beyond this commitment to learning, there are also a number of personal qualities that will help you become a better manager—as well as those you should try to curb.

Habits and patterns to overcome include:

- Procrastination. Many libraries are able to hum along for quite a while even when some managerial tasks are put off, masking the fact that their internal foundations are crumbling. Do not let a façade of well being allow you to put off potentially unpleasant tasks such as managing conflicts or making needed budget cuts.
- Impatience. Although in certain situations impatience can be quite useful in getting tasks done on a timely fashion, it has little value when dealing with library staff. As Amanda E. Standerfer, Library Director, Helen Matthes Library, Effingham, Illinois, suggests: "I would tell a new library manager to be patient. Not everything is going to work out in the first few months or years. I wanted to fix everything right away, and it just wasn't possible."
- Defensiveness. New managers sometimes develop an unfortunate tendency to take comments personally, or to jump to lay blame on others. While defensiveness may grow out of uneasiness in your new position, your staff will be more concerned about your behaviour than the reasons behind your actions. Accept that you will make mistakes; be willing to take blame as well as credit and to learn from your errors.
- Miscommunication. Effective communication goes beyond communicating clearly and providing staff with pertinent information, and includes watching your own behaviour and communication style. There is no room for sarcasm towards your staff, for example.

Habits to cultivate include:

- *Listening*. You need to pay attention to, and learn from, your staff, peers, customers, and administration. As Kari Baumann, Branch Manager, Centennial Park Branch Library, Greeley, Colorado, says: "I think the most important thing any new manager can do is to listen—to her staff, and to library staff that she doesn't supervise—to understand the organization as a whole."
- *Assertiveness and self-confidence*. Many new library managers have difficulty transitioning, not only into dealing with staff as a manager rather than as a peer, but into dealing with their own bosses and colleagues in a self-confident and effective manner. Take charge from the beginning. Start out as you mean to continue. Understand the power that you have in the organization, and do not be reluctant to use it to influence people and influence change in your library. Librarians with a tendency to be less extroverted can find this more

difficult, but a certain level of assertiveness is necessary in order to maintain your influence in the organization.

- *A willingness to be proactive*. Why wait for problems to pile up or for complaints to find you? Look for ways to improve library service, working conditions for staff, workflow, or funding, and then act on achieving your goals in these areas.
- *Communication*. The importance of maintaining open and frequent communication with anyone you supervise—or report to.
- *Lifelong learning*. Library manager can afford to stagnate in her position.

People skills are essential to any effective manager—especially in libraries!—and much of the discussion here and throughout the book reflects that fact. Of course people skills are also important in most subfields of librarianship, but they are especially necessary for managers in any library setting, type, or department.

CHARTING A MANAGEMENT PATH

The earlier you start consciously charting your career path as a library manager, the more successful you will be in your career as a whole. Some schools are proactively meeting the concerns of students seeking additional education in the management aspects of library science.

If you are just joining the profession and you have a clear vision of a library career path that includes management, you can investigate graduate library and information science programmes that offer a heavier emphasis on the administrative side of the field. Several schools now have joint programmes that offer a heavier exposure to the management aspects of librarianship; Kent State and UCLA, for example, each offer a joint MLIS/MBA degree programme, which can be especially useful to those whose career goals include management of a very large institution.

Mentors and Role Models

Earlier, the discussion focused on deciding whom *not* to emulate during your career as a library manager. Equally, if not more important, are the qualities of those you do choose to emulate. If you have lacked good managerial role models in your career so far, you can consider enrolling in a formal mentoring programme–either within your own institution, or one sponsored by a library related or other organization. Alternatively, seek out more informal mentors – online, through networking at local events, through contacting people writing on issues that interest you.

Seek out expertise wherever it lies, and be willing to ask your mentors for their support and help. Realise also that it can be useful to find multiple mentors to help you with the various facets of and different decisions involved in your position. Everyone has his or her own area of expertise, and a mentor can be anyone with experience or knowledge that you lack. Author and Webmaster Priscilla Shontz advises: "Find yourself some good mentors, either at your organization or elsewhere. This is important in any position, but in a management position you can sometimes feel very alone–especially if you manage a small library where you are the only manager. It can be incredibly helpful to have friends, mentors, and colleagues to whom you can turn when you have a question or when you just need to vent! For example, if you manage a branch library, you may want to develop relationships with other branch managers, so you can ask for advice when facing a decision or problem. Library activist suggests that new managers "find a mentor to help show you the ropes in your organization and give you pointers on management skills."

A one or two year graduate programme, of course, can be hard pressed to fit in all the coursework needed to prepare someone to become a librarian, let alone to teach management skills as well. However, the lack of practical information presented in even the most basic library management courses was overwhelmingly cited as a problem by manager survey respondents—and, given the predicted upcoming wave of library retirements, this should be a concern for schools charged with preparing future library managers to fill these anticipated upper-level vacancies.

Many respondents to the manager survey suggested that more hands on courses would have been useful, especially those incorporating role-playing, jobshadowing, and/or presentations and advice from actual working managers in different library settings. Others suggested internships or other real-world activities.

A number of library managers do take advantage of continuing education opportunities to fill in the gaps left by their alma maters, or to build up their skills in specific areas. As a manager, you will likely need to take responsibility for your own ongoing learning and professional development. There may be no one above you that will suggest you take a class, attend a conference, or otherwise push yourself professionally, whereas as a non-management librarian you may have been used to your supervisor suggesting that you engage in these activities.

Never fall into the trap of assuming that, because you have progressed to a certain point in your career, you need no further professional development. Realise also that more official professional development activities such as workshops and meetings serve as excellent networking as well as professional development opportunities, and can keep you energized and focused on your career and your profession. Cessa Vichi, a library division manager at the Josephine County Library System, says: Attending any training is always beneficial for ideas, new ways of looking at old problems, inspiration and growth as a leader.

As a leader, the responsibility for organizational/division growth falls on you. New ideas, fresh input, and different approaches are vital to learning and growing as a leader." You can locate official professional development and management training opportunities in a variety of ways, from reading your local library system's newsletter to attending ALA conferences. Also, be open to learning through your professional reading. Professional development includes all of your lifelong learning, from reading to on-the-job experience. Lifelong learning means precisely that: learning through all of your experiences, whether planned or not.

Always try to think beyond your current job, and about how you can learn, grow, and move forward in your library career. Take advantage of professional development and networking opportunities. Look at these not as an imposition on your time, but as an opportunity to reenergize, learn, and open to new possibilities. Libraries, especially today, do not remain stagnant–you need to stretch yourself to keep up! Warren Bennis and Robert Thomas note: "The ability to learn is a defining characteristic of being human; the ability to continue learning is an essential skill of leadership. When leaders lose that ability, they inevitably falter.

When any of us lose that ability, we no longer grow."2 As a librarian, you possess an inherent advantage over managers in other types of organizations. A major task of any manager is to identify and assimilate the information that will help her do her job. Who better to take on that task than information professionals? The only difference here is that, instead of compiling this information on behalf of your patrons, you are doing so for yourself and as is relevant in your own context. Most managers are made, not born, and you can use your library skills to help make your own way.

QUALITY MANAGEMENT APPROACHES

Quality management approaches can be categorised broadly into three stages according to the evolution of management control. Management can implement control before an activity commences, while the activity occurs, or after the activity has been completed. Consequently, three types of control are feedforward, concurrent and feedback. The most desirable type of management control is feedforward control that is futuredirected and takes place in advance of the actual activity.

Feedforward control is advantageous because it allows management to prevent anticipated problems rather than having to cure them later and to avoid wasting resources. Concurrent control, as its name implies, takes place while an activity is in progress. When control is enacted while the activity is being performed, management can correct problems before they become too costly. The most conventional means of control relies on feedback. The feedback control takes place after the activity.

However, a disadvantage of this approach is that the damage will have already occurred by the time that the manager has the information to take corrective actions. Consequently, feedforward control is the most economic approach and can meet the requirement of customers, followed by concurrent control and feedback control, respectively. Interestingly, quality management approaches developed and applied to assess and improve product quality can be related to types of management control from the perspective of an open system. Quality management approaches were originally developed as being product oriented. Feedback control, an inspection based quality control approach, was introduced to detect inferior products at the after production stage. Realising that quality could not be improved by merely inspecting the finished product, subsequent efforts switched the emphasis of quality management from inspection to process control: from feedback control stage to concurrent control stage.

The underlying premise regarding quality in the concurrent control stage is that quality is equivalent to meeting or exceeding customer expectations. Manufacturing products that reflect the diverse needs of customers, is more of a function of good design than of good control of a process. Therefore, quality management has gradually shifted to emphasis on the design phase: from concurrent control stage to feedforward control stage.

Quality by Inspection

The inspection based system was perhaps the first scientifically designed quality control system to evaluate quality. The system is applied to incoming raw materials and parts for use as inputs for production and/or finished products. Under this system, some quality characteristics are examined, measured and compared with required specifications to assess conformity. Therefore, the inspection based system is a screening process that merely isolates conforming from non-conforming products without having any direct mechanism to reduce defects. Reducing the damage to final products, sampling plans were developed to control product quality. Although an effective technique, a quality control system based on sampling inspection does not directly achieve customer satisfaction and continuous improvement. Producing fewer defects through process improvement is the only means of reducing defects.

QUALITY BY PROCESS CONTROL

Defects inevitably add to the production cost and waste resources. Therefore, a business strives for zero defects. The quality management system based on sampling inspections has been replaced by the approach of continuously improving the process. This concept, as pioneered by Deming, moves from detecting defects to preventing them and continuing with process improvement to meeting and exceeding customer requirements on a continuous basis. The continuous cycle of process improvement is based on the scientific method for addressing problems, commonly referred to as the Deming cycle.

Deming's approach consists of four basic stages:

- A plan of what to do;
- Do or carry out the plan;
- Study what has done; and
- Act to prevent errors or improve the process.

The planning stage consists of studying the current situation, gathering data, and planning for improvement.

Related activities include:

- Defining the process, its inputs, outputs, customers, and suppliers;
- Understanding customer expectations;
- Identifying problems;
- Testing theories of causes; and
- Developing solutions.

In the do stage, the plan is implemented on a trial basis to evaluate a proposed solution and provide objective data. The study stage determines whether or not the trial plan is working correctly and if any further problems or opportunities are identified. In the final stage, act, the final plan is implemented and the improvements become standardised and implemented continuously. This process then returns to the plan stage for further diagnosis and improvement.

The Deming Cycle can enhance communication between the staff involved and help employees to use the wheel to improve processes. Some of the specific tools used to improve processes are control charts, process capability studies, seven tools, seven new tools, and seven creativity tools. However, the appropriate tools must be applied for the specified purpose. For example, cause and effect diagrams and process flow charts could be more appropriate during the planning stage of the Deming wheel, whereas control charts may be most appropriate during the stage of checking.

QUALITY BY DESIGN

The Deming approach shifted the focus of quality management a step back from inspection to process control. The approach of quality by design makes a further step back from process to design. By definition, Quality by design implies that quality must be built in early in the development and design stage. By doing so, the final product can satisfy the customers.

Two important techniques for designing quality products are:

- Quality function deployment (QFD) and
- Failure Mode and Effect Analysis (FMEA).

Quality function deployment is a structured approach that:

- Identifies and ranks the relative importance of customer requirements;

- Identifies design parameters that contribute to the customer requirements;
- Estimates the relationship between design parameters and customer requirements and among different design parameters; and
- Sets target values for the design parameters to best satisfy customer requirements.

A QFD matrix is frequently used to translate prioritised customer requirements into identifiable and measurable product specifications and engineering requirements to reduce functional variation and costs, thereby facilitating the decision-makers in making designrelated decisions. Many investigators have successfully applied QFD in product and service design. Failure Mode and Effect Analysis is a methodical approach to examine a proposed design for possible ways in which failure can occur.

FMEA consists of:

- Identifying and listing modes of failure and the subsequent faults;
- Assessing the probability of these faults;
- Assessing the probability that the faults are detected;
- Assessing the severity of the consequences of the faults;
- Calculating a measure of the risk;
- Ranking the faults on the basis of the risk;
- Attempting to resolve the high-risk problems; and
- Verifying the effectiveness of the action by using a revised measure of risk.

In addition to providing preliminary information on reliability prediction, product and process design, FMEA helps engineers identify potential problems in the product earlier, thereby avoiding costly changes or reworks at later stages. Closely scrutinising quality management reveals that many techniques are based on experience derived from manufacturing tangible products. Whether or not quality management practices can be transferred to a service industry delivering intangible services has received considerable attention.

Many investigators confer that:

- The service and manufacturing industries differ in terms of the characteristics of quality,
- Different criteria must be used for measuring these industries, and
- The focus of quality management is rather different than similar.

The final manufacturing products can be measured objectively, while the quality can be managed by output control. Meanwhile, the deliverables of services are frequently intangible, which is difficult to measure objectively. In addition to the simultaneously delivery and consumption of services, the quality certainly cannot be managed by either output control or process control. Brophy and Coulling indicated that with the broad applications in the service sector, the sector has come to the recognition that some aspects of quality management must be approached somewhat differently in the service industry. The most distinguishing characteristic between service and manufacturing industries is that in the former, there is usually a direct interaction between the customer and the service. Libraries and information services have intensive direct interaction and also indirect contact with the customers. Because of the immediacy of the interface, libraries must develop their own framework when integrating quality management approaches into libraries.

MANAGEMENT'S USE OF MARKETING RESEARCH

In spite of the rapid growth of marketing research, many companies still fail to use it sufficiently or correctly. Several factors can stand in the way of its greater utilization.

1. A narrow conception of marketing research. Many managers see marketing research as only a fact-finding operation. The marketing researcher is supposed to design a questionnaire, choose a sample conduct interviews, and report results, often without being given a careful definition of the problem or of the decision alternatives facing management. As a result, some fact finding fails to be useful. This reinforces management's idea of the limited usefulness of some marketing research.
2. Uneven calibre of marketing researchers. Some managers view marketing research as little better than a clerical activity and reward it as such. Poorly qualified marketing researchers are hired, and their weak training and deficient creativity lead to unimpressive results. The disappointing results reinforce management's prejudice against expecting too much from marketing research. Management continues to pay low salaries, perpetuating the basic difficulty.
3. Late and occasional erroneous findings by marketing research. Managers want quick results that are accurate and conclusive. But good marketing research takes time and money. If they can't perceive the difference between quality and shoddy research, managers become disappointed, and they lower their opinion of the value of marketing research. This is especially a problem in conducting marketing research in foreign countries.
4. Intellectual differences. Intellectual divergences between the mental styles of line managers and marketing researchers often get in the way of productive relationships. The marketing researcher's report may seem abstract, complicated, and tentative, while the line manager wants concreteness, simplicity, and certainty. Yet in the more progressive companies, marketing researchers are increasingly being included as members of the product management team, and their influence on marketing strategy in growing.

LEADERSHIP AND MANAGEMENT IN LIBRARY

Leadership and management are two terms that are often used interchangeably. In fact, they describe entirely different concepts, as leadership is more than a component of the functions of management. Management is the process of administering and coordinating resources to ensure than an organisation accomplishes its mission and goals. *Library and information science* (*LIS*) has a managerial focus; librarians manage the infrastructure of a library: its collections, staff, technology, and facilities. For this reason, the interconnection between management and leadership is the domain of LIS theory and practice.

The purpose of leadership is to challenge the status quo as libraries undergo a transition in organisational culture, the services they offer, and workforce restructuring as they try to better fulfill the organisational and broader institutional mission. Management, on the other hand, prepares the infrastructure for that transition. As early as 1950s, the term *managerial leadership* was coined, but its definition was imprecise. "No definition of the phrase 'managerial leadership' has gained general acceptance. In fact, it is often referred to but left undefined" or merely equated to particular leadership theories and styles.

The term recognizes that leadership is not exclusively a top-down process between the *boss* as a leader and subordinates. This paper, which aligns with the programme in managerial leadership in the information professions at Simmons College, views managerial leadership as encompassing an examination of leaders, followers, the interaction between the two groups, and, in this context, leadership becomes a process whereby people influence others to develop, accept, and carry out a shared vision that guides future actions of the organisation.

As a result, that process is longitudinal and involves events. Because leadership is not always effective or positive, it should not automatically be assumed that goals and events are always successfully met or that staff members are sufficiently motivated or inspired to challenge themselves and others. The purpose of this paper is to build on the international research agenda that Candy Schwartz and I presented in 2008 and that illustrates that LIS research needs to go beyond a preoccupation with understanding the style, personality, traits, and other characteristics of the boss and that person's influence on organisational dynamics and performance.

LEADERSHIP MANAGEMENT

In addition to focusing on a shared vision, leadership is about giving people confidence to meet organisational expectations and to serve as change agents. It also encourages them to seek, be given, and benefit from team coaching and mentoring aimed at enhancing their knowledge, skills, abilities, effectiveness, and commitment to the transformation process. A library's staff might consist of both followers and leaders who are willing to collaborate with other institutional partners.

As well, the director, if that person is truly a leader, might be more so within the organisation than in representing the library to other stakeholders. With so many libraries organised into teams or small groups and involved in managing change; with new staff members expected to work together to plan, implement, administer, and evaluate services; and with libraries forging new partnerships at the institutional, local, and other levels, more librarians are becoming increasingly interested in knowing about and applying leadership theories, styles, traits, and roles.

They are also trying to develop their leadership potential. Within this context, there is much interest in transformational leadership and emotional intelligence, which helps leaders move beyond basic 'people skills' to understanding how one's own reactions and feelings impact how one is perceived by others.

Leaders and managers need to understand their own emotions and recognize and understand the feelings of those around them. Leaders are more successful when they pay attention to their social interactions with others in the workplace and the impact they as leaders have on those around them. It is also important for leaders to understand the impact that others' emotions have on them. When leaders are aware of the emotional side of the workplace, they are better able to create a working environment that encourages excellence.

As librarians gain an understanding of such theories, it is important to remember that, as Peter Northouse points out, leadership has 'many different meanings;' this is evident when people "finish the sentence 'Leadership is....'" Their responses might ignore social influence, add new elements, or confuse leadership with someone holding a managerial position. They might also fail to recognize that there are also spiritual, legacy, moral, ethical, charismatic, and other types of leadership. Each of these areas actually produces separate leadership theories that have been long investigated but rarely connected to LIS.

CONTEXT

Even though this paper focuses on topical areas for future research and selected methodologies, it is important to remember that methodologies do not frame a research study. Research, which engages in problem solving, is shaped by a reflective enquiry. These components, as well as the study procedures and data quality, comprise a framework in which each component should be bonded to the others through, what David R. Krathwohl calls, a 'chain of reasoning.' That 'chain,' he points out, 'is only as strong as its weakest link' and 'all links...should be built to about the same strength.' He further explains that, "as the work load is picked up by the first link and passed to successive links, the work load—and therefore the nature of each link—is determined by the previous links."

Furthermore, "where several links together join those above and below them, there may be trade offs to compensate for weaknesses. It is beyond the scope of this paper, however, to present and relate the entire chain of reasoning. Still, I would be remiss if I did not underscore the importance of the theoretical framework. Vincent A. Anfara, Jr. and Norma T. Mertz provide an excellent overview of theatrical frameworks and the impact of 'good and useful' theory on the chain of reasoning. In the case of managerial leadership, like other areas within LIS, there are numerous theories, some of which fit a given problem statement and set of objectives better than others.

One such theory might be constructive development theory, which relates directly to leadership and which offers a way to view the complex problems that organisations face from multiple perspectives. This theory describes "how adults develop more complex and comprehensive ways of making sense of themselves and their experience." Another concept relates to trust, which is an essential component in motivating or inspiring others and which is more than a trait.

RESEARCH DESIGNS IN LEADERSHIP

As a prelude to methodologies, research designs for leadership research might call for a longitudinal study and a comparison of several organisations. Widely used research designs centre on either a case study or the application of grounded theory. A case study is a means "for learning about a complex instance, based on a comprehensive understanding of that instance obtained by extensive description and analysis of that instance taken as a whole and in its context."

Grounded theory, on the other hand, "is a method for discovering theories, concepts, hypotheses, and propositions directly from data, rather than from a priori assumptions, other research, or existing theoretical frameworks." Theory emerges from, and is grounded in, the data themselves.

DATA-GATHERING TECHNIQUES

This part focuses on some of the most prevalent methodologies used in leadership research, especially within LIS. As such, it builds from Karin Klenke's work on leadership research.

It is increasingly common for researchers to apply qualitative methods. The accompanying table offers examples of some methodologies applicable to the study of leadership in LIS that will not be discussed in the body of this paper. The sources in that table came from an extensive review of the vast literature on leadership produced outside LIS.

The largest number of research studies related to leadership involves the distribution of a self report survey or questionnaire. Such surveys are often in paper and pencil format, although more recently Web-based surveys have appeared with increasing frequency. The survey might involve the use of a predeveloped, behaviour ased leadership assessment tool that is distributed to those heading the organisation or to subordinates who are asked to evaluate the director or boss as a leader or their immediate supervisor.

As an alternative, surveys might probe respondent preference for a particular leadership theory or style and ask them to rate themselves or identify the most important attributes for individuals in their position. Complementary to a questionnaire that is mailed or otherwise distributed, investigators might use personal or focus groups interviews. Responses to open ended questions might be subjected to content analysis, which "is a set of procedures for transforming non-structured information into a format that allows analysis." On occasion, biographies of people identified as leaders have been developed and their content subjected to analysis for discussions of leadership.

Available historical records, however, might focus more on their accomplishments than the story behind those accomplishments: how did the individual coopt and navigate different stakeholders and the staff to bring about that change? If a shared vision emerged, how was it developed? Some other means of data collection include an analysis of citation patterns of a body of works on leadership and a characterization of the most cited works and authors, as well as the age of the cited material. Additional insights might be gained from a consideration of the journal's impact factor and the number of copies of a work that libraries hold.

Assuming the availability of a body of independent studies focused on the same aspect of leadership and that describes the research design, the methodologies and data collection instruments used, information about the population and sample, and so on, meta analysis might be appropriate. Such analysis refers to a set of statistical procedures used to summarize and integrate those studies. It reveals sources of bias and is helpful for posing research questions for future study.

Among other things, it cannot exceed the limits of what the researchers report. Another method, known as the Delphi study or technique, is a procedure relies on the use of sequential questionnaires in which experts share their perspectives on issues. The Delphi technique is not necessarily designed to generate consensus, but it does involve a systematic refinement of prior responses. It has been applied to seeing which leadership attributes are most critical for future managerial leaders.

Concept Mapping

Concept mapping is both a process for representing data in the form of pictures or maps and a structured methodology for organising the ideas of a group or organisation. The goal is to bring together groups of multiple "stakeholders ... and help them rapidly form a common framework that can be used for planning, evaluation, or both." The maps represent the groups' thinking about a topic, show how their ideas are related to each other, and, in general, indicate "which ideas are more relevant, important, or appropriate."

Interviews and other techniques might produce datasets that might be examined by the use of concept maps. These maps provide a graphic illustration of patterns among the findings. Jan Schilling, for instance, takes interview data about negative leadership and produced maps that show the antecedents of such leadership, negative leadership behaviours, and the consequences of negative leadership.

Simulation and Scenarios

A simulation study, as G. Yukl explains, involves a realistic task that continues for several periods of time and asks participants to assume the role of top executives in an organisation and to engage in team and organisational learning. Simulation "is also relevant for understanding how collective learning occurs among people whose decisions and actions affect organisational processes and performance." Instead of doing a simulation exercise, researchers might develop scenarios that make projections for the next fifteen years; forecaster Joseph P. Martino indicates that the accuracy in predicting what will likely occur declines dramatically with a longer time frame.

Scenarios, as a prime technique of future studies, have long been used by government planners, corporate managers and military analysts as powerful tools to aid in decision making in the face of uncertainty. The idea behind them is to establish thinking about possible futures which can minimi[z]e surprises and broaden the span of managers' thinking about different possibilities.

They recommend that the number of scenarios not exceed four and that any scenario should meet criteria such as:

- *Plausibility* (each is capable of happening),
- *Differentiation* (each differs from the others and together they offer multiple futures),
- *Decision-making utility* (each offers insights into the future that help in planning and decision-making), and
- *Challenging* (each challenges conventional wisdom about the future).

RESEARCH AGENDA

The accompanying figure, which updates the depiction that Schwartz and I created, centres on three broad areas that relate to planning:

- Accomplishments (translating vision into effective organisational performance);

- People (creating an organisational climate that values staff and inspires them); and
- Transformation abilities (focusing on the change process that brings people together to accomplish the organisation's mission and goals—preparing the organisation of the future).

These areas match those that guide the doctoral programme in managerial leadership in the information professions (Simmons), which the Institute of Museum and Library Services has funded since 2005 with two multi year grants. Those areas, originally modeled by the National Centre for Health care Leadership, cover twenty five distinct leadership competencies. Under each of the broad areas, numerous topic areas emerge.

At the same time, relationships among the areas might be probed. As directors or other members of the senior management team retire or depart, their replacement might be someone who serves on an interim basis. Are such people leaders or caretakers? The answer might take into account the library but also engagement beyond the library, transformation abilities, mentoring, and talent management. Focusing solely on talent management, many businesses engage in succession management or planning, but do libraries?

Succession planning and management are not synonymous with mentoring. In some countries, if there is leadership, it might be characterized as autocratic. Such leadership merits analysis. Finally, various aspects of the figure might be probed in the present recession as libraries make significant decisions about collections and staff that will likely have a long-term impact. Turning to other topics, James G. Neal discusses 'feral library professionals,' which refers to the hiring of more people into traditional and non-traditional library positions who do not have the credentialed degree from an accredited library school programme.

Comparative case studies might analyse the emergence of leadership in organisations that employ both feral and non-feral professionals and that include staff who represent different generations. How cohesive are staff within and across departments? Do they share a common vision—do they need to share one? Studies might probe LIS educational programmes and see whether they incorporate leadership as a student learning outcome, one that reflects what students have learned throughout their programme of study and demonstrates what they can apply upon graduation.

Some other possible topics include the role of power in effective leadership, the major trends in making leadership effective, the communication networks of leaders, transformational leadership and its relationship, for instance, to

- Emotional intelligence, which deals with one's ability to manage emotions and relationships and to use this ability to advance the organisation's mission and goals. Emotional intelligence presumably requires *sense giving* or shaping how people understand themselves, their work, and others engaged in that work.

- Resonant leadership, which focuses on self awareness and self renewal, and which enables individuals to recognize and cope with work stress.
- Distributed or shared leadership, which views leadership as more than a top-down approach. Leadership moves up the organisation as well and is distributed among a number of people working in teams and groups.
- Servant leadership, which recognizes that leadership is not confined to those in formal managerial positions and who lead as a way to extend service to others. The servant leader focuses on the needs and the development of followers.

Recognizing that libraries serve multicultural communities, employ a diverse staff, and deal with myriad stakeholders, it is critical to assess different leadership theories, recognizing the strengths and weaknesses of each. Many of the prevailing theorists have not considered how multiculturalism influences what they propose. Perhaps the best illustration of this comes from Linda Sue Warner and Keith Grint, who adopt a historical perspective and compare American Indian and western approaches and perspectives on leadership. There are differences between the practice of leadership in a tribal setting and in other organisational settings.

EXAMPLE

Although library directors cannot be equated with the president of the United States and other heads of government, political commentators have identified areas in which the leadership of those aspiring to be president might be probed. Prompted by the lack of penetrating questions raised in presidential debate and the quality of the responses, David Gergen and Andy Zelleke identify a series of important questions that deal with leadership and that require answers of more than a number or brief response. Their categories and questions have been reorganised and combined with the categories that Jack and Suzy Welch would like considered.

The revamped questionnaire was pre-tested with one university library director and one library consultant. Based on their comments the questionnaire was revised. As of this time, the author of this paper is conducting a study to fine-tune the instrument and to gauge the responses of some library leaders. Instead of presenting preliminary data, this part probes relevant methodologies that might be used to address the open-ended questions and determine the relative rating of the categories. The methodology part of a hypothetical study might be based on a survey that is most likely administered in the form of an interview, either in person or by telephone.

Directors might be unwilling to devote the time necessary to complete a paper and pencil survey or be unwilling to write detailed responses to each question. It might be difficult to find a time when five to ten directors could meet and participate in a focus group interview. For additional data collection, the investigator might ask for historical documentation or visit the institutional repositories of selected institutions to gather data for event history analysis, assuming such information has been gathered and is publicly available.

Interview results might be analysed in terms of grounded theory and content analysis. The rating of the categories on a seven point scale might be visualized in terms of concept mapping, and such mapping might also apply to the responses to the various questions within a category, especially if responses can be gathered from the same scale. A follow up study might concentrate on selected categories and probe responses more deeply.

For instance, under 'Coalition Building/Advocacy,' participants might meet and be asked for an example of when they became a catalyst who brought groups with polarized opinions together so that all voices were at the table. The examples generated might be cast in terms of a concept map, or the investigator could make the topics recurring most frequently and pursue them more with the Delphi technique. A different study might recast question responses to the initial study or one focusing on selected categories as scenarios or as simulation exercises. It is also possible to take selected responses from the first study and select particular sites for in depth case study analysis. That instrument, however, is framed in such a way that the research focuses on leadership as events and assorted methodologies are applicable. Leadership, after all, "is a process, a series of activities and exchanges engaged in over time and under varied circumstances." As such, accomplishments might be viewed as events in that leadership is an ongoing, never ending process.

To gain a more complete understanding of the phenomena under investigation, it is common for studies on leadership, like other topical areas, to incorporate more than one method of data collection. Mixed methods, which are most prevalent with case studies, integrate quantitative and qualitative methods into one study and therefore strengthen the chain of reasoning presented in study findings. While it is important to expand the methodological tool-chest that researchers within LIS use, it is also important to shift from studying leaders to investigating leadership events. Many aspects of leadership presented in the figure have not been addressed, and a need emerges for a fuller body of evidence-based research relevant to change management within libraries and similar complex organisations on a global basis. It is also important that those within LIS contribute to the broader literature on leadership and that their works be recognized by those in other disciplines.

LEADERSHIP AND SERVICE PROVISION IN PUBLIC LIBRARIES

In USA and Western Europe, we do witness the same types of

developments in public libraries and we see very similar themes of discourses independent of the national and local culture in which these libraries operate. Some of the themes concern the management structure and organisation bur more important is probably the current think about service delivery in a broad sense. Service delivery concerns the activities. It is areas like collection and collection management, the allocation of resources to the different part of the collection, the interplay and relationship between national internet based delivery and the local service.

Another important theme is the effort concerning the public library and its integration into the community taking up different forms of citizen services, cooperation and partnership with the local community, but also a focus on playing a new and more active role in the cultural scene by for example emphasising learning activities, lifelong learning, internet courses and different forms for events and exhibitions. The ambition is to become a local meeting place, a third room; a common intended to generate social capital.

This discourse and many of the activities resulting from it like 23 thinks, the libraries in the second world and experiments with various forms of social technology appear to have great appeal in the library profession. However, both library statistics and numerous studies of users and their preferences give a more differentiated picture. In most countries, the public libraries face economic hardship. They witness stagnating or decreasing numbers of visitors and the issues of traditional materials also tend to decrease. The public appear to value especially the services and products that suffer due to economic pressures and the internal priority setting in libraries.

Overall, it appears—at least at the surface–that users do have a rather traditional view of the public library and their stated preferences also seems to be very traditional as they are oriented towards books and information and to a lesser degree towards new services and delivery forms. It is of course of paramount interest to investigate possible discrepancies between the discourse and the practices in the professions and the users' preferences, priorities and level of satisfaction.

There is probably no right solution to the problem, but it is of both a practical and theoretical significance to investigate which factors influence the development of the discourse and the activities in the professions and in the public libraries and is also important to be able to measure users perception of the significance and importance of the service delivery and to which degree this is connected with measures of satisfaction. The paper further discusses the factors behind the profession's discourse and practices.

The concept of an organisational recipe is introduced in relation to organisational culture as two factors that have influence on the way libraries tend to adopt different forms of innovations. Of course, leadership plays an important role and the keynote also introduces measures of the personality traits of library directors and discusses this in relation to the innovation and development process but also in relation to the 'sense' or construction the profession is creating of the user.

This paper departs from 2 different theoretical perspectives of pertinent interest for management of institutions. One of the perspectives is concerned with the question about how management information and management recipes are adopted and interpreted in organisations like libraries. The other perspective concerns the role of the directors' personality in this context especially how they acquire management information and how they value and use management information in relation to organisational change processes. This paper is built on several studies into leadership in libraries in Denmark and United Kingdom. The paper also builds on several user studies.

LEADERSHIP AND PERSONALITY

During the last couple of years, the interest in leadership and management topics has increased very much. This is also the case in library and information science. It is due to the very fundamental changes that takes place overall in the public sector. Many of these changes are connected to requirements concerning accountability, user orientation, outsourcing, quality, information technology and staff related issues. It is a widespread notion that the requirements in relation to leadership and management have become much more complex.

The complexity is connected to environmental turbulence, change processes and to the amount of vast information that leaders need to deal with. Information in the form of management tools or recipes is one way to confront the organisational problems arising from the changes. Leadership is an important element in the configuration of organisational culture and both leadership styles and the leaders approach to innovation, change, and competency development are of importance in relation to the directions of the organisation. Leaders are both part of an organisational culture but they also have the possibility to be change agents in relation to the culture. The relationship between leadership priorities and organisational culture are important.

One can argue an interesting relationship between the directors' personality and preferences and the direction and change processes in libraries and this is exactly the focus for this paper. The Revised NEO Personality Inventory is one of the most widespread personality tests based on the Five Factor model and it was employed in this investigation. Besides allowing for both a general and detailed description of personality, the test is also build up in such a way that it takes into consideration the characteristics of the specific test person in focus. Specific norms for groups of people and profiles have been developed from research to help validate the testresult. The NEO PI R measures five broad personality factors. Each of these is a summary and an average of six facets. Each of the five factors and their associated 6 facets is measured through 48 statements, implying that all 30 facets are measured through 240 statements. The result of the 240 statements is distributed into low and high scores on the 5 factors and the 30 facets, hence demonstrating a personality profile. As suggested, now turn to a short profiling of the 8 library directors.

The profiles of the directors as a whole are very congruent with modern expectations of leaders and managers. They tend to possess emotional stability. They are extroverted and open to change. They all score high on the facet assertiveness. They score high on conscientiousness. Overall, the profiles of the library directors appear to be very far away from the traditional stereo types of librarians as shy, introverted, a bit oldfashioned, nervous and timid.

The factor named openness is often considered as an important factor in relation to chance processes and it is clear that all directors except one scores high on this factor. One director is distinct from the others, scoring rather low. It is director B that scores low on 3 of the 6 facets. What is more interesting is probably that all directors score high on some of the more important facets related to get things done. All score from middle to very high on actions, ideas and values indicating openness to new ideas.

Common for all the directors have been the fact that they have been involved in change processes. These change processes have focused on both the provision of services and on organisational development implementing more flexible and democratic structures. They have all succeeded to change the libraries both internally and in relation to the users. One of the reasons that change processes have been successful overall can possibly be attributed to the assertiveness of the directors, their overall openness to experience and change and their general high degree of conscientiousness.

The organisational culture is a very important mediating factor both in relation to how information in the form of recipes are adopted and translated both also in relation to the actual possibilities the director possess for implementing change. But the style of change management varies. This can be partly explained by situational factors like the local political climate, restrictions due to the building and economy, the organisational culture and other important factors.

The relevant facets or traits that relates to interpretation and adoption of new standards are some of the traits that relate to the factors named openness and conscientiousness. The facets under openness can possibly give an indication of how willing the director is to seek and implement new recipes in the organisation and the facets related to conscientiousness can indicate how through the process of implementation is conducted. These facets will also relate to the directors' sense of the usefulness of own participating in leadership courses and development. We emphasise that it is broad hypotheses. Another more general aspect is how the directors value innovations or changes. A comparison of D with H indicates the usefulness of analysing behaviour using all the facets and not only the factors. It is evident that the profile of H indicates a person oriented towards actions and change. H also possesses a high degree of impulsiveness and a middle orientation towards ideas. H is more of a doer than a thinker and this is also the way H comes forward in the interview and in interviews with the staff.

Things must happen and failures—both own and staff failures—are accepted as inevitable. Some of the change processes are conducted nearly on the spot and many traditional activities are set in motion. In some ways, the change processes runs in a very goal directed manner but there is a high degree of acceptance of a chaotic nature of some of these processes that involves staff very much because the director delegates much based on both trust and on a disposition to take up new challenges.

The change processes that have taken place in D's library are conducted in a very different way. They are just as goal directed and strategic but they are much slower and much more deliberated and it is evident that the D places a very high value on bringing the staff along. The disposition for activity seeking is much less here than in relation to H. It results in a 'flavour' of the library as a bit more old fashioned and a bit slower or a bit more cautious in change processes.

The implicit formulated hypotheses about the relationship between personality traits and profiles indicated that the director's openness to especially intellectual experiences or practical innovations and changes influenced the process of implementation of both structures and processes of competences. It also influenced the way the recipes and standards were conceptualised in the organisation. The integration of the recipes was influenced by the perseverance of the director with cultural factors as a mediating factor.

DISCOURSES AND ORGANISATIONAL RECIPES

These figures contrast to a certain degree to the dominant discourses in the public library profession. The dominant discourses are concerned with modern topics and issues like library as a place and libraries as generators of social capital and societal trust on a more general level. In relation to services the emphasis in the discourses are on issues like lifelong learning, information literacies and integration of the physical library into the digital services. The discourse also contains strong elements of the need for permanent change for example in relation to continuing professional development.

There is also much debate on phenomena like 23 things, facebook and other digital services. A discourse is characterised by dominant themes but is also delimited by themes that do not occur and these absent themes signifies the themes in the discourse. In the 80'ies and 90'ies, the library profession had focus on collections and collection management and especially the concept of immediate availability was a central topic.

Today, these themes of discussion are missing from the professional debate. There existed also a rather interesting debate or discourse concerning the proper relationship between supply and demand in relation to the collection. It is interesting that these topics seldom are covered in the present discussion because the different digital possibilities emphasise new turns of these central concepts. Just to give a few hopefully illuminating examples one can ask questions about the links on libraries' web sites and enquire if a link is part of the collection or not.

The answer to that question is interesting because if the answer is yes it follows that the libraries have the responsibility for dead links and for the misinformation contained in some of the links. Another interesting question is the transformation of topical needs into specific needs due to the way people search the digital databases. Librarians are not discussing the increase in the selling of books and the reasons behind this interesting fact. Is it because of an increasing affluence in society or is it because of a want for instant gratification?

Many of the elements in a given dominant discourse relates to organisational recipes or standards. A recipe or a standard that becomes a trend has the following characteristics: It often originates in an academic setting but very often it is created in cooperation with the professional world—be it libraries or business. It is blueprinted by leading members of the academic and professional communities and it is taken up also by the consultancy industry.

Prestigious firm and companies use it. The recipe incorporates the promise to solve serious problems in the companies and in the institutions they are interesting to work with. They are marketed and they are frameworks for actions but most of all they are interpretable meaning that institutions can adopt them, change them according to the national and organisational culture. They are very often connected to stories of success and the story behind the recipe often takes the form of a drama.

Successful recipes tend to hit a trend in the time and use this as a kind of vehicle for its travel across boundaries and cultures. Some recipes like the balanced scorecard have a rather long life. Other—not as successful like for example business process reengineering—have a shorter lifespan. It does not mean that they are not used. It could mean that they are incorporated in the organisational operations but people have stopped talking about it.

Finally, all recipes have dimensions of both content and symbolic aspects. It is of course extremely interesting which recipes become dominating themes in the discourse of a profession. It is also of huge interest which recipes a given profession does not include in its arsenal of themes in the discourse. There is no doubt that the profession as a whole has a very determined focus on change and the need for change. The catch phrase that the libraries stand on a burning platform has been brought forward several times in the discourse and this catchphrase has been used as a kind of rationale for changes. This is of course the consequence of a special or peculiar interpretation of the environment. However, there is no doubt that the ideology of change and the need for change is deeply integrated in the professional identity of public librarians and leaders in the public libraries. It is an interesting question if the interpretation of the environment is in accordance with other indicators of changes in the environment.

USERS AND PREFERENCES

One aspect of organisational effectiveness is a system's ability to cope with users and non-users expectations and needs enabling the system to deliver services appropriate to satisfy needs and expectations. Organisational effectiveness has been one of the ultimate goals and objectives for the performance measurements endeavours for many years. Organisational effectiveness is related to processes, products or services and the customer or the user and it is normally seen as an important element in the quality of a service. The importance or significance for the users of the single services is of course a very important element for the libraries' planning process and assessment of how to proceed.

Libqual is a measurement instrument that is often used for this kind of investigation as it specifies the minimal level of service people would like. However, Libqual has not been employed in these surveys. We have simply asked people to attach the significance or importance for themselves on different services. The end result is a kind of ranking that probably is rather robust. The importance or significance is calculated on a scale from 0 to 100 and it forms the basis of the ranking. The ranking of the importance or the perception of the significance of the public libraries' services follows:

Table. The Users' Perception of the Significance of Different Services in Two Surveys

	High School	Rank	Aarhus	Rank
A kind and polite service	72	1	90	2
Distance to the library	67	2	91	1
Ambience	64	3	84	3
Collection of non-fiction	62	4	66	5
Quite and peaceful place in the library	59	5	65	6
Collection of fiction	55	6	78	4
Places for relaxation	43	7	51	8
Collection of music	41	8	46	10
Wireless network	40	9	21	14
Collection of film	37	10	47	9
Group work facilities	35	11	15	15

Computers	34	12	28	12
The Library's homepage	34	13	63	7
Study places	33	14	21	14
Exhibitions, lessons	28	15	45	11
N	978		243	

Translated into normal text, one can say that the high school students and the 'traditional public library users' prefer a kind and polite service in nice quite rooms in library with ambience not too far away and filled with books. There are differences between the preferences and significance attached to services among the two groups but rank correlation analysis shows a Spearmans Rho of 0,81 which indicate a very high degree of similarity in ranking the services. The ranking between the two groups are more or less similar, but there appears to be differences in the importance attached to the service.

One explanation for this discrepancy is simple and it is, that the group of high schools students consists of students relying heavily on public libraries and groups or segments that rarely, seldom or never use the public library. This composition of the total group tends to decrease the average figures. In comparison, the respondents from the Aarhus group were all public library users. In the 2006 investigation in Furesoe, we also asked questions about preferences and significance, but we employed a measurement tool based on forced pair wise ranking.

It is impossible to make a direct comparison, but one can look at the trends and compare these with caution. The most striking feature of the answers to this question is the similarity in preferences. The respondents were asked on a forced scale where they had to prioritise alternatives. Overall, the users preferred present openings hours more than longer opening hours with less staff service. The preferred more books in favour of longer opening hours or music.

The preferred more film than more music. They preferred a broader range of literature more than additional copies of the popular books. We did not find any differences in pair wise preferences in relation fiction versus non–fiction, computers versus more reading places or more reading places versus more places for relaxation or social interaction. The conclusion is that users–even the young age group—want more documents. It is a very clear first priority.

We do see that this priority and preference increase with age, but it is still a very striking result that young people that rely heavily on and use the library's collection of film and music much prioritise books and documents more if they had to choose. The preferences and the prioritising are probably an expression of the perception of what a public library is—and ought to be. It is obvious that the structure of preferences in relation to public libraries is rather traditional. The nationwide study of high school students also showed some interesting features of the significance they attached to the services in relation to different demographic factors.

Table. The Students' Perceptions of the Importance of Services and Facilities in Relation to Demographics

	Type High School			Gender		Study Year		
	G	B	T	Female	Male	1	2	3
A kind and polite service	77	69	63	76	66			
Distance to the library	74	61	61	72	61			
Ambience	68	61	59	67	60			
Collection of non-fiction	70	54	52	66	56	56	61	68
Quite and peaceful places in the library	63	55	51					
Collection of fiction	61	49	49	63	44			
Places for relaxation						49	44	36
Collection of music						45	36	38
Wireless network						45	40	35
Collection of film Group work facilities						41	35	28
Computers				32	37			
The Library's homepage	37	28	33			28	36	37
Study places						38	30	29
Exhibitions, lessons								

First of all, there appears to be differences in perceptions of significance and importance dependent on the type of high school. There are 3 types of high schools in the country. The general high school is the classic one. In the table it is called G. There is also a high school oriented towards business topics called B and at last a technical high school called T. The general picture is that the high school students from the general school place more significance on most of the library services than students from the other two hig schools do. We also notice marked differences between male and female high school students.

Female high school students tend to value the collection of fiction an non- fiction much more than the male students. It is also interesting to note that the students through their study process tend to place less significance to the library as a place to be and work in. However, overall the ranking of the single services is not hugely affected by this segmentation, but the segmentation indicates that the different groups have very different preferences and strength of preferences attached to the single services.

LIBRARIES AND POTENTIAL USERS: METHODOLOGICAL APPROACH, THE CASE OF GREEK LIBRARIES

Libraries in the fast communicative environment they live, implement three spaces of interaction:

- Between librarians who decide the offered services, the resources, the manuals and every necessary equipment for users satisfaction and the exploitation of the service.
- Among users and librarians who are responsible. The communication aims to identify the users' needs and the relevance of the resources to them.
- Between Library and users community as a whole. Users receive modified information that can be used to their work. This is the step that library proves its usefulness and illumine its image.

Libraries are social places, where individuals, teams, social groups interact. Social theories, behaviourism, sociopsychological analyses drive to the recognition of special characteristics of libraries and of every target group they refer. Libraries are also one of the key factors that can impact the development and the prosperity of the social entity they refer. Consequently, we can say that they involve competitiveness and entrepreneurship.

They take into account the following factors before decision making:

- Target focusing;
- Strategic planning;
- Efficiency and effectiveness;
- Resources saving;
- Cost benefits analysis.

The coupling of these different options, social and business, designates the communication methods and the policies that libraries choose on occasion. The synthesis and the identity of the unity that we call 'library users' is a continuing changed variable, as it strands upon the dynamic of human mobility, potential individual needs, and behavioural rules of societies. Users can turn into non-users, actually without caution, but not without any cause. Equally non-users could turn into new, enthusiastic users.

THE RESEARCH AND THE METHODOLOGIES

The questionnaire consists of items that derived from:

- The subject as come up for discussion in the literature;
- The marketing plans of business;
- The adjustment of them to library context.

Needless to say that the findings analysed by qualitative methods. There is an integrated combination of qualitative and quantitative methods, what is referred as mixing methods. Libraries need to know the synthesis and the characteristics of the population they refer to, in order to successfully appeal them. The major problems on this face the public and the special libraries, which the target groups are fuzzy and random. The social stratification is a matter of research of specialized organisations that collect data on the population structure, family synthesis, economic activities, education, leisure etc. The data is completed by using qualitative methods like interviews of opinion leaders, structured observation, discussions with famous public people. The target is to be ensured that the concept, the structure and the procedures of a service are harmonized to the target group.

MARKETING AND LIBRARIES

Marketing is the wide range of activities involved in making sure that you're continuing to meet the needs of your customers and getting value in return. These activities include market research to find out, for example, what groups of potential customers exist, what their needs, are, which of those needs you can meet, how you should meet them etc. Marketing also includes analysing the competition, positioning your new product or service pricing your products and services, and promoting them through continued advertising, promotions, public relations and sales.

Marketing is connected with library's operation itself. Value added works such as cataloguing and classification corresponds to the product packing, embodied also the concept of the product: in this case is knowledge, research, information, entertainment. Shelving, Abstracting and Indexing, bibliography compilation correspond to the promotion. Regarding the users training programmes, the location of material in the library correlates with marketing practices, such as study of consumer behaviour, product promotion etc.

The mission and the objectives of libraries are modified according to the conditions; services, procedures, rules and operation follow the change. Consequently the Marketing Mix changes too. To catch the alterations, a marketing plan is necessary in order to define the policies, the promotional practices. On the other hand and because of the 4P balance differs for every target group, it is necessary the research on the groups of population that are the potential clients of the library.

4 Ps of Marketing Mix of libraries:

- Product is the value that librarians add through their knowledge, expertise, and informational, organisational, and retrieval skills. Product is library's services. Collections consists the basis of the 'product', but the main one is an *Idea, an intangible product,* in which the tangible good, the services and the processes are incorporated;
- Place is the space of the library, either physical or virtual. Place is an important factor that can appeal the potential users. Another factor relevant to this is the location of the building, how easily accessible is it. Relevant to this point is the mention that the place nowadays is both place and space, equally physical and virtual;
- The Price of library services or products consists of both the staff time spent in ensuring that resources and services are available and accessible and user's time in finding and using resources efficiently. Libraries do not Price their activities and decisions. However they assess the cost of services, of acquisitions, of operation. The main interest of libraries is the best exploitation of their resources, the advancement of their services, the improvement of their quality, without increasing of their cost;
- The communicative policy of the library is the Promotion policy and its part of the strategic marketing. Promotion consists every positive action, even the politeness of the staff, but in practice, promotion targets to explain to users and non-users why they need the library in their everyday life.

THE SURVEY AND THE RESULTS

The questionnaire contains questions for collecting quantitative information, questions for seeking behaviours and attitudes scaled to 4 degrees. The third unity contains questions on the organisational level of the library, its resources, its finance and fund raising. The stratification of the sampling of libraries who participated to the survey is analog to the number of libraries that belong to every type. The questions and the analysis follow the structure of a marketing plan.

Mission and Goals of the Library

The diagrams show the weak idea that Greek libraries have on the strategic management:

- More than half of the libraries have a fuzzy idea of their mission;
- Only 37, 5 per cent has written specific explicit mission.
- Only 11,4 per cent writes down the strategic plan, shared to the whole staff; and
- 21,5 per cent of libraries share the plan to employees relevant to the its content.

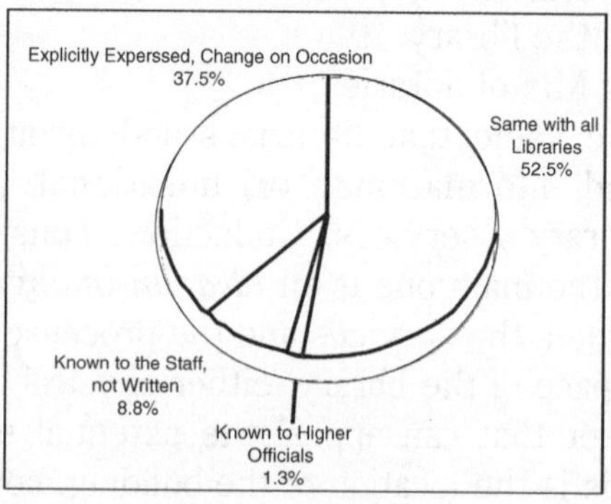

Fig. Library's Mission

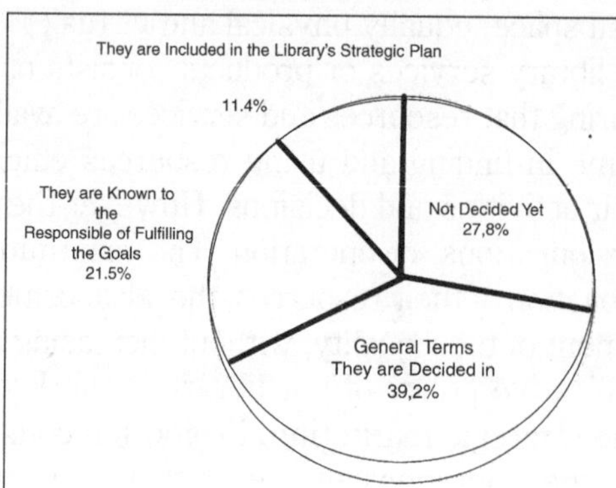

Fig. Means for Achieving Library's Goals as they are Ordered by its Purpose and Strategy

Furthermore, as usual, the 56 per cent of Libraries deny to set economic goals, but the 57, 5 per cent of libraries set non-economic goals, which they achieve and sometimes they overcome. Needless to say that an economic goal is not a business goal: it could be a cost effective goal, or the better exploitation of the resources or the decrease of operational expenses etc. Libraries are negatively biased on economic and public relations actions. Marshall mentions some causes for academic libraries that seem to be common to every kind:

- Argument that academic libraries have a captive audience in members of the academic community who need to use the library in order to be successful in their academic areas of teaching and research;
- Library funding is not a concern because it is linked to overall institutional funding;
- Promotion is not a part of the library's purpose;
- Promotion of the library and its services will crate expectations and demand that are beyond the library's capabilities;
- Reliance on the university's communication or development office to perform a public relations role will suffice.

Product (Life Cycle, New Life Design)

Because of the lack of strategic thought and promotional vision, libraries gave the following answers:

- 69 per cent declare that the strategic planning is unofficial, and
- 54, 5 per cent answer that there are no procedures for the creation of new services.
- Not users but other factors determine the orientation and establishment of new services.
- The questions on the life cycle of the services reveal that libraries mainly operate as traditional organisations and low communicated.

Market (Target–groups)

- Most of the libraries (86, 8 per cent) know their population and their mobility;
- They study the attitude of people; and
- They try to form a special policy for every group.

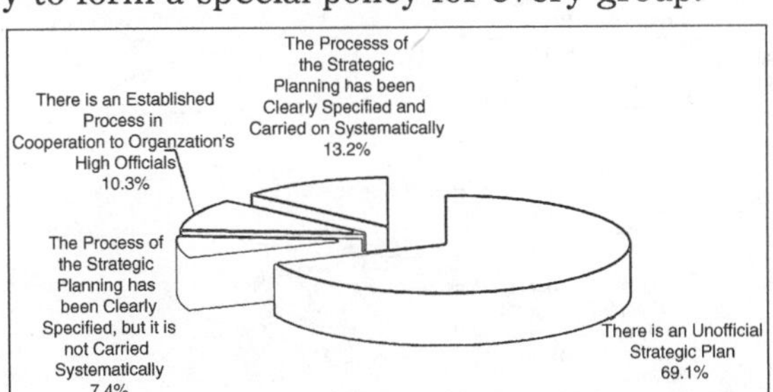

Fig. Is there Any Strategy for Developing Library Services

The kind of libraries that answered explain it:

- 44,3 per cent does not examine the target group, and
- 30 per cent systematically focuses on numerous groups of the population.

The Library's Image and the External Relationships

As it is clear up to now, libraries operation is mainly collection oriented than users centred. The modernization steps parallel to technology, without harmonizing processes, management, and services. They use technology without innovative processes.

The following answers confirm the lack of a strategy for appealing new groups of population and new users.

- Only 1,4 per cent collects systematically data on users' and groups' behaviour; and
- 7, 8 per cent focuses on the appealing of new target groups.

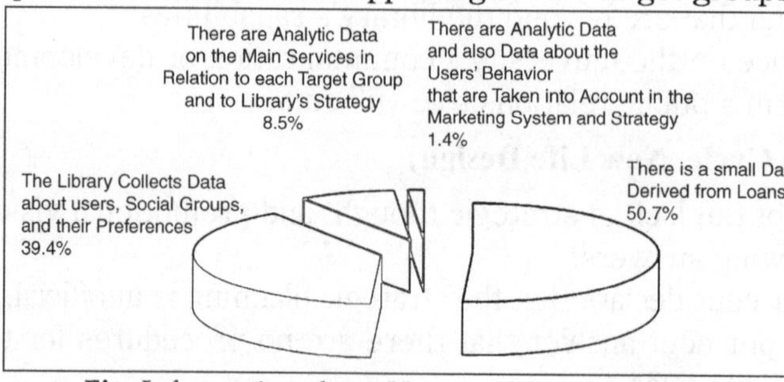

Fig. Information about Users and Potential Users

External relationships:

- 8,3 per cent agree that strategic alliances increase the users and advertise their services, and
- 52,8 per cent agrees to evaluate cooperation proposals that could cause the increase of the users;
- Lack of active, systemic promotion of the library;
- Uninterested in communication.

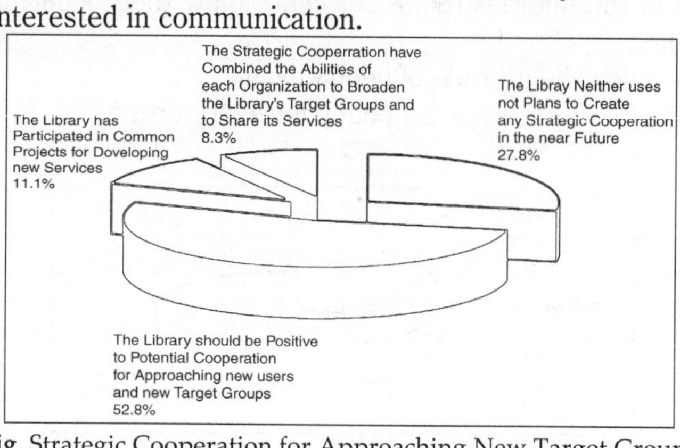

Fig. Strategic Cooperation for Approaching New Target Groups

Nevertheless, half of the people that participate to library's events use the library, become members. The opposite valid also: the majority of the members are interested in library's events. That means that users' attitude is positive, but how many people use it? That's the crucial question. That's the main problem of libraries: not the whole people who need libraries use them.

THE LIBRARY MANAGEMENT QUALITY

A great number of scientific, reference, educational, methodical and practical publications is devoted to the quality of library activity in Russia. One of the most characteristic tendencies is the active interest to management, especially quality management that explains the fact of formation of new management concept in the sphere of library science. Modern management researches show a great significance of rational information processing for achieving strategic and operative aims. The quality of information defines the quality of management because information covers all spheres of management.

Being the most important function of management process, information must meet the following requirements: authenticity, accuracy and completeness, efficiency and regularity, its conformity with management level. Management of documentation as function of management is realised in the conditions of decision making process to achieve the aim. That is why documentation management is closely connected with the problems of management, organisation structures, the problems of design of information systems management, their implementation and operation, with automation of managerial procedures and processes.

Urgency of the problem consists in support of the processes of documentation information management due to more effective technologies of its processing including analytical components and the connection of management functions with documents, their servicing. The development of new management technologies plans systematic approach to the decision making process on the base of flexible information analytical integrated management system.

DOCUMENTS MANAGEMENT

The organisation of work with documents is a very important part of management processes and taking managerial decisions influencing efficiency and management quality. From the point of view of information technologies documentation information management activity and the management activity itself—as a subsystem of an integrated technological system of library. So, the library management is characterised as technological process that supposes regularity of management. In management activity a document is a tool, means or method of management. The whole documentation is closely connected with the concrete management function for which it is created. It allows, in Larin's opinion with the help of systematic analysis to identify the content of managerial documents and to connect it with the definite management function. Optimal system of internal legal regulation helps to provide successfully and realise substantially the local legal regulation of general principles of activity, some decisions and concrete aspects of library operation. The complex of internal regulated documents, being formed in each library objectively consists of a package of separate interrelated and mutually complementary blocks. The documents, included, reflect legal organisational and technological sides of professional activity, fix aims, order and conditions of library functioning as informational, educational and cultural institution.

Pilko suggests to classify the complex of documents regulating the activity of the library for convenience according to the following functions: organisational—administrative documentation, scientific—methodical documentation, normative documentation and technological documentation. At the present stage in the system of library management the whole range of documents concerning different types and kinds of documentation systems and being a part of documentation support of management.

INFORMATION MANAGEMENT SYSTEM

The use of information technologies in the sphere of management gives opportunities of more effective and rational organisation of information processes, increase of their flexibility and dynamics expansion of the range of analysed factors when making decisions. 'Perfect' information system of management must automate all or the majority of protective kinds of activity in the frames of integrated information space and in interrelation of automated functions. It is more optimal to use the system which is the part of the architecture of the system of complex library automation that implies the use of joint technologies of management automation and documents circulation. The creation of the system of automated management of documents or service database in the library is a very complicated organisational technical task, administrative office automation being the main, basic platform within information library system. Designing database, one should orient on the use of standard management system of data and technology 'client–server' which allows to combine operative work with archiving documents.

Automated system in the library:

- Provides coordinated work of all departments;
- Simplifies work with documents, increases its effectiveness;
- Increases labour efficiency due to shortening time for creation, documents processing and search;
- Increases efficiency of access to information;
- Allows to delimit the competence of access of workers to information.

The implementation of such system in the library will optimize the activity of the library in whole, to get analytical information for using and taking important managerial decisions. Without any doubts, the system will influence on effectiveness of library activity as well as on increase of professional personnel training, the culture of the use of modern information technologies.

DATABASE OF REGULATING DOCUMENTATION

For solving intersystem tasks of the library one can suggest the module of service database of regulated documentation as foundation of effective library management. Designing technological project of database we relied on methodical basis and regulations considered by Pilko and Voroisky. The main source when forming database is regulated documents of library.

Database supports the main functions of documents processing on line which include: documents development and custody; search of documents according to different parameters, input, support and custody of any kind of documents; control over implementation of documents; protection and management of separation of rights for access.

Database includes the complex of functional means realised as a programme modules helping to plan work, to get interim and resort valuation of separate operations, to control and, if necessary, to correct the plan or process. The idea of centralised storage of e-documents is also obvious: integrated database in server keeps documents safely, systematizes them and finds necessary information very quickly. Not the least of the features of the system is unification of the most widespread types and kinds of documents in management, development and use of patterns. Database is corporate storage of regulating documents of the library. In includes the catalogue of organisational efficient, regulatory–methodical and technological documentation, unified forms of documents, documents archive, office documents of departments or separate workers. Through interface of database, installed in all computers, the workers of the library get access to hierarchy of folders and operations concerning design and search of documents. The search of documents is realised through folders navigation.

Creating a new document a database offers users to identify its belonging to concrete theme by classifier and to use standard sheet, pattern. Information, formed by users in the process of selecting data, is displayed as a reference in matrix format, graphic material, fulltext document or pattern. Different functional and practical tasks are solved by the method of contiguous look of database modules and data selection or seriating. The tasks can be operational analysis of technological processes; valuation of resort support of processes; valuation of work content of library production.

Managers of a library, having full access to all documents, can control the process of creating office documents any time. The analysis of report documents formed in database, gives opportunity to correct the library activity, to improve organisational structure, character and content of implemented works, personnel, provision with financial, material and other resources.

3

Advantages of Stock Verification in Library

INTRODUCTION

A library should also take note of some advantages in carrying out stock verification. *Firstly,* periodic stock verification and write-off of resultant loss helps to reduce unnecessary escalation in book value of assets. *Secondly,* physical verification also helps in replacing relevant, useful and on demand documents with new copies wherever lost or mutilated. *Thirdly,* stock verification is the time to introduce new ways of arrangement of stack, modified or new lending system and other procedures.

Fourthly, if a library calls back all issued out documents for stock verification purpose, it can provide an opportunity for its users to browse the entire collection after verification. This very much counters the otherwise bias of less useful books lying on shelves all through the year. *Fifthly,* stock verification helps to review the precautionary measures already taken in preventing loss and mutilation as well as to identify any deficiencies in the existing procedure of maintenance of library and vigilance.

Stock verification helps as a way of identifying and discarding obsolete volumes. Normally in an active collection of a well organised library, loss of on demand books are only noticed in day to day working. Other incidental benefits of stock verification include identification of damaged and worn-out documents for repair or rebinding, keeping shelf list and other records up to date, rearrangement and cleaning of stack, better acquaintance of collection and popular documents by library staff, etc.

METHODS OF STOCK VERIFICATION

As far as methods of carrying out stock verification are concerned the parent organisation may involve or may not involve external persons in the team of stock verification and may decide to exclude certain types of material in the library. The rest of the methodology of verification depends on the provisions already made in the design and organisation of library records. There are a number of methods followed for stock verification. The most crude method is to numerically count the number of documents and it practically does not serve any purpose except to know the number of documents lost.

The old and fairly crude method is to physically check and tally documents on shelves with accession register. This method is not only cumbersome and time consuming but also require the entire register to be kept while checking. It may also lead to spoiling the register with tick marks. However, with the advent of new ways of reproduction of accession register now the original register can still be saved. Another accession number based scheme which also has the disadvantage of keeping the entire register is to have prewriting/typed/printed cards carrying accession numbers in blocks of 100 numbers while physically checking the documents on shelves.

In both these methods the simultaneous working of number of batches depends on availability of number of copies of accession register or its surrogate and if more than one copy of accession register is used the results of checking needs to be consolidated from different copies/batches. All these not only make it cumbersome but also lead to waste of time and efforts. It is also possible now with the proliferation of personal computers to just key in all accession numbers as and when checked to consolidate the loss in terms of missing accession numbers.

The most economical and fast way of entering accession number is to use a mobile bar code/wand reader to scan accession numbers of books from the bar code stickers in the books. But bar code system is yet to pickup in this country. The most popular and fairly reliable and quick manual method is to verify stock based on shelf list. This method requires an up to date shelf list. All these methods presuppose closing library for verification purpose.

Yet another shelf list based method which does not require closing down the library but ensures reasonably economical, quick and dependable stock checking is to have two card systems. In this method two different colour book cards are prepared for each document and one of them is maintained as shelf list card and the other kept in book. At the time of stock verification these two book cards are exchanged. This method allows for simultaneous working of many batches as both shelf list and documents are arranged in the same sequence and also allows for rectifying errors of stock verification at a later date.

RESPONSIBILITY AND WRITE-OFF OF LOSS

After accepting and probably implementing wherever possible the additional precautionary measures against loss of library documents the ordeal does not end. No precautionary measure without fully undermining the service function in an open access library can ensure total elimination of loss. A negligible number of perverted, possessive, habituated persons responsible for loss and mutilation are likely to continue inspite of liberalised services and strict vigilance. Further what has already been lost and what is going to be discovered as lost in the future stock verifications need to be explained to and got write-off by the competent authority. At this stage the question of who is responsible for loss of library documents often surfaces with an indirect hint at librarian or librarian together with his staff though most of special libraries and information centres are directly or indirectly managed by non- librarians either in the form of committees or as officer incharge. In some libraries, the librarian may be directly held responsible for the loss.

Loss of moveable property, stores and consumable is a universal phenomenon. Individuals, insitutions, departments, public and private enterprises incur loss of many types of moveable property, stores and consumables. An individual library user, who looses a book borrowed from the library pays the 'replacement cost' to the library, rightfully and sometimes vengefully feels that what is lost by librarian should be made good by librarian. But he conveniently forgets to distinguish librarian as individual user from librarian as a functional head of the library.

In no other area of loss like that of minor equipment and consumable in any organisation so much of fuss about responsibility of loss arises as it happens in loss of library documents. As such stock verification is covertly viewed as a tool to punish librarians. Librarian in the process of providing service to users antagonises those who loose documents borrowed in their names and earns a psychological dislike or hatred by recovering the 'replacement cost' of documents. It is extremely rare to see a situation in an organisation where recoveries are made for loss of minor equipment and consumables even though they are issued in the names of individuals for keeping in their exclusive possession.

Compared to the magnitude of losses in many types of stores items in an organisation, the loss of library documents is meagre. Secondly the stores items including smaller equipments would have been kept under exclusive possession in lock and key and there may not be a need to share them with others. Infact, many times books issued to individual departments are also lost. Further all other types of items are subjected to strict security with gate passes. On the other hand, documents in an open access library are meant for shared use by many.

Library staff is not meant to keep custody of library documents alone. This comparison of the circumstances in which loss of library documents occur with that of stores items clearly shows that loss in libraries are inevitable. For argument sake, an antiservice attitude can be taken by a library and advocate for having security guarded closed access library with gate pass system. But it takes away the essence of library services.

Results of stock verification should not be used to impose restrictions. In any organisation, if librarian and his colleagues have to take the full responsibility for the loss of documents and make good the loss from their salary, it is obvious that he and his colleagues who share the responsibility be given a 'risk allowance' on line with allowances given for jobs like that of cashier in offices in addition to providing freedom in amending the policies and procedures of library to minimise loss.

However, the more reasonable way of clearing the deadlock of responsibility is to treat the loss of library documents like any other loss in the organisation and the competent authority write-off the same unless the situation warrants an enquiry about negligence and dereliction of duty on the part of librarian and library staff. The rules governed by the institution would indicate the financial powers and limits for write-off and the extent of loss allowed.

For example in case of Goverment of India institutions, librarian in the rank not below that of a Deputy Secretary to the Goverment of India or Head of the Department who has financial powers can write-off loss of library documents to the extent of financial powers and monitory limits. A loss of 3 volumes per 1000 volumes issued/consulted in a year is proposed as reasonable limit for loss unless the loss is attributable to dishonesty or negligence on the part of librarian. Loss of a book of the value exceeding ₹200/ and the books of–special nature and rarity shall invariably be investigated and consequential action taken.

Further rare books and books of special nature may be kept under closed access. There is also a provision in the rules that there should not be any objection to the disposing of mutilated/damaged/obsolete volumes to the best interest of the library as long as it is based on recommendations of a three member committee appointed by the Department.

In practice, many authorities have a peculiar way of looking at new policies, procedures, services including write-off of loss. They wish to know what is the situation in Y&Z libraries nearby and how they have acted. Unfortunately the authorities of Y&Z libraries would have desired to know the situation in X&Z and X&Y libraries, respectively. This kind of conservative and risk less attitude prevails in many places. Lastly, there is also a dishonest way of handling this occupational hazard of library stock verification being practiced by some libraries by way of declaring the loss as much less than actual and hence defeating the very purpose and advantages of stock verifications.

PRECAUTIONARY MEASURES AGAINST LOSS

Having carried out stock verification in a library, the very first question to be asked is that 'are the existing precautionary measures against loss of library documents enough? and `is there any scope to take further precautions?'. Here again the preventive and precautionary actions normally cost much more than the value of loss. The usual precautions taken at the time of planning a library is to operate with one exit cum entrance, not allowing personal belongings inside the library and covering all windows of the building with suitable wire mesh or metal grills to avoid passing books through windows.

Additional precautions like a check point at exit gate with a person and/or vigilance manpower including security guard, magnetised document checking/ burglar's alarm and other electronic book security system, CCTV, insurance against loss, etc. cost substantially to the organisation in addition to being not fool proof. What additional precautions are to be taken depends on how much additional expenditure the organisation is willing to incur.

Here two things need special mention. Firstly some of the costs like salaries of vigilance/checking staff are often invisible. Secondly, any physical check by a security guard in reputed institution may not only bring resistance from users but also makes an ugly show.

Apart from intensifying vigilance, another positive approach propounded is to liberalise services like extended library hours during examination time, liberal or subsidised xerox service and liberal lending of books marked 'not to be issued'.

It is natural to raise a question as to how library books are lost that too in research institutions where majority of the users are from higher strata of society. Mysteriously, it becomes almost impossible to pin point at any individual or set of individuals. Nor it is easy to catch redhandedly such thieves. Where they are caught also, surprisingly the legal process is so fragile that it becomes difficult to establish a theft.

Any way librarian is not a police officer. While discussing various security methods Pierce says "... maintaining the security of library materials has changed from a minor irritant to a major problem.

Many libraries have discovered that they are loosing more than one per cent of their collections each year vandalism, arson and wanton destruction have become more common in libraries and will probably continue and even possibly increase".

An analysis of types of books lost and the distribution of value of books lost as against the strength of collection and average cost of books acquired should provide some guidelines about type and nature of books lost the need for vigilance, the need for change in arrangement and organisation of collection. Such analysis with some useful ratios like loss to use/consultation, loss to stock, loss per user per year, etc. would be quite useful. One such analysis of loss of ISRO Satellite Centre (ISAC) Library for the year 1987-88.

It has clearly indicated that text books and other popular books in the area of office rules, electronics, computer science, etc. costing far less than the average cost of book acquired are lost. Further, for every 1000 documents in stock on an average 3.67 documents are lost. As against Goverment of India guideline of allowing 3 books for every 1000 circulated/consulted, ISAC library has lost only 0.58 document. Lastly the value of loss of ISAC library is just 80 per cent of the incidental revenue earned in the form of nominal overdue charges levied by library.

STOCK VERIFICATION AND PROCEDURE TO WITHDRAW BOOKS

LOSS OF PUBLICATIONS

- Some loss of publications is inevitable especially in the context of open access practice in libraries. The librarian has a role as information manager and not just a custodian. Therefore he/she should not be held responsible for the losses.
- Loss of 5 volumes per 1000 volumes issued and/or consulted in a year may be taken as reasonable.
- Loss of a book of the value exceeding ₹.2000.00 for books published in India and ₹.10,000.00 for books published abroad and books of special nature and rarity shall invariably be investigated and consequential action taken. The Director will write off all such losses. The base values suggested for Indian and foreign books shall be reviewed every five years.
- A publication may be considered as lost only when it is found missing in two successive stock verifications and thereafter only action be taken to write off the publications by competent authority.
- If the loss of book is more than the permissible extent, the causes of such loss may be investigated by the competent authority and the remedial measures be strengthened.
- Occasional loss/damage of issues of periodicals is inevitable during postal transit. If the payment is made directly to the publisher, then sometimes it is not possible to get the replacement. In such cases, the non-receipts/ damages be considered as loss for write-off.
- Librarian may write off the loss of books, volumes, etc. mentioned in the proceeding paragraph provided the total value of all such books, etc. does not exceed the monetary limit prescribed the Delegation of Financial Powers Rules, 1978 for Head of a Department in respect of deficiencies and depreciations in the value of stores included in the stock and other accounts. In the event of the total value exceeding the monetary limit specified above, the loss of books shall be written off by the competent authority as specified in the Delegation of Financial Power Rules, 1978's.
- There may be no objection to the Librarian disposing of mutilated/ damaged/ obsolete volumes to the best interest of the library. However, the disposal of such volumes should be made on the recommendations of a Library Advisory Committee to be appointed by the competent authority which shall decide whether the books mutilated/damaged/obsolete are not fit for further use.

PROCEDURE FOR WRITE-OFF

- List the documents not found during stock verification
- Library staff to make all possible efforts to locate the document not found during stock verification (the process can go up to six months but not as an exclusive task)
- Prepare pre-final list of the documents not found and publicize
- Compile a final list of documents not found
- Compare with the list of earlier stock verification to identify common entries
- Compare losses with borrowing/ consulting/ photo copying statistics
- Put up the list of common entries to the Director along with justification for the losses (open access, limited staff, inadequate security system, large number of students visiting library, losses within permissible limits, etc.)
- Get approval from the Director
- Issue OM
- Make necessary entries in the accession register, write-off register, assets register, etc
- Remove records from databases
- Close file.
- Improve the system with additional precautionary measures

PREVENTIVE MEASURES

Some preventive measures are listed below:

- Follow closed access to the rare books and specialized collections.
- The exit/entry to the library be monitored
- Sealing of windows with wire mesh, installation of wicket gate, adequate vigilance in the stack room(s), provision of adequate lighting, use of electronic or magnetic gadgets for detection of the theft, closed circuit television monitoring system, introduction of identity/ membership cards for identification of users, etc., can be adopted.
- Inadequate staff in the library is also one of the reasons for the losses.

REFERENCE SERVICE

Library houses all important reference sources like Encyclopaedias, Dictionaries, handbooks and Manuals, Statistics, Yearbooks. The collection ranges from general to subject specific sources. All the reference sources are housed in the Ground floor Reference section. Users can also contact staff on duty for any assistance. Library also has access to online reference sources which may be accessed from the library web site.

INFORMATION LITERACY/LIBRARY ORIENTATION

Library will conduct Information Literacy/User Education/Orientation programmes to all in the beginning of the academic year. Besides this, these awareness programmes should be conducted when requested by users from time to time.

INTER–LIBRARY LOAN

Library maintains an inter –library loan arrangement with leading local libraries like IIT Mumbai, Homi Bhabha Centre for Science Education and Research TIFR), Mumbai University, SNDT University, IGIDR, etc. Apart from this library also has membership with DELNET. Hence, all possible efforts must be made to make available the learning resources needed for the faculty and students.

PHOTOCOPYING SERVICES

Presently library maintains two heavy duty photocopying machines. Two operators are appointed to provide photocopying service in shift basis.

UGC-INFONET SERVICES

The SDTM Library is one of the members of INFLIBNET UGC-Infonet Digital Library Consortium since 2003. UGC has set up this programme to promote use of electronic databases and full text access to e-journals by the research and Academic community of the country.

Online databases are accessible via the Library Homepage, which provide access to full-text scholarly research articles beyond the physical wall of the library:

- Access to more than 7000 full text scholarly journals online
- Nine online databases in the field of social science: Project Muse (389 journals); Oxford University Press (202 journals); JSTOR (729 journals); Springer Link (1236 journals); Taylor and Francis (1076 journals); JCCC (Gateway Portal); ISID; Cambridge Journals Online (279 journals); Wiley Interscience (502 journals) available under the UGC Infonet services
- Library subscribe to Sage Online Journals (240 journals); Emerald Management Xtra (160 journals); ABI/INFORM Complete™ (2950 journals); indiastat.com (statistical database); World Bank Databases (GDF+WDI+e-Library)
- IP Based access to all e-Resources
- Statistical usage reports of e-resources

DOCUMENT DELIVERY SERVICES

TISS Library has been recognized as one of the Twenty Two Document Delivery Centres established by UGC-INFLIBNET, Ahmedabad. The Centre will deliver, on demand, the copies of research papers from 4000 and odd print journals subscribed by these 22 centres apart from 7000 and odd full text e-journals, conference proceedings and other materials. Access to all these journals has been provided through JCCC gateway portal. Users can also submit an online request in JCCC for the article from both print and e-journals.

DIGITAL LIBRARY SERVICES

A State-of-art Digital Library provides seamless access to various CD-ROM Databases, Electronic Theses and Dissertations, In-house Bibliographic and full text Databases, Institutional Repository, MK Tata Centre Archive etc.

Major CD-ROM database collections includes ProQuest, Wilson Social Science Abstract, Popline, ABI/INFORM etc:

- Access to Electronic version of Indian Journal of Social Work and Sociological Bulletin on Library intranet
- Digitisation of library materials including Rare and Out of Print books but in demand
- Digitisation of Theses and Dissertations submitted to the institute
- External Digitisation projects
- Scanning and printing facility for the students

CYBER LIBRARY

The SDTM Library has set up Cyber Library with over 100 Pentium computers working in a networked environment through connectivity provided by ERNET India using 2 Mbps High Bandwidth Leased Line. It was inaugurated and thrown open to the students on 12th November, 2008 during the ILA International Conference from 12-15 November, 2008 organised by the library in collaboration with Indian Library Association. The Online databases like Project Muse, Springer Link, JSTOR, Blackwell will provide access to full text journals through UGCInfonet E-Journals Consortia. In addition, SPSS and SAS computing facilities will also be accessible to the scholars.

Salient features of SDTM Cyber Library:

- Cyber library in a networked environment with 100 computers using a dedicated 2 Mbps leased line
- Open 24×7 and 365 days a year
- Both reading and computing facilities
- Laser printing facility
- Access to full text online journals through UGC-Infonet E-Journals Consortia and other library e-resources.
- IP based Web Cameras for surveillance to enhance security of the library resources

Cyber Library-Acceptable Use and Code of Conduct:

- Do Not Connect Your Mobile To Computers.
- Do Not Install Any Software Without Prior Permission Of IT Team.

- Do Not Download Movies OR Songs.
- Do Not Remove LAN Cord, Keyboard And Mouse From The Computers.
- Do Not Save Any Document On The Desktop.
- Kindly Scan Your Pen Drive, CDs OR DVDs Before use.
- Keep Your Mobile On Silent Mode.
- Eatables are not allowed inside the Cyber Library.
- Take Care Of Your Own Belongings.
- Turn Off The Computer After Your Work Is Completed.
- All Drives Will Be Formatted After Every 15 Days by IT team Without Any Intimation.
- IT Team Will Not be Responsible For Any Data Loss
- Kindly Co-operate With IT Team For Minimum Downtime Of The Computers.
- Please Inform To IT Team In Case Of Any Computers Problem.
- Please Keep The Cyber Library Clean.
- Keep Silence In Cyber Library.

LICENSES AND FAIR USE OF E-RESOURCES

The INFLIBNET Consortium subscribes to thousands of electronic journals including full text electronic resources and bibliographic databases for its member institutions. All electronic resources available through the Consortium are governed by license agreements.

The terms and conditions for using these resources are spelled out in license agreements that are signed with each publisher by the INFLIBNET Consortium on behalf of its member institutions.

The licenses for electronic resources impose two types of restrictions on its usage, namely:

- Who can use these resources; and
- How the resources can be used.

The first restriction defines authorized users for e-resources, which generally includes students, faculty, staff and onsite visitors of a subscribing institution. The second restriction deals with how these resources can be used. It is the responsibility of individual users to ensure that e-resources are used for personal, educational and research purposes only. Most of the agreements entered into by the Consortium and publishers specify items that users are prohibited to do.

Some of them are as follows:

- Systematic or programmatic downloading, retention, and printing are prohibited. For example, you cannot download entire issue of a journal or print out several copies of the same article.
- Electronic distribution of content is also restricted although the

specific restrictions vary from publisher to publisher. It may be permissible to forward an article to another colleague in your own institution by e-mail, however, transmitting an article to someone outside of the institution, or to a large group of recipients, a mailing list, or an electronic bulletin board, is not allowed.

- If you are teaching a class, you can print out a copy of an article from an electronic journal and include it in your course pack. However, do not make multiple copies for circulation. Copyright laws protect published material in any format so that it cannot be copied except in accordance with fair use. Providing access to material for educational purposes falls within the realm of fair use.
- Please ensure that the resource is used for educational and research purposes and not for commercial purposes.
- Providing electronic links on your course web pages to the Library's licensed resources is permitted but you cannot post the PDF of an article on your web site. The publishers' main concern is that people outside of your campus network should not be able to access resources licensed by your institution. However, a researcher can post a pre print of an article written by himself.
- As with any kind of scholarly communication, a researcher can use phrases or quotes from other articles and cite the source of information. However, a researcher is prohibited from using large chunk of information from an article or from a chapter in a book.

What Happens if the Licence is Violated

Publishers track the use of their electronic resources in terms of number of downloads made by subscribing institution. Misuse, if any, is notified to the subscribing institution with details of kinds of violations and institution is expected to take action.

The publisher also suspends the access to e-resource pending suitable action by subscribing institution. The access is stopped not only for journals where license agreement was violated but for all journals by the same publisher. Moreover, the access is suspended not only for the individual violator but for the entire institution.

Conditions of Use and Licensing Restrictions for Electronic Resources

The Consortium subscribes to thousands of electronic journals and bibliographic databases for use by authorized users in member institutions. The terms and conditions for using these resources are spelled out in electronic resource license agreements with each publisher.

It is the responsibility of individual users to ensure that the use of electronic resources does not breach the terms and conditions specified in the license agreements.

Licences vary from publisher to publisher; however, the general principles are as follows:

- Permitted:
  - Viewing, downloading, copying, printing and saving a copy of search results
  - Viewing, downloading, copying, printing and saving individual articles
  - Using e-resources for scholarly, educational or scientific research, teaching, private study and clinical purposes
  - Sending a copy of an article to another authorized user (*i.e.* current faculty, students or staff)
  - Posting the URL to the publisher's version of the article on a class web site (publisher links will allow only authorized users access)
- Not Permitted:
  - Use of robots or intelligent agents to do systematic, bulk or automatic downloading is not permitted
  - Systematic downloading or printing of entire journal issues or volumes, or large portions of other e-resources is not permitted
  - Using e-resources for commercial gain is not permitted (*i.e.* reselling, redistributing or republishing licensed content)
  - Transmitting, disseminating or otherwise making online content available to unauthorized users (*i.e.* sending to mailing lists or electronic bulletin boards) is not permitted
  - Posting the publisher's version or PDF of an article to an open class web site is not permitted (instead, post the URL to the article which will allow only authorized users access)

Breaches of the license agreement with publishers could result in the suspension of access to the resources for the member institutions. Generic license agreements for all publishers specifying all the terms and conditions of the following databases are available at their respective web site.

e-Resources under UGC-Infonet Digital Consortium:

- Project Muse (389 journals)
- Oxford University Press (202 journals)
- JSTOR (729 journals)
- Springer Link (1236 journals)
- Taylor and Francis (1076 journals)
- JCCC (Gateway Portal)
- ISID (Industrial Development Bibliographic Database)
- Cambridge Journals Online (279 journals)
- Wiley Interscience (502 journals)

e-Resources Subscribed by SDTM Library:

- Sage Publications (240 journals)

- Emerald Management Xtra (160 journals)
- ABI/INFORM Complete™ (2950 journals)
- indiastat.com (statistical database)
- World Bank Databases (GDF+WDI+e-Library)

Computer Access Acceptable Use and Code of Conduct

Only registered members of the Library are authorized to use the Computers, Internet facility or to access e-Resources. Prior to such authorization, the students must sign and return the Library Registration Form acknowledging their responsibilities and the consequences of violation.

Students are expected to observe network etiquette by being polite. Students are prohibited from pretending to be someone else; transmitting obscene messages or pictures; revealing personal addresses or telephone numbers either their own or another person's; or using the network in a way that would disrupt use by others. The following policy for acceptable use of computers, networks, and system resources, including the Internet and e-resources, shall apply to all TISS administrators, faculty, staff, and students.

All technology equipment shall be used under the supervision of the site administrator. Any user who violates any condition of this policy is subject to disciplinary action or administrative sanctions.

In addition to any other disciplinary action taken, the Technology Department reserves the right to terminate access to system resources for any user who violates these guidelines:

- Every user in whose name a system account is issued will be responsible at all times for its proper use.
- Users shall not let other persons use their name, logon, password, or files for any reason
- Users shall not use others' system accounts or try to discover another user's password.
- Users shall not erase, rename, or make unusable anyone else's computer files, programmes or disks.
- Users shall not use computers for any non-instructional or non-administrative purpose, including, instant messaging, online shopping, or personal use of streaming media such as online radio stations or video broadcasts.
- Users may not install, download, copy, or distribute copyrighted materials such as software, audio or video, files, graphics, and text without the written permission of the administrator.
- Users shall not use the computers for illegal purposes, in support of illegal activities, or for any other activity prohibited.
- Users shall not write, produce, generate, copy, propagate, or attempt to introduce any computer code designed to self-replicate, damage, or otherwise hinder the performance of any computer's memory, file

system, or software. Such software is often called a bug, virus, worm, Trojan Horse, or other name.

- Users shall not use computers to purposefully distribute, create, or copy messages or materials that are abusive, obscene, sexually oriented, threatening, harassing, damaging to another's reputation, or illegal.
- Users shall not use computers to purposefully access materials that are abusive, obscene, sexually oriented, threatening, harassing, damaging to another's reputation, or illegal. In the event that accidental access to prohibited materials occurs, users are expected to immediately discontinue such access and report the incident either to Library staff or to the administrator.
- Users shall not intentionally damage the system, damage information belonging to others, misuse system resources, or allow others to misuse system resources.
- Users shall not alter or vandalize computers, networks, printers, or other associated equipment and system resources. Alteration or vandalism includes, but is not limited to: removal of parts, intentional destruction of equipment, altering system settings or software, installing unauthorized or unlicensed software or programmes, attempting to degrade or disrupt system performance, or attempting to make system resources unusable.
- Users shall not use computers for the forgery or attempted forgery of e-mail messages. Attempts to read, delete, copy, or modify the e-mail of other system users, deliberate interference with the ability of other users to send/receive e-mail, or the use of another person's e-mail account is prohibited.
- Users should not use library network for sending and receiving a large number of personal messages, including using group e-mail distribution lists to send non-administrative or non-instructional messages to other users.

NATIONAL CENTRE FOR SOCIAL SCIENCES INFORMATION AND DOCUMENTATION

The TISS library with its valuable collections both in terms of quality and quantity in the field of social sciences, social work, health sciences act as a nodal centre of major source of information in the field of social sciences in India as well as abroad. This Centre's vision is to bring world class information services to the academic community of India in the field of social science.

The main mandate is to provide full range of documentation and information services in the area of social sciences apart from the core subject of Social Work, which will accept request from other user libraries via post, telephone, e-mail or fax and delivers the information. The centre is also providing 50 research students space for retrieving information, analysing data with all IT infrastructure from India and abroad with residential facility from the institute.

Salient features of the Centre are:

- Provide seamless, network access to worldwide scholarly information resources of relevance to the academic community, facilitating improved learning, teaching, research, collaboration and information sharing
- Provide orientation and training to the academic community in making effective use of electronic information sources, tools and services
- Dedicated Data Centre for e-journals, full text CD-ROM databases in the field of social sciences
- Training Centre for Research Scholars from NGO's, Institutions who are involved in Social Science Research and dissemination of information

PHYSICAL AMBIENCES

- *Cleanliness:* Library is a central resource department that is the backbone of all academic programmes of the institute. Students and faculty would be spending their considerable time in library premises pursuing their research and studies. Hence, it is very much essential that library has a checking system in place to monitor the cleanliness and hygiene of the library premises like regular sweeping, cleaning and mopping of all floors, and washrooms.
- *Electricity and Water and Ventilation:* Library will ensure that these essential things are working at all times and users would not be put to any inconvenience.
- *Floor Plan and Direction/Guideposts:* Library shall have floor plans designed and proper directions/guideposts for people to move around the library looking for resources/services.

4

Digital Library from "Project" to "Production"

Digital libraries are in a period of exploration and rapid development. While our sense of what they are or should become varies, for the sake of this discussion we assume a definition consistent with that articulated by Don Waters, the Director of the Digital Library Federation:

Digital libraries are organizations that provide the resources, including the specialized staff, to select, structure, offer intellectual access to, distribute, preserve the integrity of, and ensure the persistence over time of collections of digital works so that they are readily and economically available for use by a defined community or set of communities.

While experimentation and research are essential to the development of effective digital libraries, it is ultimately formally defined and institutionally supported *organizations* that will ensure the viability of digital collections.

Wendy Lougee, the University of Michigan's digital library programme director, has suggested that we can apply a kind of human developmental model to the four distinct stages of digital library development, beginning with Infancy and culminating in Maturity.

Infancy is marked by learning through projects. Projects not only facilitate learning, but test resistance to ideas, find opportunities and resources and barriers, and eventually create stable building blocks. In Adolescence, we see peer modeling and the exploration of best practices: here, the digital library has begun to look outward both to other institutions, but also to methods and formats that will ensure longevity and interoperability.

The third stage of development, which she calls the digital library as Young Adult, is where we find the organizations that I wish to explore in this paper. In this stage of development, we find an increasing focus on collaboration, especially for the establishment of standards and architectures for interoperability. Maturity is marked by the presence of a fully functioning digital society, a market economy, and rich collaboration and knowledge environments such as those found in UARC.

The relatively intense focus on digital libraries in the last few years has resulted in a handful of well-developed production support organizations. Although experimentation for materials such as video continues to be important, these organizations have all successfully moved beyond the early stages marked by projects, work in isolation, and developing support for basic formats and methods.

In fact, these stable digital library production organizations exhibit a new set of characteristics that are an important part of their productivity and livelihood.

- They are not only engaged with the digital library community, but are fully integrated into their larger organizations (such as university libraries).
- These relatively mature organizations have moved beyond a focus on "projects" to a mode where they are deploying and supporting classes of systems—systems into which more content can be added.
- The production organizations reflect a high level of investment by the larger institutions in which they are situated. This investment is consistent with a recognition by the institution that the digital library is critical to its mission.
- Finally, and significantly, these organizations undertake *open ended* maintenance and development of the collections and access systems they support. While it is a certainty that the methods and strategies for maintenance will evolve, setting a term on the duration of responsibility for a collection can only contribute to a process of trivializing the collections of the digital library: these digital library collections are, in effect, our perpetual responsibility.

The University of Michigan's Digital Library Production Service is an operation that exhibits these characteristics. The discussion that follows is one that attempts to illustrate the value of these characteristics by exploring the organization of DLPS and three model systems that it uses to provide a high degree of functionality and cost effectiveness in building the digital library.

BACKGROUND

The Digital Library Production Service is part of a larger University of Michigan Digital Library Initiative, led by one of the University Library's three Associate Directors. The catalyst for the UM Digital Library Initiative was the 1991 Information Symposium, an effort to address campus issues with regard to networked information.

That Information Symposium, involving a broad cross section of the University faculty, culminated with a number of recommendations. The campus should attempt to:

- Bring together library and technology expertise

- Develop visible projects
- Create an "Information Community" (*i.e.*, principles of access and support)

Eventually, in support of these goals, the heads of the three principal information organizations on campus, the Information Technology Division, the School of Information, and the University Library, committed joint funding for a Digital Library Initiative. This funding included support for the creation of a programme director position and funding for projects that would have campus impact.

Even this commitment was situated in a set of larger accomplishments, which allowed the formalization of goals for campus digital library initiatives. Prior to the Information Symposium, the University Library had begun to embark on some preliminary and perhaps formative efforts to build digital library components.

Wide area access to non-bibliographic information sources *i.e.*, to the data themselves, rather than metadata became a focal effort of the University Library in the late 1980's. The University of Michigan Library put in place a modest programme of support for statistical data files, began exploring delivery of GIS data, and then ultimately put in place a formal access system for text encoded in SGML. The Library had begun to build systems for storing and accessing library collections in electronic formats.

After the Information Symposium, beginning in 1992, the University Library undertook a number of initiatives that laid the groundwork for future work and future relationships. Some of these, like the Library's Gopher server, were unremarkable in their use of technology, but played important roles in information provision and partnerships.

Others, like the UM implementation of TULIP, put in place significant pieces of infrastructure that would later prove instrumental in the University's development of digital libraries. The Library's Gopher server was remarkable in at least one respect, its aggressive approach to putting collection material online. Although it had previously undertaken similar efforts prior to Gopher, the new mechanism allowed Library staff to mount collections like statistical information from the Commerce Department in ways that reached extremely broad audiences.

The strong presence of the Library's Gopher on campus also contributed to early cooperative efforts with the University's computing organization, ITD. TULIP's contributions were even more profound, if less visible. Although Michigan's was one of several Elsevier TULIP implementations, at the University of Michigan TULIP spawned a development effort that saw the creation of FTL, the search engine now used by JSTOR, and tif2gif, Doug Orr's optimized GIF generator for TIFF G4 images, now used by the University of Michigan Making of America system.

A broad, campus wide partnership has played a powerful role in moving the concept of digital libraries forward at the University of Michigan. As mentioned earlier, the Library's Gopher project played an important role in establishing a partnership between the University of Michigan's Library and the Information Technology Division.

Like Gopher, the TULIP effort contributed to bringing the Library together with another campus entity, the School of Information. These partnerships were formalized in 1993, and Wendy Lougee was appointed the director of campus wide digital library efforts.

That partnership is a powerful presence today in the University of Michigan's digital library work, with management and advisory committees composed of representatives from each of the organizations, and multi-organizational funding for initiatives. A number of significant UM digital library efforts began in 1994. Among these is the now organizationally independent JSTOR, which grew rapidly in size and scope, and now plays an important role in shaping our expectations about archiving and retrospective conversion.

Another major initiative appearing in 1994 was the UM Humanities Text Initiative, which served to expand the earlier UMLibText effort and provide a significant WWW presence for the University's SGML-based text collections. Also appearing in 1994 was the University of Michigan's NSF/NASA/ARPA funded digital library effort, focusing not on production technologies, but on the role of agent technologies and distribution of responsibility for the digital library. The breadth of these 1994 initiatives provides some indication of the fruitfulness and variety of the evolving environment at Michigan. This growing proliferation of significant digital library activities—activities that had moved well beyond the "experimental" and had begun to reach wide audiences—that contributed most to the recognition of a need for a digital library production organization. Between 1994 and 1996, while the activities mentioned above continued to grow, new efforts at Michigan were introduced, and along with them new models and formats.

Among the significant efforts undertaken were UM's local image system developed for the Museum Education Site Licensing Project (MESL), the UM Making of America development, and negotiation of the Elsevier journal content that would later go into the PEAK system. These initiatives will be discussed in greater detail later, but they brought to the digital library environment at Michigan a variety of significant new elements.

Not only were new formats or methods introduced (continuous tone images in the case of MESL, and preservation oriented monograph conversion in the case of MOA), but several of these efforts helped to highlight the absence of a formally defined organization to support the effort. In 1996, the partnership's support expanded and the resources were identified to create a digital library production service.

THE OLE PROJECT

The project is an initiative of the Duke University in the USA. The Project, begun in 2008 with funding from the Andrew Mellon Foundation and has involved a multinational group of libraries in the USA, Canada, Australia and UK with the objective of developing the design for an *Open Library Environment* (OLE), an alternative to the current model of an Integrated Library System. The goal is to produce a design document to inform open source library system development efforts, to guide future library system implementations, and to influence current Integrated Library System vendor products.

The aims of the Project are to:

- Adopt a transformational design approach to create a flexible, interoperable system that goes beyond replicating the concepts that underlie legacy LMS.
- Develop and use open, flexible technology to produce a community sourced alternative to current LMS and *electronic resource management* (ERM) systems.
- Automate core library functions in a way suited to modern workflows and one that interoperates with business and content applications beyond the library.

OLE is a framework and platform that goes beyond the monolithic LMS through its ability to utilize other systems and deliver valuable new services. At the same time, OLE allows institutions to avoid redundancy of data, and reduce purchase and integration of add on components to their current ILS in order to carry out library business. The OLE places the library's business in context within the fabric of the institution and the research process, rather than keeping it a separate, siloed operation. The Australian National Library, one of the partners in the OLE Project, articulated a service framework based on a *services oriented architecture* (SOA). In the SOA sense of the word, a service is a set of capabilities offered by a service provider through a service definition that makes the capabilities discoverable by a service consumer. The implementation of the service is "opaque" to the consumer, and the invocation of a service itself may seek out the SOA defined capabilities of another service provider. Importantly, the services may be locally owned or those under the control of others. The articulation of SOA requires service definitions and agreed protocols and schemas. Thus standards, in this case, web services based, will be required to be defined. This is where bodies such as the DLF and NISO have made their presence felt.

The OLE framework has also suggested a predominantly SOA-based model and has the following characteristics:

- *Flexibility:* Supports a wide range of resources; accessed by a wide range of customers in a variety of contexts; provides structures for extending and adding new types of resources, customers and contexts.

- *Community Ownership:* Designed, built, owned, and governed by and for the library community on an open source licensing basis; sustained by the community with the assistance of a thriving vendor marketplace; evolves over time through transparent processes that enable and respond to input and innovation from the community.
- *Service Orientation:* Developed using the methods of *Service Oriented Architecture* (SOA) and implemented with web services to be a modular and technology neutral framework that ensures the interoperability of library business systems and accommodates a diversity of solutions without the risks posed by single source providers. Further, it can be customised to support local needs.
- *Enterprise Level Integration*: Designed to adapt to and integrate with other enterprise systems such as research support, student information, human resources, identity management, fiscal control, and repository and content management.
- *Efficiency:* Provides a modular application infrastructure that integrates with new and existing academic and research technologies and business processes for improved efficiency and effectiveness of the institution; meets current and future business needs of the community.
- *Sustainability:* Creates a reliable and robust framework to identify, document, innovate, develop, maintain, and review the software necessary to further the operation and mission of libraries.

The OLE Project draft final report provides an open source reference implementation of a set of technology services that that allow libraries to carry out their backend business operations, and therefore to replace their current ILS. However, OLE will also support functional capabilities that go beyond the existing ILS core. Each OLE component will be highly modular and use standards based interfaces, allowing an institution to mix and match OLE components with other, existing campus and library systems if desired—including both open source and commercial systems.

This will allow institutions to install only selected portions of OLE, or to adopt a phased replacement strategy. The OLE will not build the front end or resource discovery functionality of today's ILS's, but will instead provide support for several open source front end projects, as well as any commercial alternative that is willing to use OLE's standards based interfaces. OLE also expects its services to be delivered through non-library interfaces such as smart phones, learning management systems, campus portals, and other institutional products that involve resources and/or support from the library. The Abstract Reference Model for OLE shows the relationship between OLE middleware, OLE components, entities acted on by OLE, and third party components, such as Identity Management, Institutional Repositories, and Course Management

Systems. The OLE Reference Model is an abstract representation of the OLE framework. As such, it describes the high level *functional components* that will form OLE. Each of these components is made up of a number of workflows and/ or processes.

A workflow is a series of activities that involve people, business processes, and software that achieve a library business goal. For example, the OLE component *Describe Entity* is comprised of the processes *Obtain Metadata*, *Create Metadata*, *Modify Metadata*, *Delete Metadata* and *Expose Metadata*. Additionally, the reference model shows examples of *third party components* with which OLE will interoperate. These are reusable services, not developed or supplied by OLE, that fulfill an OLE business process.

The components that straddle the boundary between OLE and third party components represent the functions that will be provided partly by OLE and partly by third party components. The reference model also includes the *entities* that have so far been identified as belonging in the OLE framework. These are resources, collections, persons, organizations, and services. Finally, the bottom portion of the Reference Model illustrates the software that will manage and connect OLE components. It is this *middleware* that will provide interoperability with third party applications. An important point to note here is that the OLE Project used the ideas of the Australian NLA and also aligned its framework with a higher level framework such as the framework for Education and Research or e-Framework.

Similarly the OLE project aligns itself also with one or more services defined by the DLF. In other words, OLE will use the results of parallel activities both within the public domain as well as those of commercial vendors which conform to the principles of web services SOA is an architecture philosophy or framework that breaks down business processes into several generic services. Business processes or workflows, a *service usage model* (SUM) and protocols and schemas are defined. The framework also assumes that there is a Workflow Engine and a Rules/Policy Engine.

The Workflow Engine manages the modeled business processes whereas the Rules Engine modifies the workflows based on local policies. In other words a library using the OLE framework can customise the Rules Engine to suit its policy, which then modifies the Workflow Engine suitably for its purpose. This way, there will be no need for a library to reinvent commonly used workflows via a service layer but at the same time have the possibility of modifying the workflow with an appropriate change in the Rules Engine. The fact that workflows are defined within generic services, allows that two or more tasks may use the same service layer to accomplish different tasks.

This will ensure reusability of software and re-purposing of software, two key advantages of SOA. For instance, the Deliver Entity component describes processes that track the request and supply of a resource. It includes processes that initiate and receive the request, identify the user requesting the resource, check and verify the user's credentials, and determine availability and terms of use of the resource requested. A message is sent to the user whenever a condition is not met. The resource is supplied if all conditions are met. Another important feature of the OLE Project is that a Build Project is proposed following the planning phase which was completed in July 2009.

The Build Project will be a Community Sourced Project. It means a project that will be funded by a consortium of institutions that will sign an agreement and contribute financial/human resources in the building and testing of the The OLE planners have recommended becoming a project within the Kuali Foundation.

The Kuali Foundation, which directly supports administrative community source software projects in the higher education sector, was designed as a lightweight administrative organization and can provide administrative functions for OLE at a fraction of the cost of building an entirely new entity. In addition, the SOA middleware that Kuali has developed will play an important role in the OLE Build Project. The Build phase of the project is expected to begin soon after the funding proposal is given to and approved by the Andrew Mellon Foundation.

The advantages of building the software as a community sourced project are that it will:

- Provide sustainability over the course of product development
- Promote innovation and shared knowledge
- Allow Interaction with the broader academic and research library community to ensure that the delivered software is matched to as wide a set of needs as possible.
- Provide the ongoing support needed once the software is ready for use.

Assuming that funding is approved by the donor and contributions by Build partners, the first full release to partners, consisting of the full infrastructure and basic set of services needed for ILS replacement, as well as for the enhanced functionality specified by the OLE design, and accompanied by workflow/ customization templates for research universities and liberal arts colleges is expected by Jan 2012.

The Build Project will leverage the results of other initiatives:

- Existing systems, *e.g.* shared database feeds, open ERM data from e-publishers.
- Existing Discovery Tools
  - WorldCat Local
  - LibraryFind
  - VuFind
  - extensible Catalog toolkits

The Project will also outsource the coding to organizations in Bulgaria and India.

When complete, OLE will allow libraries to:

- Discontinue their current ILS and several ancillary systems necessary today to manage scholarly content, and to continue their business functions through OLE or through the enterprise integration of OLE with Identity Management, Enterprise Resource Planning systems and Virtual Learning Environment systems.
- Provide interoperability with institution wide applications. This will allow the library to leverage rather than duplicate enterprise functions.

The OLE will also be format agnostic for collection and resource management thereby dissolving differences between physical and electronic resources. What makes OLE different from current monolithic LMS products is that libraries take on only the services and workflows they need through workflow managers and engines.

Libraries that don't need certain services can turn them off or adapt them to the workflows that better fit their needs. It is not as if only OLE is alone in choosing to go the SOA route. As already pointed out, the Education and Research Framework and the Kuali Foundation have already used SOA based software and paradigms in their projects. What makes the OLE approach different from the model used in current offerings of LMS products is that the latter emphasize internal functional integration while the former advocates the freeing of the LMS via use of external services and tools using commonly agreed business processes, protocols and data models so that a library can choose to use those services, processes, etc., that it requires rather than committing itself to a complex internally integrated product. Since the release of the final draft report, some vendors have criticized the approach spelt out by the OLE project for contradicting itself: first by stating that the OLE Project was to... "guide further library and to influence current Integrated Library System vendor products" and second by stating that... "a proposal to carry the project forward into the next phase of building the software".

The criticism is that the project has not spelt out the business model that will support development based on the demand, market share expected, the existing competition, risks that institutions would be willing to take in investing in the build project. In spite of the criticism, the support OLE has received, the meticulousness with which the OLE Project's planning phase has been conceived and implemented and the fact that over 300 libraries in four countries participated in the exercise is indicative of the importance that was attached to the project and the consensus on using a totally different approach to designing and implementing LMS functions and beyond. The impact of OLE is bound to change the face of LMS, whether via the OLE Build Project or via vendor's adopting the principles and ideas that are undoubtedly sound.

The DLF Discovery Interface Task Force Recommendations

The DLF in 2007 created a ILS Discovery Interface Task Group to:

- Analyse issues involved in integrating *integrated Library systems* (ILS's) and discovery applications, and
- Create a technical proposal for accomplishing such integration.

A set of revised recommendations was released in December 2008. The task force recommendations were preceded by a careful analysis of the premises that should drive the task force's work.

The premises include the following:

- OPAC interfaces currently provided by most LMS's cannot by themselves meet the demands of users in a world where the availability and sophistication of digital resources and web applications has increased significantly.
- This does not reflect on badly designed interfaces; it reflects the fact that users now need a wider variety of capabilities than any one software package can be expected to provide.
- These trends imply that the ILS needs to become a platform that supports appropriate interfaces for discovery applications living on top of it instead of trying to do everything on its own.
- Some ILS vendors provide proprietary methods for accessing their underlying data stores, *e.g.* API tools accessible only for a special fee to trained users, or direct SQL queries against the ILS's database
- These methods do provide the hooks into the ILS but making library resources more widely usable requires a larger, standards based API.
- To enable outward integration ILS's should adopt a more standardized method for providing API access to the data store
- There is need to move away from traditional library centric protocols like Z39.50 towards an XML based web services API model.
- Such a model will enable developers outside of the library community to more easily access the information stored within the ILS, creating opportunities for greater integration with non library applications, *e.g.*, course management tools.

The task force recommendations comprise a set of Abstract functions and bindings that should be satisfied by APIs and/or protocols at different levels of interoperability.

The work of the DLF task force is for the benefit of developers of open source and commercial LMS vendors and will no doubt be used by the OLE Project in its build project. The future of LMS discovery interfaces will be bound by the standards and protocols that have been articulated by the DLF and a national standards body such as the NISO.

THE NISO BEST PRACTICES FOR DESIGNING WEB SERVICES IN THE LIBRARY CONTEXT

In a parallel move but not confined to discovery interfaces, the NISO too has come up with broad principles which may guide the design of web services of the following categories:

Discovery Services

Web services to discover metadata, full text or a service; web service to create and maintain a directory.

Locate Services

Web services to communicate requests and circulation transactions between peer circulation systems, *e.g.*, between members of a consortium of libraries.

Requesting Services; Delivery Services; Common Services

Like the DLF-DI task force recommendations, NISO guidelines are targeted to developers of LMS products. The OLE build project, no doubt, will take notice of the NISO guidelines and to that extent there is a common thread that will bind these apparently independent initiatives in the years to come. Both the DLF and NISO speak of 'Services', clearly indicating that the future of library applications will be firmly founded on the principles of SOA.

THE EXTENSIBLE CATALAOG (XC) PROJECT OF THE UNIVERSITY OF ROCHESTER

The XC Project is to design/develop a set of open source applications that will:

- Provide libraries with an alternative way to reveal their collections to library users.
- Provide easy access to all resources across a variety of databases, metadata schemas and standards
- Enable library content to be revealed through other services that libraries may already be using, such as content management systems and learning management systems.
- Make library collections more web accessible by revealing them through web search engines.

As can be seen the objectives of the XC as indeed the OLE initiatives spoken of earlier are similar. However, the XC's uniqueness lies in the fact that it has developed and released various Tool Kits as open source implementations.

The following tool kits have been released:

- OAI. This will allow integration of XC with an existing ILS and digital repositories.

- NCIP. This tool kit will allow RFID functionality to be enabled within An existing LMS
- Learning Management.

The following tool kits are under development:

- *Metadata services* four types of metadata will be available to XC: bibliographic, holding, item and authority data. The tool kit will also have live access to circulation status, authentication mechanisms, and native ILS circulation request functionality.
- *Drupal Tool Kit* XC will offer a number of user interfaces including one that is embedded into the Drupal CMS
- A tool kit that will be embedded into the Blackboard Learning Management System

Toolkits will incorporate unanimously agreed upon standards for searching through library resources including faceted browsing interface and compliance with the *Functional Requirements for Bibliographic Records* (FRBR) which lays stress on the usefulness of bibliographic displays rather than just the matching of search terms with catalogue records.

The fact that XC is open source will provide possibilities for customization, although this may be a theoretical advantage since the cost of such customization is not known. The XC Project and its tool kits are already recognized by the OLE Project as resources that can be leveraged in its Build Project plan. To this extent the work will contribute to the future of LMS and open source initiatives in this area.

Web Scale Service Proposal of OCLC

In an announcement made by OCLC in 2009, they have proposed to offer "the first Web scale, cooperative library management service." This will ultimately, it is hoped, bring into WorldCat Local the full complement of functions traditionally performed by a locally installed *integrated library system* (ILS) via the web.

In this, the OCLC will be using the WorldCat database, undoubtedly the world's largest bibliographic database of over a billion records plus OCLC's "cloud", or bank of servers and communications infrastructure. OCLC's vision involves shifting increasing portions of activity managed library by library through locally or consortially implemented automation to the network level, under its global WorldCat infrastructure. OCLC plans to work with the more than 1,000 libraries and partners that are currently using OCLC library management systems in Europe and Asia Pacific to help build the new service.

Like in the full version of WorldCat, WorldCat Local users search against the massive WorldCat.org database, with their local library's holdings presented first in result lists. The proposal envisages the use OCLCs' enriched WorldCat Local with article level content including the material from its Article First service plus a vast body of articles from EBSCO to those who subscribe to First Search and EBSCO host. Other providers may be added in course of time. WorldCat's meta search enhancement will allow search also of a library's licensed content. The WorldCat Navigator will enable consortial borrowing.

OCLC plans to move circulation and acquisitions functions in time:

- Circulation is planned to be implemented via a web based client
- Acquisitions through WorldCat Local will include functionality of the ILS print acquisitions module and an *electronic resource management* (ERM) system.

These moves could bring the local ILS in use at the libraries which may use this web scale service, redundant. Since the users of OCLC are among the biggest libraries in the world, their influence on the rest is bound to be significant.

However, there are also concerns about the OCLC proposal:

- A library using the OCLC cloud services route, will be exposing themselves to the risk of giving away to OCLC control of how all their data is used and shared
- The planned OCLC system would probably appeal mainly to smaller to medium sized institutions. Large libraries may not like to compromise on functionality and customization to be "web scale," as OCLC is describes it.
- Developing country libraries, many of whom are not members of OCLC will not find the option appealing
- The plan is presently confined as being applicable to a few ILS vendor systems

DLPS ARCHETYPES: SYSTEMS, NOT PROJECTS

The University of Michigan Digital Library Production Service is working to define classes of systems, and to put in place mechanisms to support these classes. These systems represent archetypes, and each collection is assessed to determine whether and how it might fit existing systems.

We are careful not to *force* a particular body of material to fit one of the existing systems, but when it is possible, we are able to achieve those previously mentioned economies of scale much more effectively. This approach also results in other significant advantages.

- By approaching support for the digital library in this way, we are able to draw on significant format expertise within DLPS.
- We are able to deploy collections in an environment of ongoing support and planning. Each class represents a model or framework for continuing expansion rather than a standalone system that could be orphaned.
- DLPS staff members are able to participate more effectively in national

or regional cooperative efforts, sharing models and expertise. These larger efforts enrich DLPS efforts at the same time that DLPS contributes to the larger digital library community.

As we continue development of these classes, we are frequently able to see opportunities for consolidation or expansion. A powerful example of this refinement process was encountered in 1998.

The HTI, in cooperation with SGML Systems, deployed each new collection in its native SGML encoding, re using access mechanisms previously developed wherever possible. Although DLPS principles of re-use were in wide evidence, the large number of legacy systems for text collections had become a significant problem when we wanted to add new features.

Each new feature assumed a foundation of code that may or may not be in existence, depending on when the collection was put online. A strategy was articulated for encoding all such collections in a common format, and building a single piece of code to provide all of the functionality needed for all of the text collections.

If the collection was predominantly drama and HTI wished to provide searching on speakers and speeches, this subroutine would be invoked; otherwise, in cases where it was inappropriate to the collection (or speaker and speech were not encoded), speaker/speech searching would not be made available.

The approach was christened GUMS (General Unified Markup System), and early work on moving to implement collections and systems using GUMS has been very successful. There is a clear sense, however, that we must undertake an ongoing activity, parallel to the work of extending the current systems, to refine and document of the current set of classes.

THREE SAMPLE MODELS

The principles elaborated earlier are clearly visible in many of the collections or services within DLPS. Each of the following three examples benefited from previous work within DLPS, and each forms a class, as well as a system to which more content can be added.

Making of America and Encoded Text Systems

The system built for the first University of Michigan Making of America collection was designed to fully support preservation oriented conversion methods and provide a gateway or even bridge to the high quality access systems developed for the Humanities Text Initiative.

The history of the UM MOA development effort is documented elsewhere, and a more lengthy treatment of the technology used is also available. The UM MOA system has been extraordinarily successful, both as an architecture within the DLPS digital library efforts, and as a digital library resource for a broad range of users. Of primary importance in the UM MOA architecture is support for the products of a Library Preservation process. Images in the system are 600 dpi bitonal, TIFF G4 files. No derivatives (*e.g.*, GIF or JPEG images) are created or stored, except at the time of viewing request. When a user requests a page, the system generates a GIF or PDF derivative in real time and without any appreciable delay (typically less than one second).

Four levels of resolution in GIF are made available to users, taking into account the wide range of displays and network connections; a 600dpi PDF version is also made available, primarily for printing. While the number of pages—approximately 3 million by late 2000—is relatively small compared to a typical research library collection, its large size, expected continued growth, and continuing changes in desktop technology (including networking) argue against storing anything but the master images online.

Use patterns also suggest that as long as we are able to generate appropriate derivatives in real time, based on user demand, we will significantly minimize the requirements for management. Of course there are still concerns about the appropriateness of TIFF G4 as a preservation quality surrogate for pages, but the University of Michigan Library believes that this format provides a high quality surrogate for most printed materials.

Page images from the Preservation conversion process are subsequently treated by automated Optical Character Recognition (OCR), and the OCR is associated with the page image using a simple form of SGML.

The extensibility of the MOA system has in fact been tested through our OCR processes: two generations of OCR have been applied to all of the materials without the need to change the system architecture. Current OCR technology used by DLPS is a voting system, providing the MOA system with a significantly high quality of character representation than typical OCR.

The system exhibits approximately 99.8 per cent accuracy for nearly all content bearing pages (*e.g.*, excluding pages with engravings and textual pages such as the title page and advertisements). The SGML applied to the text is XML-compliant, and provides information such as image location, page type (*e.g.*, table of contents), "confidence" of the OCR, and page number.

The automatically generated SGML in MOA is also largely consistent with the Text Encoding Initiative (TEI) Guidelines, allowing a full integration with DLPS' encoded text efforts. While certain attributes such as those mentioned above (*e.g.*, OCR "confidence") have been added to the MOA SGML Document Type Definition (DTD), it is otherwise entirely consistent with the TEI.

This has allowed DLPS' encoded text operations in HTI to extract individual texts and upgrade them, correcting OCR and applying fuller encoding. Because the MOA system is fundamentally TEI-compliant, it can accommodate both the loosely encoded texts and texts with more detailed encoding.

As resources are available to HTI, materials can be enhanced in MOA, ensuring better retrieval and higher levels of functionality for users. Extensibility is critical for a system of this size and importance. The UM MOA system has been designed to be augmented in a variety of ways without significant overhaul.

For example, DLPS has regenerated OCR for MOA without interruptions in service, thereby improving retrieval. Texts can be augmented by HTI, as discussed above. New texts can be added as Preservation resources allow, and all indexing and preparation of Web pages is automated.

The underlying body of materials can remain largely unchanged while work on enhanced interfaces takes place—a process that took place between November 1998 and January 1999. We believe that the MOA system is a model of scalability and extensibility.

The success of the MOA archetype has been multifold. It has allowed us to add materials, a process now underway with MOA4 (2.3 million additional pages). It has helped reduce HTI costs, providing a readily accessible surrogate for the encoding process; in 1998-1999, HTI will add 100 more texts to the American Verse Project collection.

HTI works with the MOA system and contract services to keep its overall cost down and ensure future integration of its products with a Preservation surrogate. Perhaps most significant among MOA's successes, however, is the level of use by a broad range of users.

While the printed source materials were largely unused (most had not circulated in more than ten years), in their online format they are searched some 100,000 times each month, and approximately 100,000 page images are displayed. The constant stream of positive user responses comes from genealogists, philologists, and academics alike.

Image Services

The system built by DLPS Image Services provides a high degree of functionality for a variety of images of objects ranging from art and architecture, to artifacts, to manuscripts. It is also a model for federating diverse collections, respecting the autonomy and heterogeneity of the source collection while creating a union collection for mainstream users.

Image Services uses a mapping strategy for its metadata, keeping the native field names and data but simultaneously "tagging" each field with a corresponding value in a sort of Dublin Core scheme.

This allows Image Services to provide collections in two ways: first, as a highly functional version of the database maintained by the contributing organization (*e.g.*, the University of Michigan Museum of Art); and second, with generic field labels common to all of the images in the system. Thus, for example, the Museum of Art might use the field label "Artist," while the History of Art Department might use the field label "Source." Having selected only the Museum of Art data online, the user would be presented with search options for "Artist," and data would be displayed accordingly.

However, if the user search across the entire collection, the Dublin Core value "Creator" is presented to the user as a search option and in the display of records. This, along with features for tailoring display and functionality ensures that a contributing organization such as the Museum of Art will enjoy the benefits of a powerful and highly functional system for their data.

Trying to bring together a wide variety of administratively separate collections on campus is challenging, but we believe that the incentive of a cost effective, inexpensive, highly functional host service (rather than, for example, administrative mandates) has been very effective in creating a unified database managed by DLPS.

DLPS Image Services uses a unified database to ensure a high level of performance and flexibility. Indeed, many of the collection providers maintain local management systems that could be brought online successfully.

The diversity of systems, including Oracle, FileMaker, Embark, and others, would present a serious challenge to creating a distributed search feature. Instead, data are extracted from each of these systems on a periodic basis, and are then ported into the DLPS Image Services system.

Using the methods described above, Image Services is still able to provide access to each collection as if it were an isolated, separately managed collection; the federating approach does not force a lowest common denominator effect.

Instead, the significant resources of DLPS can be leveraged to provide faster search mechanisms, low cost RAID, and around the clock maintenance of the database. These too are effective incentives to organizations when considering whether to mount their data through a central campus agency such as DLPS.

The Image Services system is very rich in functionality. Primarily to satisfy the variety of needs created by the diverse collections, Image Services has built its system using a template system. By specifying (and possibly even creating) a different template, one can make the system appear radically differently.

For example, the primary interface presented to users is a search interface, with results appearing as a collection of thumbnails with associated descriptive information. Each thumbnail and descriptive label is, of course, a link to a fuller resolution view and more descriptive data.

However, by invoking another template such as that for "slide shows," the system can be made to appear as a set of larger images in a pre-selected and set sequence. Another templates provides an interfaces for comparison of multiple images, critical for use of art and architectural images. Each high resolution image is ultimately displayed with a pan-and-zoom interface.

Users can take advantage of low network speed connections or low end displays by sending relatively small segments of high resolution images across the network, and panning directionally to view more of the image. This feature has been extremely useful to a wide variety of users, including our Papyrologists, who use the system to work with extremely high resolution images of papyri, and are rarely equipped with computing resources to be able to bring up the full resolution image.

The approach taken by Image Services is extremely scalable. Adding other collections incurs only small, marginal costs (*e.g.*, RAID and time to process the new collection) rather than requiring us to build a new system for each.

We are also able to add new functionality easily, adding "modules" or subroutines to the current middleware rather than re-writing the programmes each time. At the same time, the system provides a high degree of functionality for a wide variety of users, including those who own and maintain the collections represented.

Peak

The PEAK system is, in the simplest terms, a mechanism for delivering the entire body of Elsevier Science's journals to a dozen institutions, with varying levels of access within and across institutions.

It is, however, an excellent example of the value of a production organization in an academic research institution. The University of Michigan was able to use DLPS to leverage production technologies in support of the research mission of the University.

Although alternatives were available to using a locally developed system, those alternatives would not have allowed us to use the Elsevier materials to learn about the economic decisions of users and institutions when using current journals.

Critical to our being able to support the research mission was our ability to use known technologies to bring the journals online. The University of Michigan had prior experience with the Effect Specifications (*i.e.*, Elsevier's format for delivering image, OCR, and metadata) during the TULIP experiment, and as mentioned earlier, UM developed several significant tools to make the TULIP journals available.

Notably, Ken Alexander had developed the search engine, FTL, which was subsequently used and refined in JSTOR, and Doug Orr had developed tif2gif to enable real time generation of GIF derivatives from the TIFF G4 images. The use of these tools in previous environments (*e.g.*, TULIP and the early days of JSTOR development at UM) allowed us to look past these critical hurdles and instead to focus on supporting the research model.

The availability of the known technologies also allowed us to invest energies in putting in place database mechanisms for authentication and for subscription/purchase control information, as well as new methods for compression to handle the large amounts of material.

Material began to arrive in late summer, 1997. Within a few months, the system was ready for use at the University of Michigan, and by the beginning of 1998, it was released to the subscribing institutions.

With Elsevier's cooperation, Michigan contracted with eleven other institutions to deliver the 1,200 journals with some very unique subscription models. Using a model dictated by Prof. Jeff Mackie Mason, four types of access were put in place:

- *Free*: Older materials (*i.e.*, pre-1997) were made freely available to all project participants. All project participants were also permitted free access to bibliographic and full text searches, with no charges levied for viewing citations or abstracts.
- *Traditional subscription*: As its name suggests, this model corresponds directly to the familiar subscription by journal title. A traditional subscription to a journal title permits unlimited access to the articles within that journal for the subscriber or subscribing institution.
- *Per-article purchase*: When access to an article is purchased by a user, the user has unlimited access to that article. While at one level, this is a fairly unremarkable feature, Mackie Mason's additional stipulation that this access should not be time bound added the burden of using a database to associate a user identity with an article identity. This ensured that that the user who purchased access to an article would continue to have unrestricted access to the online article for the duration of the project.
- *Generalized subscription:* The generalized subscription is the most novel and most challenging addition to PEAK. A generalized subscription consists of a number of "tokens" that can be spent on articles. An institution would purchase "bundles" of tokens, or generalized subscriptions. When tokens are available, they are spent on behalf of users for articles not covered by other subscription models. For example, if a user attempted to read an article from a journal not in an institution's traditional subscriptions, a generalized subscription token would be spent on that article. The article would then be available, without restrictions, to all other users at the institution. Again, the PEAK system must collect information about individual article access permissions, and associate them with users from each institution.

The research model further complicates these methods for access, where all methods for access are not available to all institutions, and not all institutions choose to take advantage of all methods available to them. This creates a complex matrix of users and materials, a matrix that must be available and reliable for the system to function properly. Please note that publications analyzing the results of this research will follow. We have already learned important lessons, however, and are working to share data on use with the participating institutions.

In implementing PEAK, our production technologies *and especially our production organization* allowed us to extend the digital library more fully into the University's mission of research and teaching. Independence from Elsevier was critical in order for us to be able to test these models, and the body of Elsevier materials was equally important to ensure that users would have a valuable body of materials that would draw them into the research environment.

The ultimate control and flexibility of the local production environment allowed the University of Michigan to perform research that would probably not have otherwise been possible, or could not have been performed in ways that the researcher stipulated.

MODELS CONCLUSION

These model systems help us to understand the value of a production organization in building the digital library. They also amply demonstrate each of the principles or ideals proposed as critical for the functioning of a digital library production organization.

- None of these systems would be possible without the full integration of DLPS into the Library, and indeed the University itself. Politically and procedurally, the fact that DLPS is a part of the University Library ensures a range of outcomes, including effective preservation oriented conversion and deployment (in the case of Making of America), online strategies guided by information professionals (in all of the systems), and integration of online resources with subscription and acquisition procedures (especially in the case of PEAK).
- Each of these systems is or represents a "class" of information, with consistent characteristics and support. Each is easily extensible through the addition of features or migration of code, and each continues to grow (in size) without revision of the underlying mechanisms. The imperatives of DLPS have ensured that we have invested in these models and long term value, rather than hastily deploying "stovepipes" of separate and inconsistent systems without integration.
- The investments made in the systems (and support for them) reflect a high level of investment consistent with the institutional mission. The quality of the underlying resources, for example, is extraordinarily high, just as the underlying metadata are extraordinarily rich. The staff resources (20 FTE) are primarily base budget resources, and staff skills are very high.

- All of the systems were constructed so that they could be supported in an open ended fashion (*i.e.*, as much as it is possible to say this, in perpetuity). Capture formats are all standards based and high fidelity; in fact, most are suitable for creating replacement copies of original publications. In nearly all cases, the "archival" version of the digital surrogate is also the online version.

These models are all cost effective and sustainable, and represent model systems for DLPS, with a significant emphasis placed on long term support and extension.

The progress of digital libraries will depend increasingly on the creation of production organizations, particularly within libraries.

The digital library cannot thrive on a proliferation of experimental projects, projects that will tend to undermine the viability of collections and work against cooperative architectures. In order for the digital library to thrive, we must begin to see a shift from "projects" to "archetypes." A focus on archetypes rather than projects is only possible in a production organization because of the need for continuity and re-use of resources in a coordinated, planned way.

The effective digital library production organization must be fully integrated into campus' academic mission, and especially into the mission and functions of the library. This can only be done by situating the digital library production organization *in* the library.

Too many of the processes and resources needed to support the digital library are a part of libraries; the principles for information organization and management are an essential part of librarianship.

Success in creating digital library production organizations like those I describe here will also lead to an increased probability that we will successfully federate digital library resources. The holistic approach creates not only economies of scale, but also important opportunities for integration.

At Michigan, this approach is leading to the elaboration of an architecture where every digital object is managed in highly functional ways that ensure the long term maintenance of that object. This architecture also brings these resources together in ways that are transparent to the user, but which ensures tight integration of multimedia resources. A focus on overall architecture is essential, and again can only ensue from testing hypotheses in production organizations.

Finally, sustainability is one of the key issues of the digital library, and an issue that also argues for the presence of the production operation. Certainly, as an ideal, many of us can readily embrace the notion that decisions must be made with regard for long term value of the digital object. It is only through a permanent production organization—an organization with funding in a base budget, with open ended appointments for staff, and with long term responsibility for maintenance and migration—that this ideal can be supported.

PRODUCTS AND SERVICES

Adapting IT for library applications is an ongoing process, right from procuring or developing IT enabled information products through computer aided processing and management to delivering IT-enriched services. Library professionals in India are already exposed to the different offshoots of IT for library organization and information services.

LIBRARY AUTOMATION PACKAGES

The availability of a wide variety of library automation software to suit the varied needs of libraries themselves is a reflection of the progress libraries have made in automating the operations of procuring, processing and providing information sources. Procurement is the end of the story for many other software/databases used in a library, whereas library automation systems will open a floodgate of issues. What the vendor provides is a structure to build information concerning the collection and users, to conduct various aspects of organizing the collection and offering information services.

Thus software needs to be evaluated for its suitability for the target library before purchase. This may include case studies from other libraries using the software, evaluation of hardware and operating system required, computer awareness among staff and users, network as well as computer infrastructure in the institution, and above all estimation of cost and charges for after sales support. Using suitable software for library automation will significantly reduce manual operations and enable professionals to dedicate more time for professional jobs.

CD-ROM AND ELECTRONIC DATABASES

Due to the poor communication infrastructure prevalent in India and to the immense costs involved, online database services were used only by few institutions. The distribution of the same content of online data repositories subsequently in CD-ROMs made it affordable to a larger number of institutions. While the library automation package gave search and access facility to information sources present in the local collection, CD-ROM databases attempted consolidated access irrespective of holdings to the bibliographic data of publications in a discipline. CD-ROM databases have also freed library professionals from conducting searches and allowed the end user to conduct the searches. CD-ROM is so common nowadays that a library holds a good number of them not only for bibliographic, numeric and full text databases, but also those received along with printed books and other reference sources. Managing and serving these high capacity discs was a problem earlier due to the stand alone software required, whereas the onset of networking and harddisk cached solutions provides an effective and functional way to enable access to them through the intranet.

WEB

Since the 1990s, the Internet has changed the dissemination of information, such as electronic copies of traditional paper based journals and conference proceedings, free electronic only refereed journals, haphazard copies of all kinds of material on home pages and a handful of electronic preprints archives. Most libraries in India now have a web site and they use the site to present the basic strengths of the library and to host services such as the OPAC and Web access to electronic information.

The 'size of the catalogue card' and the field lengths of primitive database technology are surpassed in the Web era. Types of information resources on the Web also vary from authentic primary information about the latest research results to ephemeral product catalogues. Issues worth consideration are often the content of the sites that are deleted, modified or changed to new machines without proper redirection and the extraction mechanism through search engines, when a flood of sources is retrieved against a query, of which few are relevant. The Internet and Web demonstrate that a large amount of electronic information can be hosted in a decentralized fashion in a cost effective manner. The Web has also freed the user's dependence on library resources for finding information related to address and contact details of a person/institution, contents pages of books, journals, etc.

As far as possible, especially for reference and information services, looking at the Web has become an innovative trend in the reference service to complement dated print sources. Many publishers visibly feel the benefits and reach of the Web, and have considered it as an alternate medium for delivering information sources; some publishers even permit unrestricted access of tables of contents and abstracts of their primary journals. As a result of these initiatives, the 'print and distribute' paradigm is challenged by 'distribute and print' paradigm.

CONSORTIAL LICENCES

The term 'consortial licences' designates library groupings to negotiate access rights to electronic information with publishers and vendors aiming at enhanced access to more resources at better pricing. "Consortia can be a means to introduce products to a previously untapped market" for vendors and "consortia provide shared expertise, access to new electronic and print resources, professional development, new sources of funds, and safety in numbers" for libraries. In contrast to earlier library collaborative arrangements such as ILL and resource sharing, the publisher and trade community are parties in the consortial agreements.

In resource sharing, libraries concentrate on collaborative subscriptions by avoiding duplication, where as in consortial licenses, the emphasis is to strike the 'best deals' even if the library suffers some duplication. The publisher community experience is that increased subscription costs lead to a reduction in the total number of subscriptions, further raising the subscription cost every year. Publishers also found it difficult to enforce ownership rights with electronic sources, even after adopting the latest technology tools and forcing libraries to sign the toughest of the legal clauses.

The good marketing wisdom of the publisher and trade community prevailed to open up information access rights through consortial licenses for a large part of the product spectrum to at least those libraries or groups of libraries which procure products beyond a certain threshold value. The *Indian National Digital Library in Engineering Science and Technology* (INDEST) is the first and the major consortium in India. It is under the aegis of the *Ministry of Human Resource Development* (MHRD). Before the creation of the consortium, access to electronic journals in these institutions remained at 60 per cent of subscribed titles, but the number of online journals has increased 10 times after the establishment of the consortium.

The rates for access offered to the consortium are lower by 50 per cent to 90 per cent depending upon the category of institution and the consortium paid only 11 per cent of the list price to access these resources. Info net, another consortium, floated by the *University Grants Commission* (UGC) for Universities, is also gaining strength. Similar consortia are also operational for research institutions under the Council of Scientific and Industrial Research (CSIR) and the Department of Atomic Energy (DAE).

DIGITAL LIBRARIES

Libraries in India are engaged in the development of prototypes of digital information resources, as influenced by developments in other countries. There are certain types of content which lie inaccessible or less used in their present physical forms that can be put to more visible and enhanced use through digitization. Also heavily used content presently available in limited numbers of copies can be identified for conversion to electronic format. The linear text in many of the print sources presents difficulties for providing a hypertext approach or a multimedia feeling, for simulating learning by doing; sustaining attention and interest for long duration calls for using electronic technologies to enable content to be more functional.

The static content in printed sources fails to attract users who are increasingly exposed to the widely appealing features of broadcasting and IT-intensive presentation tools. Multimediaenabled digital information will be useful to a large percentage of illiterate and older population also. There are cases such as papers in journals and conferences in print form that never get their deserved visibility and often end up with out reaching the target population. The digital dissemination of this content may lead to very effective teaching and more focused research in most areas.

To demonstrate the efficacy of digital libraries and collections, libraries must be able to identify materials in the public domain, sources generated in house, and similar materials to overcome the constraints of copyright. Digital library (DL) development needs a two pronged strategy to digitize local content as well as to devise options for providing access to external resources obtained as free or as part of existing subscriptions or access licenses.

The typical academic or research library in house digital library on an Intranet must include the following components:

- Consortial access to electronic journals and electronic databases;
- Free/paid Web access to journals subscribed in print format;
- Subject gateways and virtual libraries;
- Free/paid e-books from publishers and portals;
- Intranet access to bibliographic and full text databases, and CD-ROM publications;
- Local archiving of free and paid e-books;
- LAN serving of e-supplements of purchased books;
- In house digitization of copyright owned and copyright free printed books in the collection;
- Born digital in house publications such as research reports, annual reports, convocation reports, teaching materials, theses and dissertations, in house journals, proceedings of conferences, seminars, workshops, etc., conducted by the institution;
- Preprints and post prints of research papers sent for publication to journals, conferences, and books, especially with respect to the Open Archives Initiative gaining ground to provide further access to research published in toll journals and to make the results of publicly funded research available to those who need them;
- Publications in the public domain, such as government publications, publications from non profit institutions, etc.

But many libraries are unable to provide these components due to lack of awareness or due to the hurdles invariably faced by libraries in India. The lack of interest on the part of parent institutions and the absence of action plans or priorities is the major hindrance. Though computer and communication infrastructure is improving, their availability for information work is not appreciated in many organizations. Paschoud commented how several of the speakers and many of the delegates at the International Conference on Digital Libraries (ICDL) 2004 conference in New Delhi focussed on addressing what most European libraries would consider very basic issues such as network/ Internet connectivity and management.

Even in places where infrastructure is available, there is an acute shortage of competent labour to take up the task of digitizing local content and evolving digital information repositories. The students, faculty, curriculum and training methodology at the disposal of library schools have to be improved visibly to meet this challenge. Coupled with this is the need for continuing education for retraining the working professionals. Institutions, individuals, or private publishers have rights over content, and motivating them to ease these rights when they are not inclined towards digitization is not a simple task. Levying charges for access is a distant proposition; instead sponsorships from institutions, government bodies and library suppliers can be explored.

Even when hosted as a free facility, enough security mechanisms must be evolved to prevent any trespassing by hackers. Selecting useful content requires careful review and evaluation by subject experts, as digitization will only help to preserve the record, and not its enhanced and continued access. Internet bandwidth in India has to be sufficiently augmented to allow faster access to Web content as more content is being hosted on the Web. The different funding agencies, research councils and institutions are not currently offering monetary support to the desired extent for digital library development.

FORMATION OF DIGITAL LIBRARY PRODUCTION SERVICE

ORIGINS

The University of Michigan Digital Library Production Service was formed in 1996 through a commitment of resources from the four organizations then guiding the campus Digital Library Initiative. The Information Technology Division allocated a substantial sum from its personnel budget (and many early DLPS staff were hired from ITD).

The newly formed Media Union, home to the University's advanced and robust Computer Aided Engineering Network (CAEN) computing organization, provided DLPS with hardware and software, staff support for hardware, and use of a climate controlled facility with around the clock support. The School of Information and the University Library provided a combination of staffing, hardware, and space (as well as funds for renovation of the space).

Additionally, the University Library fully funded all digital collections and most of resources necessary for creation of new materials. Formed from resources from the four organizations, DLPS works with each to ensure that it is meeting the goals set out by each. For example, DLPS supports major collections used by faculty and students in Schools and Colleges programmatically linked to the Media Union.

DLPS was established with clearly defined areas of responsibility. Not only would it provide long term support to the growing array of production digital library operations (*e.g.*, the Humanities Text Initiative) at the University of Michigan, but it would undertake a process of articulating and implementing a number of higher level goals. DLPS was made responsible for defining near term digital library architectures for the campus, primarily refining those mechanisms it had already put in place, and extending them to create a more fully integrated environment.

Similarly, it would work to take lessons learned in previous efforts to define appropriate document or data structures for the digital library. This goal was seen as essential for ensuring that our investments made in digitization would have enduring value.

DLPS was also made responsible for application development and maintenance in those primary areas of responsibility (*e.g.*, bitonal page image systems, continuous tone colour image systems, and encoded text systems).

As new formats such as video evolve, it is expected that DLPS will take responsibility for them as well. Finally, DLPS was charged with responsibility for basic operations such as data loading, and ensuring that servers and software have appropriate levels of maintenance.

FUTURE OF LIBRARIES

Throughout the history of the world, libraries have been important institutions for the cultivation and preservation of humanity. Libraries are the repositories for humanity's knowledge; they are our past, our present, and our future. Cultural relevancies and temporal developments have always been deciding factors for determining the kinds of information collected.

The Egyptians, the Greeks, and the Romans developed some of the greatest libraries known to the world, expanding far beyond the clerical and economic data stored in Sumerian libraries, to include many more forms of knowledge. Over the centuries, libraries continued to transform themselves to reflect the ever changing needs of users.

Today, libraries are much more than storehouses for books, journals, and newspapers, and include other forms of electronic data, however, one thing that has not changed is the universe of information is forever expanding and is continuing to do so at ever increasing speeds.

Presently there is so much information in print that it is impossible to expect that individual libraries will have the funds to acquire, or the space to store, all of it. Has anything really changed?

Almost one hundred and fifty years ago, Charles Jewett expressed concern that without one great library that everyone could take advantage of, there could never be the great dissemination of information and access to scholarly knowledge he envisioned.

Can anyone say that a gifted student living in an outport in rural Newfoundland has access to the information he or she may need to reach their potential or even be aware that various books and research exist? The same can be said for an intellectual living in Chernobyl.

Jewett also believed that many books would not be written if their authors knew in advance that other very similar books already existed, and as a result, many writers would spend their time on more constructive projects. He also insisted that scholars needed to use the latest available data to produce worthwhile literature and to stay on top of recent trends.

Of course, that is the niche that academic journals fill, but the question must be asked again, has anything really changed at all? Many libraries cannot afford to purchase all of the increasing numbers of journals published each day, and in fact, there are universities who do not have a budget big enough to subscribe to the journals for which their own professors write.

Jewett's panacea was a union catalogue that would provide an interlibrary loan service to anyone who was interested. An admirable idea, and as we know, the Library of Congress and the National Library of Canada were later founded. But is the technology now available to fulfil Charles Jewett's vision for universal access to all the knowledge that the world has to offer?

The terms *digital libraries* and *virtual libraries* are being used everywhere today. Are they the answer to some of the problems being experienced by traditional libraries, or do they create problems that will never outweigh their benefits? Can any common vision be seen for the future of libraries?

This essay will try to answer these questions, while presenting some of the most recent literature written on the topic. Libraries have arrived at a critical point in their history. The direction they take will hopefully be based upon careful consideration, keeping in mind both the near and distant future. What is decided upon in the next decade or so could mean the difference between carving a niche in the new frontier of an information society, and the dissolution of an institution that has been around in some form or another since the dawn of writing.

The Question of Terminology

The first consideration is to decide whether to discuss the terms *digital libraries* and *virtual libraries* separately or not. The initial research using *Library Literature* gave some insight. When requesting a single search for *virtual libraries*, the response was that the preferred terminology is *digital libraries*.

Many writers use the terms *electronic*, *digital*, and *virtual* interchangeably; some are on a quest for the ultimate library without walls that they call the Virtual Library; and still others see it as a futile dream that cannot be attained.

The technology that makes these terms more than the futuristic desires of men like Vannevar Bush has not been around for very long. Bush was writing at the end of World War Two and could see that the explosion of information resulting from the war effort would have to be organized and retrievable to be of any use to humanity.

Nevertheless, many different challenges had to be overcome before any prototypes could be developed, including a reduction in the size of computers (the ENIAC prototype weighed thirty tons), and the creation of an effective networking system. Both requirements have been met in the last forty years through the availability of powerful microcomputers, with higher speed modems, and the explosion of the Internet caused by the development of graphical browsers.

Cheryl LaGuardia, Coordinator of the Electronic Teaching Centre, Harvard College Library, maintains that the virtual library was promised since the 1970s, but "it became a contradiction in terms: there was no reality to it; it receded further with every hard look you gave it".

LaGuardia believes that the virtual library that could possibly close the doors of traditional institutions is nothing more than a "romantic pie-in the sky techie pipedream". For her, virtual libraries will never be, while digital library technology can succeed and become a part of the mainstream by supplementing resources with important digital products.

Since these technological possibilities are so cutting edge, it is only realistic to expect that the terminology is equally so, and misunderstood by many. There are no fixed definitions or rules yet for the vocabulary surrounding electronic libraries, and it is quite possible that these information resources may take on a completely new name, when and if they become entrenched in society.

For now, one can only muddle through and let each writer stand on his or her own merit, while providing interesting views on a bright new frontier.

Digital and Virtual Libraries

The digital library was one of the main topics at the OLA's Super Conference II in Toronto in February 1996. The Director of Information Services for the University of Calgary, Alan MacDonald, began his discussion with an attempt to define digital libraries, asking if they are the same as virtual libraries, Internet libraries, electronic libraries, and libraries without walls.

For him, the terms are interchangeable, with the only criteria being the ability to transmit over the Internet and receive information from it as well. Additional requirements stipulate that this must be true for anyone at anytime, without the use of an intermediary librarian.

MacDonald cites the online searching of bibliographic databases in the early 1970s and the introduction of online catalogues as precursors to the digital library, as well as CD-ROMs.

He says that it was not until the graphical browser was introduced a few years ago that digital or virtual libraries became possible, but the challenges do not end there: We must not lose sight of the guiding principles that transcend the technologies and modalities of the day imperatives such as: the Alexandrian desire to preserve; the Medieval desire to share collectively; the democratic desire for the empowerment of knowledge; Panizzi's desire to organize systematically; and Vannevar Bush's desire to retrieve effectively and conveniently.

Decisions involving storage and retrieval procedures are noteworthy, as well as the fragility of storage media (it will not be the first time that libraries have to consider moving information around: push cards and beta videotapes have come and gone.), the integrity of the materials, and copyright legalities.

Walt Crawford maintains that copyright dilemmas and economic realities will assure that digital libraries will not adversely affect most publishing houses to any great degree.

In *Living Books and Dynamic Electronic Libraries*, Philip Barker offers his vision of digital and virtual libraries. For him, both are types of electronic libraries, but that is where the similarities stop. Digital libraries cannot contain any conventional books according to Barker because digital storehouses hold only digitized forms.

In these new libraries reader workstations and mechanisms for remote access will be necessary for users and will include newspapers, journals, and books that are electronic. Barker distinguishes virtual libraries as those that use the technology of virtual reality (VR) to work.

Virtual libraries will allow users to manoeuvre in a library setting, with access to virtual librarians, virtual books, and virtual indexes. He cites *Treasures of the Smithsonian*, published in 1993 on CD-ROM, as an example of what the future holds for libraries.

Writing in *Information Technology and Libraries*, Howard Harris uses the terms virtual, digital, and electronic interchangeably and forecasts that it will take the next fifteen to twenty years for the technology of virtual libraries to be integrated into library services.

Libraries may already be offering access to a variety of databases, full Internet services, and "internet based digital information" and they will be expected to offer more virtual library services in the future. There will be dilemmas associated with the allocation of funds for both traditional and virtual library services, and challenges as to what guidelines should be followed.

Conflicts should be expected and librarians need to prepare to bridge the troublesome gaps and help to rebuild their libraries in keeping with the virtual age. Librarians have to continue to upgrade their skills and learn to use new search tools for the creation of an innovative library "in which a significant number of the users and the materials that they use may not be housed in the library".

Other writers have defined virtual/digital libraries as those that collect a variety of documents, magazines, and books in a machine readable format, which can only be accessed digitally. What this means is that a user can read and study materials that do not have any physical connection to them.

Gary Harden writes that electronic library services are here to stay, and it is up to librarians to map out a plan, become better educated in the new technologies, and embrace the opportunities that are sure to be offered to everyone (. How many people have had the opportunity to see the Nuremburg Trial Papers before now?

Project Janus is Columbia University Law School's digital library prototype. Its claim to fame is that it was the first library in the world to provide virtual library service through a supercomputer. Besides offering users the latest in copyrighted editions, it links to tens of thousands of books and the university's archives. Virtual libraries will play a valuable role in the availability of restricted collections and contribute to their preservation.

In many ways, Kay Cloyes' article *Journey from the Vision to Reality of a Virtual Library* offers a synthesis for most of the literature on digital and virtual libraries. These new libraries of the not so distant future have names ranging from online, digital, electronic, desktop, virtual, and information superhighway. Virtual libraries can be as limited as online public access computers or as sophisticated as the technology will allow. What they have in common is that "a virtual library implies electronic integration of new services with traditional library services".

It is a way of using technology to give library users the latest and best information that is available electronically. Cloyes points out that high costs and maintenance requirements must be carefully considered and planned for.

Rising costs in one area of a library may have to be offset with cuts in other services. The point is to investigate all of the options that are now presenting themselves, and take advantage of the experiences of other libraries that have started similar virtual library projects.

The other major consideration is for library planners to decide how libraries for the 21st century will look. Margaret Beckman's *Library Buildings, or Virtual Libraries?* raises many issues in relation to how library buildings can integrate the new technologies and plan for future implementation.

Very basic instructions are given for the capability to convert book stacks into areas that can accommodate digital library resources, such as workstations, printers, and computers, along with the needed electrical requirements. Provisions should be made for future loading capacities for floors in the range of 250 pounds per square foot, and the use of non-glare and task lighting.

Finally, library users will need more room for their personal computers, and may expect the latest in ergonomic chairs to allow them a comfortable environment for hours of work.

Important Digital Projects

Gary Cleveland, Network Specialist for the National Library of Canada, explains that "phrases like virtual library, electronic library, libraries without walls, and most recently, digital library have all been used interchangeably to describe this broad concept". He also points out one of the common hazards of researching in the area, by saying that writers are using many different definitions to describe digital libraries. Included are the depictions of digital libraries as computer repositories, collections of objects in digital form, and one that the National Library of Canada finds quite realistic:

It is a library that carries out the traditional library functions of collection, preservation, and access provision, while integrating to an increasing degree, digital media and remotely accessible digital library services.

So digital libraries do not have to remain without walls, they can operate under the same directives and perform the same functions, as they integrate another new media type into a traditional setting.

Nevertheless, as Cleveland states, it will be much more challenging than the introduction of videotapes ever was because of the fluidity of digitized information and its lack of a medium. Adding digital information requires online databases, and a great addition to the numbers of library computers available, but it does not stop there, and considerations have to be made for the copyright dilemmas that will certainly come up.

Libraries are beginning to collect information in digital form that they may never be able to offer to library users if copyright barriers are not resolved. Coupled with these restrictions are those involving cost of services.

Libraries try to offer most of their services free (some apply user fees to some of the new databases already), and historically they were built on Andrew Carnegie's vision of the provision of an equal level of service to all sectors of society, despite financial status. Will only the privileged be able to take advantage of such an important information technology?

The NLC has a variety of digital projects underway right now. One called *Out of this World: Canadian Science Fiction and Fantasy*, and another that provides an overview of the life and times of classical musician Glenn Gould.

One of the more fascinating is *North: Landscape of the Imagination* that reveals the north of Canada from an artist's perspective. The digital collection was put together using the NLC's books, magazines, manuscripts, paintings, and music of the North.

All of the digital information is put in digital storehouses that Cleveland describes as "fragile, with limited lifespans" 3). Libraries may have to move the preserved information from one system to another, updating as the technology improves. What is impossible to know is how much money it will cost, and how much information will be lost to obsolescence.

There are also a number of significant American digital projects that should be discussed. Funded by the United States Congress, the Library of Congress, and both private and corporate sponsors, the National Digital Library is a consortium of fifteen of America's largest research libraries and archives, who are creating digital libraries.

Included are Cornell, Yale, Harvard, and Pennsylvania State, and they are converting documents of all kinds to digital form for public accessibility across the Internet. The Library of Congress' personal contribution is called *American Memory*, which uses archival materials and primary sources to depict topics like the Civil War and American Architecture.

Also deserving of mention is the prominent research development called the Digital Libraries Initiative Projects that are being funded jointly by the National Science Federation (NSF), the Department of Defence Advanced Research Projects Agency (DARPA), and the National Aeronautics and Space Administration (NASA).

The initiative incorporates six research universities that are developing digital storehouses of information for the Internet. Their aim is to make retrieval, processing, and searching user friendly and more organized.

The University of Michigan is digitizing earth and space materials; the University of Illinois is designing a digital library for engineering and science literature; the University of California at Berkeley is involved in environmental studies; Carnegie Mellon University's team is working on the access and retrievability of digitized math and science materials from video archives; and the University of California at Santa Barbara's Alexandria Project is designing a digital library for spatially indexed information like maps, atlases, and gazetteers.

Only very few research libraries are fortunate enough to have such collections of any size, and since the available digital forms are not very accessible, the Alexandria Project is attempting to put them online, with distribution across the global Internet.

Finally, Stanford University does not follow suit with the others and instead stipulates that it will be using their four million dollar grant to develop the technology for an "integrated Virtual Library that will provide access to large numbers of emerging information sources and collections".

The Library of Virginia completed Phase 1 of its Digital Library Project by scanning more than 600 000 images, including a collection of rare family bibles. Phase II and III will add one million archival and historical images to their collection. Last year, San Francisco's $137 million library was opened.

Labelled the *Library for the 21st Century* it has installed rooms for multimedia conferencing, multimedia workstations, three hundred high speed computers, and the new computerized database is multilingual. Director Ken Dowlin says they are ready for the explosion of digital materials, but adds that the book collection is numbered at more than one million.

Finally, an interesting project sponsored by the School of Information and Library Studies at the University of Michigan is called the *Internet Public Library*.

Opened in 1995, it is researching ways to incorporate public library traditions with Internet resources, and is investigating how librarians can find their niche in a digital world through retraining. The interface of the *Internet*

Public Library gives the visitor options for reference, youth, librarian services, and education, which has a virtual children's room and an exhibit hall.

The links include social service information sites, and teen help resources. In *Building Virtual Libraries*, Janet Balas talks about the possibility of building virtual libraries that include traditional library services.

Considerations for the conversion of huge volumes of materials for use in a digital library are staggering as the monumental project carried out by Case Western Reserve University and sponsored by IBM has shown.

The impetus for the project came from a group of Latin American scholars who wanted access to the Vatican Library for research, but were hampered by the reality of travelling to Rome and gaining admittance. The faculty members of the Pontifical Catholic University of Rio de Janeiro asked for access through the Internet.

The Vatican Library has a priceless collection of rare manuscripts, books, and pictures, including early copies of Aristotle and Homer. For F.C. Mintzer and his colleagues, their goals were fivefold: to create and capture, to store and manage, to search and access, to distribute, and to use rights management for the project.

The Vatican gave its consent only with the assurance that the environmental conditions would be carefully monitored while the scanning took place to protect the items, and it also insisted upon some form of digital protection for the online materials. It took a team of six, one year to reach their goal of 20 000 images, scanning an average of eighty items a day.

The consortium has definitive ideas about digital libraries since their project was deemed a success, and documents some of the many problems experienced as a learning tool for others. Besides the difficulties of developing multi server systems; the faithful capture of colour; and copyright protection concerns, there is the whole area of how to create the proper tools that scholars will need to locate and study images.

The team also ran into problems with deciding how different materials should be presented to users and the challenges of handling fragile and valuable materials for scanning purposes. They see digital libraries as having the same fundamental requirement of providing information as traditional libraries do, but the technology allows for additional services that provide a new realm of possibilities for users.

Mintzer is quick to add that there are no digital libraries in existence to date, because that "implies a massive amount of managed information, only many prior projects that have contributed to our knowledge of them". He forecasts that large scale digital library service will be in place for universities within five years and for the public in ten.

Other important work in this area is being carried out by the University of California at Berkeley, under the project name: Berkeley Digital Library

SunSite. An example of their endeavours is *California Heritage*, which provides thousands of digitized images of Californian history from their archives.

A common vision is offered in the latest literature. Researchers, librarians, computer experts, and library school academics may have slightly varying conceptions of what electronic libraries will look like, how they will function, their physical surroundings, and the extent of their infiltration into traditional libraries.

Nevertheless, all agree that expanded electronic library service is needed, possible, and will resolve some of the problems that are fundamentally affecting libraries today. With limited funds and a lack of storage space, libraries are experiencing some of their worst times in recorded history and find it increasingly difficult to maintain large self sufficient collections for users.

Libraries, such as Weldon at the University of Western Ontario are even sinking with the weight of books, many of which will never be seen on the public stacks again. Having electronic versions of materials such as, encyclopaedias, reference resources, and journals, which have skyrocketed in price, would be quite beneficial for libraries.

The other added bonus that digital versions of these carry is that many people can use the items at the same time, and their authors can easily update the information contained within them. This is one reason why CD-ROM versions are by their very nature, not as valuable a resource librarians have to keep buying the updated versions.

The other interesting theme that runs through a lot of the literature is there is no general denunciation of the technology by librarians, even though librarians' jobs and workplaces will undergo quite drastic changes.

Librarians know that many problems associated with fund allocations, copyright laws, fragile storage and obsolescence, authentication, and protection of digital information resources have to be faced and overcome, but they intuitively understand the value that it can bring to the lives of library users.

Users have always come first for the men and women who dedicate their lives to the dissemination of information. Some people may worry that libraries will go the way of the horse and carriage, but Walt Crawford has words of wisdom on the introduction of digital information. He says:

Libraries have never been the sole, or even the primary source of information for people. Good libraries serve many niches, but they never served as universal sources, and they never will. by and large, the new complements the old. Print did not destroy the oral tradition, radio did not destroy newspapers.

Television changed radio, newspapers, and movies but didn't destroy any of them. Home video changed the motion picture business but motion picture studios take in more money than ever.

Libraries will find their niche, if they remain flexible and continue to provide exemplary service in whatever format that users desire. There will definitely be people who prefer to walk into a library to borrow a book, rather than download every book they want to read. As well, there will be many who can never hope to have the technology at home to access a truly Virtual Universal Library.

5

Price Collection in Library

STATUTORY BASIS

The collection of producer price indices, which had previously been voluntary, was moved to a statutory basis in 1991. The move was to improve the quality of the overall and component indices and ensured a greater response to recruitment forms, particularly in areas such as aerospace and shipbuilding, where companies were previously reluctant to provide data because of the complicated nature of their industries. Price collection in Great Britain is statutory under the Statistics of Trade Act 1947; and since, 1993 has also been statutory in Northern Ireland under Article 5 of the Statistics of Trade and Employment Order 1988.

PRICES REQUESTED

At the time of recruitment to the home PPI, ONS request that companies supply price quotations for items which have the following attributes:

- Are representative of the company's production in the relevant heading which is a six digit code within the 1992 Standard Industrial Classification.
- Are manufactured and sold within the UK. The definition of UK manufacture is that the nature of the good must be changed within the UK. As examples, assembly of imported parts within this country would be included, but not a simple repackaging of an imported good.

Prices are then requested on a monthly basis:

- The prices quoted should represent a price which would be achieved in a significant proportion of UK sales, after discounts and excluding VAT.
- The product must be quoted on the same basis each month *i.e.,* the same product and same terms of sale.
- The product and terms of sale must be described in enough detail to ensure consistency each month.
- The price must be recorded at the time at which the product is

ordered. PPIs are published on this basis but for such purposes as deflating turnover in certain industries, PPIs are lagged so that they relate to time of delivery.

- Prices are ex works price, *i.e.,* excluding any delivery charge outside the factory.

The most recent price history is returned to the contributor. Prices should be recorded as well as the date of any change. A contributor may choose to supply data in the form of a price index. Prices may be supplied up to three months ahead. The price averaged over the month as a whole is then calculated by the ONS.

Excise Duties

The headline PPI includes excise duties on such items as tobacco, petroleum products and alcoholic drinks. For analytical purposes, an additional all manufacturing PPI excluding excise duties is published in the PPI First Release, so manufacturers in these industries are asked to provide prices both including and excluding excise duties, and indices are published on both bases. Since, 1998, the series excluding duty have been used for deflation in the national accounts, in line with international guidelines.

Average Prices

Generally, contributors are discouraged from simply providing average prices covering all transactions in a particular month. Experience has indicated that such average prices tend to be very volatile and can be affected by an occasional very large order. Such fluctuations reflect changes in customer mix rather than genuine changes in prices. For this reason, contributors are asked to quote prices for a similar transaction each month, though there are industries such as the manufacture of construction materials, *e.g.,* bricks or cement, where average prices are accepted as a preferable alternative to unrealistic list prices.

Charge out Rates

It is difficult for contributors in particular industries such as ship building and repair, to provide quotes as so much of their work is one off in nature which means it is difficult to quote for the same product over a period of time. In such cases, hourly charge out rates give an approximation to the trends for the product or service itself, whilst keeping the compliance costs to a minimum.

However, they can lead to distortions in not allowing for productivity increases over time and excluding any price movements in the raw materials involved. There are exceptions but this method of pricing is generally best avoided if possible.

Where labour charge out rates are used, ONS staff are advised to:

- Ensure they cover one specific type of a constant mix of labour.

- Avoid industries where productivity gains or development are likely to be rapid.
- Avoid industries where the materials element in prices is high.
- Ensure the quoted rate reflects what the customer actually pays.

Rates per tonne of material are more likely to be satisfactory than labour charge out rates, but ONS staff are asked to:

- Ensure the rate is what the customer pays after discount.
- Include the cost of the material and ensure this is specified precisely.
- Ensure quotes cover specific products or product types.
- Ensure the working of the material is the predominant element in the product being quoted for. Design charges should be excluded.

IMPORT PRICE COLLECTION

Prices of imported raw materials and semi manufactured goods are also collected as part of the PPI system. Contributors are selected from a list of importers supplied by Customs and Excise. They can either be manufacturers in their own right or may operate as importers who then sell on to manufacturers; in the former case they should represent the price they typically pay for the product quoted, in the latter case they should record the price they would charge to a UK manufacturing company. They can either be manufacturers in their own right or may operate as importers who then sell on to manufacturers; in the former case they should represent the price they typically pay for the product quoted, in the latter case they should record the price they would charge to a UK manufacturing company.

Export Price Collection

Export prices are collected on a separate form from the home PPI.

The crucial differences are:

- Goods must be manufactured in the UK and destined for export.
- Quotes are requested for both EC and non-EC destinations
- Prices should be supplied in the currency which their overseas customer pays.
- The ideal definition is FOB but other terms are acceptable, on the grounds that trends on the various definitions should be similar. Prices should be provided on a consistent basis—*i.e.,* the same good to the same destination. Prices to another part of the same company are generally avoided, but will be accepted if necessary. In such a case, export prices as quoted on the company's INTRASTAT form or Customs documentation are acceptable.

Field Officers

A recent innovation is the use of a field officer to liase with contributors to ensure that the prices they provide meet the specified criteria. Such field officers have been used successfully in other countries, particularly the USA and France, and it is planned to increase their use in this country as resources permit over the next few years.

Published Sources

A few price quotations are obtained from published sources rather than direct from companies. Examples are prices for imported metals, which are obtained from the London Metal Exchange and for meat which come from the Meat and Livestock Commission.

CALCULATION OF INDICES

Price Relatives

The next stage after collecting prices for a specific good from companies is to derive a price relative, which is the pure price for an item divided by its price in a base year, currently 1995. Algebraically, the price relative at time t is equivalent to $\frac{P_i * 100}{P_b}$. The price relative in general follows the same movements as the price of the item but allowance is made for changes in specification. Around 2,400 specification changes were undertaken in the home PPI during 1996.

Laspeyres Indices

Producer price indices are base weighted indices—that is to say they are weighted according to the sales or purchases in the base year, currently 1995.

The simplest form of a Laspeyres index is:

$$\frac{100 * \sum Q_b P_t}{\sum Q_b P_b}$$

where Q and P are the quantities and prices respectively of products—the subscript b denotes 'in the base period' and the subscript *t* denotes 'in the current period'. The base year is updated every five years, so that 1995 = 100 PPIs were published for the first time in October 1998. Until recently, the base year underlying the PPI was actually one year earlier than the reference year, *e.g.*, the PPI for 1985=100 was based on weights relating to 1984. However, the base year and reference year have coincided from 1995 when the indices based on 1990=100 were reclassified from the 1980 SIC onto the 1992 SIC.

Gross and Net Sector

PPIs are measured on two different bases—gross and net of inter sector sales. As an example of the concepts, the motor industry is comprised of many companies supplying parts to a few car manufacturers who then produce the final product for sale to the customer. The gross sector output of Division 34 would include both the sales of the parts and the sale of the finished cars. The net sector output of Division 34 would measure only the finished product and exclude the intervening stages. All sales of capital goods are regarded as final products, and so are not netted out. Most countries calculate PPIs on a gross basis, and the UK supplies PPIs on this basis to EUROSTAT. However, the high level output price indices given prominence in the First Release are on a net basis. The argument for the latter presentation is that this is the measure which best reflects manufacturing inflation on the rest of the economy.

Since, inflation affecting the output prices of intermediate goods will implicitly be factored into the output prices of finished products, the gross sector approach can be seen as duplicating the contribution of the manufacture of intermediate goods. Gross sector indices, however, also contain valuable information, and are used to deflate the total turnover of industries, which by definition are on a gross basis. Apart from the highest level indices in the First Release and tables of Business Monitor MM22, the rest of the indices published since, October 1998 have been on a gross sector basis.

Level of Detail Collected

Contributors are initially asked to select a representative quote at the 6 digit SIC(92) level. PPIs are calculated at the 6 digit SIC (92) level and are grossed to the 4 digit class and higher levels. Items are numbered within the 6 digit heading they are recorded, so that for example a washing machine would come within SIC (92) code 297113 with the ten digit code of the form 2971130001.

EXPORT PRICE INDICES

EPIs are collected at the 6 digit Combined Nomenclature (CN) level published annually by HM Customs and Excise. This is also known as the Harmonised System (HS). For publication purposes and for deflation in the national accounts, the indices are aggregated to a three digit CN level. For the purposes of deflating turnover for export, EPIs are converted to SIC(92) by the Balance of Payments branch of ONS, who forward them on for deflation of the export component of the Index of Production.

Import Price Indices

IPIs are collected using the 6 digit CN, but published according to the Standard International Trade Classification (SITC). The detailed relationship between CN and SITC is shown in *Guide to the classification for Overseas trade Statistics* published annually by HM Customs and Excise.

Reconstitution of Indices

A reconstitution of an index occurs when an item is to be deleted or added to an index. This is distinct from a specification change, where a contributor changes the specification of an item for which prices are supplied, but the weights of the item are unchanged. In a 'recon', the weights of an item are changed, together with other changes to ensure weights continue to add up to 100 per cent. A multiplication factor is applied to ensure that the value of the reconstituted index four months prior to the most recent calculated month are unchanged.

Derivation of Weights

The PPI is at present re-weighted every five years. The most recent results were first published in October 1998 with 1995=100. The weights used in the PPI system have two main sources:

PRODCOM

The value of sales in the base year is extracted from the PRODCOM enquiry. PRODCOM, an acronym for Products of the European Community, collects data on sales from some 25,000 contributors annually under a EUROSTAT directive. An attempt is made to exclude the value of exports from the weight at index level. However, due to the lack of data, total sales including exports are used to calculate each contributor's weight at item level.

To reduce variability at index level, sales from two years are used to derive weights. It is important to note that the weights within the PPI are product based, while the turnover figures underlying the Index of Production (IOP) are based on the main industrial products of particular companies. For IOP purposes, adjustments are made to the PPIs to allow for this difference in coverage and also the fact that PPIs relate to time of order while IOP relate to time of delivery.

Purchasing Data

Data on manufacturing companies' purchases of materials and fuel were obtained from quinquennial Purchases Enquiries, until recently. The last of these was collected in respect of 1989. To minimise contributors' costs, information on purchases is now collected as part of the Annual Business Enquiry (ABI). Particular industries are targeted on a rotating basis so that all industries are covered in a five year period.

Input Output Tables

Input indices are calculated from ONS's Input Output Tables, which use ABI and PRODCOM data as sources. As a result, input indices shown in table of Business Monitor MM22 are calculated no lower than Input Output Group level. To derive weights for the high level net sector indices, it is necessary to exclude transactions between industrial groupings. These are also derived from the Input Output tables. A methodological manual explaining these tables was published in 1997.

Import Price Indices

A contributor's weight in the import price index system is derived from the value of a company's imports in particular 6 digit CN tariff headings as obtained directly from the company. Weights at tariff code heading and above are derived from the total imports recorded in the Customs and Excise Returns in the base year.

Export Price Indices

A contributor's weight in the export price index system is derived from the value of the company's exports at a six digit CN heading for EU and non- EU destinations separately. This is in general taken from the Customs and Excise returns in the base year confirmed by the company if necessary. Weights for EPIs above 6 digit headings are taken from the Overseas Trade Statistics for the base year.

Seasonal Adjustment

To assist economic analysis, four high level PPIs are published in seasonally adjusted form. On the output side, these are the indices for all manufacturing excluding excise duties, and manufacturing excluding the food, beverages, tobacco and petroleum industries. On the input side, the indices for all manufacturing and manufacturing excluding food, beverages, tobacco and petroleum industries are seasonally adjusted to take account of volatile seasonal movements, especially in electricity and food input prices. The US Bureau of the Census seasonal adjustment package is used. Once a year, full results are taken on board for the most recent three months, but otherwise only the most recent two months figures and the month a year before the current month are revised.

SAMPLE RECRUITMENT

HOME PPIS

The sampling frame of companies for domestic PPIs is the production survey in the base year at the time at which recruitment takes place. For 1990, it was the Quarterly and Annual Sales Enquiries (QSI/ASI) while it has been the PRODCOM enquiry for 1995, which will continue in future base years. Until recently, sampling has been on a cut off basis—so that only the largest firms in each industry are selected for new recruitment, though in the past, when recruitment was on a voluntary basis some small firms were selected, some of whom are still in the sample. The contributor coverage at the all manufacturing level amounts to some 44 per cent of production.

Import Price Indices

Importers of raw materials and semi manufactures are recruited to the IPI panel by selection of the largest importers in specific headings recorded on Customs and Excise returns.

Export Price Indices

Exporters are recruited to EPIs by selection of the largest exporters in specific 6 digit CN. So whilst agents can be recruited for the IPIs, they are not recruited for the EPIs; only exporters who are also manufacturers are included in the panel.

Prices Supplied by other Government Departments

Other government departments provide indices for a few industries, as follows:

- *Department of Trade and Industry (DTI)* provides indices for energy industries, including electricity, gas and petroleum, based on DTI's monthly surveys to companies in those industries.
- *The Ministry of Agriculture, Fisheries and Food (MAFF)* provides monthly prices on many of the outputs from UK agriculture purchased by UK manufacturing industry. These prices are either taken from MAFF surveys or from the Meat and Livestock Commission, the Home Grown Cereals Authority or the National Farmers Union.
- *The Department of the Environment, Transport and the Regions* calculates price indices for output of construction.

Trade Associations

In the past, when the PPI was a voluntary survey, data for certain industries, such as brewing, were provided by trade associations. In recent years, the trend has been to move away from such quotes and to recruit data directly from companies. Very few quotes are now collected from trade associations.

New Price Quotes

The base price for an item is the price in the base year, currently 1995. If a new item is recruited after the base year, a notional base price is set so that the initial price relative for the item is calculated to be the same as its parent index. For instance, suppose a new manufacturer of washing machine is recruited in January 1999. If the value of the item's first stage parent index 'cloth washing and drying machines' 2971130000 under SIC (92) stands at 120.0 at that time, and the price of the washing machine is £300, then the base price will be assumed to have been £250 in 1995, so that a price relative of (300/250)*100 =120.0 in January 1999 is calculated—the same as its parent index. From that point on the price relatives for the new item will be calculated relative to a notional base price for that item of £250 in 1995.

NEW SAMPLING SCHEME FOR HOME PPIS

The methodology used to calculate the PPI has been reviewed and between 1999 and 2000 a new sample design is being introduced. Once this design has been fully phased in a new estimator will be introduced. This will require an extended parallel run and is not likely to be introduced until late 2001.

The main elements of the new sampling scheme are:

- Sampling from Prodcom;
- Using an optimal allocation; and
- Sample rotation.

Sampling from Prodcom

The new PPI sample will be chosen from those companies selected for Prodcom. This will ensure that the most up to date information for products and sales will be available for the sample. The sampling units for the PPI sample are contributor product pairs, which are created by matching contributors to the products they produce. For instance if a Prodcom contributor made five products then five contributor product pairs would be created.

Optimal Allocation

To ensure that the PPI sample gives the best results possible within its limit of 9,000 price quotes a month an optimal allocation has been calculated using data from 1996 Prodcom.

The objectives in calculating the allocation of price quotes between six digits were:

- Minimising the sampling error of the all manufacturing index;
- A maximum of 9,000 price quotes in total;
- Providing the highest quality four digit indices possible;
- Each six digit index to have at least three contributor product pairs;
- Each four digit index to have at least five contributor product pairs;
- Broadly the same resources should be needed for monthly calculation of the PPI.

The allocation calculations were statistically complex. In very simple terms the allocation of price quotes for a stratum within a six digit was related to:

- The squared value of sales;
- The number of contributor product pairs; and
- The variance of the prices for the product.

The higher the relative value of any of these, then the higher the allocation. To minimise the sampling error for the overall index, each contributor provides only one price quote per product. The only exception to this is where the optimal allocation was greater than the number of contributor product pairs available from the Prodcom sample. In these instances contributors were asked to provide two or three price quotes for a product.

Effect of New Sample

Using the optimal allocation to select a sample from the contributors to the 1996 Prodcom survey showed two main effects on the sample. The first was that it increased the number of contributors from 3,700 to just under 7,000 but with the same total of 9,000 price quotes. As a consequence, more of the contributors were providing fewer price quotes. 70 per cent of the new sample provide just one price quote in total compared to 38 per cent of the present sample. The sample has also been re-balanced to better reflect current production.

The total number of price quotes for most products has remained fairly stable, but there are a few indices that have gained or lost a large number of price quotes. These include a large decrease in price quotes for navigation instruments and large gains for computers, motor vehicles and aircraft. Comparing the sample selected from 1996 Prodcom with the current panel showed that out of the present 9,000 price quotes from around 3,700 contributors, 2,000 price quotes were retained.

Phasing in the New Sample

The 7,000 new price quotes to be recruited to the PPI sample are too many to obtain in one exercise.

Recruitment of new price quotes will therefore be done in three 'waves', each comprising of a set of four digits:

- The first wave requires about 3,000 new price quotes to be recruited between June and December 1998. The new quotes will be run in parallel with the current sample from February 1999 for a few months during which time the PPI will be published using the current sample. Once the impact of the new sample has been assessed it will be linked into the PPI. The length of time the parallel run can be carried out may be limited by the resources available;
- The second wave of 1,000 new price quotes will be recruited between January and June 1999, and will be linked into the PPI indices after July 1999, depending on the results of the parallel run in the first wave. This wave will be selected from 1997 Prodcom;
- The third wave of 3,000 new price quotes will be recruited between June and December 1999, and will be linked into the PPI indices after February 2000, depending on the results of the parallel run in the first wave.

This wave will probably be selected from 1997 Prodcom, although there is a chance that 1998 Prodcom might be used if the timing of Prodcom results and PPI selection can be brought closer together. It is important to note that the updating of the sample will have no impact on back data.

Sample Rotation

The proposed method of rotation for the PPI is to select the sample afresh from each year's Prodcom sample. Contributors who have been dropped from the Prodcom sample will no longer be available for the PPI, but their replacements will be available. Selecting a new sample each year will retain a large proportion of the contributor product pairs in the PPI sample, but will allow rotation for the smaller contributors. It is proposed to introduce rotation for the PPI once the new sample has been fully introduced.

The main benefits of rotation for the PPI are that it will:

- Pick up new products and new contributors;
- Pick up existing companies making a product for the first time;
- Update company structures once a year only, and provide sales figures if structures have changed;
- Fill in gaps in the sample caused by contributors dropping out; and spread the burden of completing forms between smaller contributors.

DATA COLLECTION

Qualitative researchers may use different approaches in collecting data, such as the grounded theory practice, narratology, storytelling, classical ethnography, or shadowing. Qualitative methods are also loosely present in other methodological approaches, such as action research or actor network theory.

Forms of the data collected can include interviews and group discussions, observation and reflection field notes, various texts, pictures, and other materials.

Qualitative research often categorizes data into patterns as the primary basis for organizing and reporting results. Qualitative researchers typically rely on the following methods for gathering information: *Participant Observation, Non-participant Observation, Field Notes, Reflexive Journals, Structured Interview, Semi structured Interview, Unstructured Interview, and Analysis of documents and materials*.

The ways of participating and observing can vary widely from setting to setting. Participant observation is a strategy of reflexive learning, not a single method of observing In participant observation researchers typically become members of a culture, group, or setting, and adopt roles to conform to that setting.

In doing so, the aim is for the researcher to gain a closer insight into the culture's practices, motivations and emotions. It is argued that the researchers' ability to understand the experiences of the culture may be inhibited if they observe without participating.

Some distinctive qualitative methods are the use of focus groups and key informant interviews. The focus group technique involves a moderator facilitating a small group discussion between selected individuals on a particular topic. This is a particularly popular method in market research and testing new initiatives with users/workers.

One traditional and specialized form of qualitative research is called cognitive testing or pilot testing which is used in the development of quantitative survey items. Survey items are piloted on study participants to test the reliability and validity of the items. In the academic social sciences the most frequently used qualitative research approaches include the following:

1. Ethnographic Research, used for investigating cultures by collecting and describing data that is intended to help in the development of a theory. This method is also called "ethnomethodology" or "methodology of the people". An example of applied ethnographic research, is the study of a particular culture and their understanding of the role of a particular disease in their cultural framework.
2. Critical Social Research, used by a researcher to understand how people communicate and develop symbolic meanings.
3. Ethical Enquiry, an intellectual analysis of ethical problems. It includes the study of ethics as related to obligation, rights, duty, right and wrong, choice etc.
4. Foundational Research, examines the foundations for a science, analyses the beliefs and develops ways to specify how a knowledge base should change in light of new information.
5. Historical Research, allows one to discuss past and present events in the context of the present condition, and allows one to reflect and provide possible answers to current issues and problems. Historical research helps us in answering questions such as: Where have we come from, where are we, who are we now and where are we going?
6. Grounded Theory, is an inductive type of research, based or "grounded" in the observations or data from which it was developed; it uses a variety of data sources, including quantitative data, review of records, interviews, observation and surveys.
7. Phenomenology, describes the "subjective reality" of an event, as perceived by the study population; it is the study of a phenomenon.
8. Philosophical Research, is conducted by field experts within the boundaries of a specific field of study or profession, the best qualified individual in any field of study to use an intellectual analyses, in order to clarify definitions, identify ethics, or make a value judgement concerning an issue in their field of study.

DATA ANALYSIS

INTERPRETIVE TECHNIQUES

The most common analysis of qualitative data is observer impression. That is, expert or bystander observers examine the data, interpret it via forming an impression and report their impression in a structured and sometimes quantitative form.

CODING

Coding is an interpretive technique that both organizes the data and provides a means to introduce the interpretations of it into certain quantitative methods. Most coding requires the analyst to read the data and demarcate segments within it. Each segment is labeled with a "code" – usually a word or short phrase that suggests how the associated data segments inform the research objectives. When coding is complete, the analyst prepares reports via a mix of: summarizing the prevalence of codes, discussing similarities and differences in related codes across distinct original sources/contexts, or comparing the relationship between one or more codes.

Some qualitative data that is highly structured (*e.g.*, open end responses from surveys or tightly defined interview questions) is typically coded without additional segmenting of the content. In these cases, codes are often applied as a layer on top of the data. Quantitative analysis of these codes is typically the capstone analytical step for this type of qualitative data.

Contemporary qualitative data analyses are sometimes supported by computer programmes, termed Computer Assisted Qualitative Data Analysis Software. These programmes do not supplant the interpretive nature of coding but rather are aimed at enhancing the analyst's efficiency at data storage/retrieval and at applying the codes to the data. Many programmes offer efficiencies in editing and revising coding, which allow for work sharing, peer review, and recursive examination of data.

A frequent criticism of coding method is that it seeks to transform qualitative data into quantitative data, thereby draining the data of its variety, richness, and individual character. Analysts respond to this criticism by thoroughly expositing their definitions of codes and linking those codes soundly to the underlying data, therein bringing back some of the richness that might be absent from a mere list of codes.

RECURSIVE ABSTRACTION

Some qualitative datasets are analyzed without coding. A common method here is recursive abstraction, where datasets are summarized, those summaries are then further summarized, and so on. The end result is a more compact summary that would have been difficult to accurately discern without the preceding steps of distillation.

A frequent criticism of recursive abstraction is that the final conclusions are several times removed from the underlying data. While it is true that poor initial summaries will certainly yield an inaccurate final report, qualitative analysts can respond to this criticism. They do so, like those using coding method, by documenting the reasoning behind each summary step, citing examples from the data where statements were included and where statements were excluded from the intermediate summary.

MECHANICAL TECHNIQUES

Some techniques rely on leveraging computers to scan and sort large sets of qualitative data. At their most basic level, mechanical techniques rely on counting words, phrases, or coincidences of tokens within the data. Often referred to as content analysis, the output from these techniques is amenable to many advanced statistical analyses.

Mechanical techniques are particularly well suited for a few scenarios. One such scenario is for datasets that are simply too large for a human to effectively analyse, or where analysis of them would be cost prohibitive relative to the value of information they contain. Another scenario is when the chief value of a dataset is the extent to which it contains "red flags" (*e.g.*, searching for reports of certain adverse events within a lengthy journal dataset from patients in a clinical trial) or "green flags" (*e.g.*, searching for mentions of your brand in positive reviews of marketplace products).

A frequent criticism of mechanical techniques is the absence of a human interpreter. And while masters of these methods are able to write sophisticated software to mimic some human decisions, the bulk of the "analysis" is non-human. Analysts respond by proving the value of their methods relative to either a) hiring and training a human team to analyse the data or b) letting the data go untouched, leaving any actionable nuggets undiscovered.

DATA ANALYSIS AND PROCESS

Analysis of data is a process of inspecting, cleaning, transforming, and modeling data with the goal of highlighting useful information, suggesting conclusions, and supporting decision making. Data analysis has multiple facets and approaches, encompassing diverse techniques under a variety of names, in different business, science, and social science domains.

Data mining is a particular data analysis technique that focuses on modeling and knowledge discovery for predictive rather than purely descriptive purposes. Business intelligence covers data analysis that relies heavily on aggregation, focusing on business information.

In statistical applications, some people divide data analysis into descriptive statistics, exploratory data analysis (EDA), and confirmatory data analysis (CDA). EDA focuses on discovering new features in the data and CDA on confirming or falsifying existing hypotheses. Predictive analytics focuses on application of statistical or structural models for predictive forecasting or classification, while text analytics applies statistical, linguistic, and structural techniques to extract and classify information from textual sources, a species of unstructured data. All are varieties of data analysis.

Data integration is a precursor to data analysis, and data analysis is closely linked to data visualization and data dissemination. The term *data analysis* is sometimes used as a synonym for data modeling.

TYPE OF DATA

Data can be of several types

- Quantitative data data is a number
  - Often this is a continuous decimal number to a specified number of significant digits
  - Sometimes it is a whole counting number
- Categorical data data one of several categories
- Qualitative data data is a pass/fail or the presence or lack of a characteristic

THE PROCESS OF DATA ANALYSIS

Data analysis is a process, within which several phases can be distinguished:

Data cleaning is an important procedure during which the data are inspected, and erroneous data are—if necessary, preferable, and possible—corrected. Data cleaning can be done during the stage of data entry. If this is done, it is important that no subjective decisions are made. The guiding principle provided by Adèr (ref) is: during subsequent manipulations of the data, information should always be cumulatively retrievable.

In other words, it should always be possible to undo any data set alterations. Therefore, it is important not to throw information away at any stage in the data cleaning phase. All information should be saved (*i.e.*, when altering variables, both the original values and the new values should be kept, either in a duplicate data set or under a different variable name), and all alterations to the data set should carefully and clearly documented, for instance in a syntax or a log.

The most important distinction between the initial data analysis phase and the main analysis phase, is that during initial data analysis one refrains from any analysis that are aimed at answering the original research question. The initial data analysis phase is guided by the following four questions: The quality of the data should be checked as early as possible. Data quality can be assessed in several ways, using different types of analyses: frequency counts, descriptive statistics (mean, standard deviation, median), normality (skewness, kurtosis, frequency histograms, normal probability plots), associations (correlations, scatter plots).

Other initial data quality checks are:

- Checks on data cleaning: have decisions influenced the distribution of the variables? The distribution of the variables before data cleaning is compared to the distribution of the variables after data cleaning to see whether data cleaning has had unwanted effects on the data.
- Analysis of missing observations: are there many missing values, and are the values missing at random? The missing observations in the data are analyzed to see whether more than 25 per cent of the values

are missing, whether they are missing at random (MAR), and whether some form of imputation is needed.

- Analysis of extreme observations: outlying observations in the data are analyzed to see if they seem to disturb the distribution.
- Comparison and correction of differences in coding schemes: variables are compared with coding schemes of variables external to the data set, and possibly corrected if coding schemes are not comparable.

The choice of analyses to assess the data quality during the initial data analysis phase depends on the analyses that will be conducted in the main analysis phase.

QUALITY OF MEASUREMENTS

The quality of the measurement instruments should only be checked during the initial data analysis phase when this is not the focus or research question of the study. One should check whether structure of measurement instruments corresponds to structure reported in the literature.

There are two ways to assess measurement quality:

- Confirmatory factor analysis
- Analysis of homogeneity (internal consistency), which gives an indication of the reliability of a measurement instrument. During this analysis, one inspects the variances of the items and the scales, the Cronbach's α of the scales, and the change in the Cronbach's alpha when an item would be deleted from a scale.

INITIAL TRANSFORMATIONS

After assessing the quality of the data and of the measurements, one might decide to impute missing data, or to perform initial transformations of one or more variables, although this can also be done during the main analysis phase. Possible transformations of variables are:

- Square root transformation (if the distribution differs moderately from normal)
- Log transformation (if the distribution differs substantially from normal)
- Inverse transformation (if the distribution differs severely from normal)
- Make categorical (ordinal/dichotomous) (if the distribution differs severely from normal, and no transformations help)

One should check the success of the randomization procedure, for instance by checking whether background and substantive variables are equally distributed within and across groups. If the study did not need and/or use a randomization procedure, one should check the success of the non-random sampling, for instance by checking whether all subgroups of the population of interest are represented in sample.

Other possible data distortions that should be checked are:
- dropout (this should be identified during the initial data analysis phase)
- Item non-response (whether this is random or not should be assessed during the initial data analysis phase)
- Treatment quality (using manipulation checks).

CHARACTERISTICS OF DATA SAMPLE

In any report or article, the structure of the sample must be accurately described. It is especially important to exactly determine the structure of the sample (and specifically the size of the subgroups) when subgroup analyses will be performed during the main analysis phase. The characteristics of the data sample can be assessed by looking at:
- Basic statistics of important variables
- Scatter plots
- Correlations
- Cross tabulations

FINAL STAGE OF THE INITIAL DATA ANALYSIS

During the final stage, the findings of the initial data analysis are documented, and necessary, preferable, and possible corrective actions are taken.

Also, the original plan for the main data analyses can and should be specified in more detail and/or rewritten. In order to do this, several decisions about the main data analyses can and should be made:
- In the case of non-normals: should one transform variables; make variables categorical (ordinal/dichotomous); adapt the analysis method?
- In the case of missing data: should one neglect or impute the missing data; which imputation technique should be used?
- In the case of outliers: should one use robust analysis techniques?
- In case items do not fit the scale: should one adapt the measurement instrument by omitting items, or rather ensure comparability with other (uses of the) measurement instrument(s)?
- In the case of (too) small subgroups: should one drop the hypothesis about inter group differences, or use small sample techniques, like exact tests or bootstrapping?
- In case the randomization procedure seems to be defective: can and should one calculate propensity scores and include them as covariates in the main analyses?

ANALYSES

Several analyses can be used during the initial data analysis phase:
- Univariate statistics

- Bivariate associations (correlations)
- Graphical techniques (scatter plots)

It is important to take the measurement levels of the variables into account for the analyses, as special statistical techniques are available for each level:

- Nominal and ordinal variables
  - Frequency counts (numbers and percentages)
  - Associations
- Circumambulations (crosstabulations)
- Hierarchical loglinear analysis (restricted to a maximum of 8 variables)
- Loglinear analysis (to identify relevant/important variables and possible confounders)
  - Exact tests or bootstrapping (in case subgroups are small)
  - Computation of new variables
- Continuous variables
  - Distribution
- Statistics (M, SD, variance, skewness, kurtosis)
- Stem and leaf displays
- Box plots

MAIN DATA ANALYSIS

In the main analysis phase analyses aimed at answering the research question are performed as well as any other relevant analysis needed to write the first draft of the research report.

EXPLORATORY AND CONFIRMATORY APPROACHES

In the main analysis phase either an exploratory or confirmatory approach can be adopted. Usually the approach is decided before data is collected. In an exploratory analysis no clear hypothesis is stated before analysing the data, and the data is searched for models that describe the data well. In a confirmatory analysis clear hypotheses about the data are tested. Exploratory data analysis should be interpreted carefully. When testing multiple models at once there is a high chance on finding at least one of them to be significant, but this can be due to a type 1 error. It is important to always adjust the significance level when testing multiple models with, for example, a bonferroni correction. Also, one should not follow up an exploratory analysis with a confirmatory analysis in the same dataset. An exploratory analysis is used to find ideas for a theory, but not to test that theory as well. When a model is found exploratory in a dataset, then following up that analysis with a comfirmatory analysis in the same dataset could simply mean that the results of the comfirmatory analysis are due to the same type 1 error that resulted in the exploratory model in the first place. The comfirmatory analysis therefore will not be more informative than the original exploratory analysis.

STABILITY OF RESULTS

It is important to obtain some indication about how generalizable the results are. While this is hard to check, one can look at the stability of the results. Are the results reliable and reproducible? There are two main ways of doing this:

- Cross validation: By splitting the data in multiple parts we can check if analyzes (like a fitted model) based on one part of the data generalize to another part of the data as well.
- Sensitivity analysis: A procedure to study the behaviour of a system or model when global parameters are (systematically) varied. One way to do this is with bootstrapping.

STATISTICAL METHODS

A lot of statistical methods have been used for statistical analyses. A very brief list of four of the more popular methods is:

- General linear model: A widely used model on which various statistical methods are based (*e.g.* t test, ANOVA, ANCOVA, MANOVA). Usable for assessing the effect of several predictors on one or more continuous dependent variables.
- Generalized linear model: An extension of the general linear model for discrete dependent variables.
- Structural equation modelling: Usable for assessing latent structures from measured manifest variables.
- Item response theory: Models for (mostly) assessing one latent variable from several binary measured variables (*e.g.* an exam).

FREE SOFTWARE FOR DATA ANALYSIS

- ROOT- C++ data analysis framework developed at CERN
- PAW- FORTRAN/C data analysis framework developed at CERN
- JHepWork- Java (multi-platform) data analysis framework developed at ANL
- KNIME- the Konstanz Information Miner, a user friendly and comprehensive data analytics framework.
- Data Applied- an online data mining and data visualization solution.
- R- a programming language and software environment for statistical computing and graphics.
- DevInfo- a database system endorsed by the United Nations Development Group for monitoring and analysing human development.
- Zeptoscope Basic Interactive Java-based plotter developed at Nanomix.

NUCLEAR AND PARTICLE PHYSICS

In nuclear and particle physics the data usually originate from the experimental apparatus via a data acquisition system. It is then processed, in a step usually called *data reduction*, to apply calibrations and to extract physically significant information. Data reduction is most often, especially in large particle physics experiments, an automatic, batch mode operation carried out by software written ad hoc. The resulting data *n-tuples* are then scrutinized by the physicists, using specialized software tools like ROOT or PAW, comparing the results of the experiment with theory.

The theoretical models are often difficult to compare directly with the results of the experiments, so they are used instead as input for Monte Carlo simulation software like Geant4, predict the response of the detector to a given theoretical event, producing simulated events which are then compared to experimental data.

PROCESSING AND DATA VALIDATION

Contributors return price movements by means of a pre-printed form containing the most recent details provided to the ONS. These are sent to contributors at the beginning of each month. They return their latest prices, and may provide future prices if they know the position for the three months ahead. The form asks contributors to check if the specifications are still up to date and representative and to amend accordingly. Forms for companies in Northern Ireland are despatched via the Department of Economic Development in Belfast.

Data Validation

There are two tests which staff use to check price movements on the home PPI with contributors:

- *Monthly Movements Outside the Range 2.5 to +5 per cent*: These are known as 'dubious' price movements and are only input after checking with the contributors. Any information given by the contributor is included on the computer system. For the more volatile export and import price indices wider gates of -7.5 to +7.5 per cent are used.
- *Monthly Movements Outside the Range -25 to +25 per cent*: These are known as 'incredible' price movements. These are also queried with contributors. Unlike 'dubious' price movements, these must be specifically confirmed on the computer system with an explanation—otherwise they will be rejected.

As well as these checks before returns are input, there are also the following checks at later stages. Indices which move by more than 5 per cent are highlighted in prints following the two monthly calculation runs. Reasons for such movements must be shown on the printouts and circulated to internal users of the data. 'Too stable' letters are sent to contributors whose prices are recorded as not having moved for a set period, currently around eighteen months.

Data Collection by Telephone

Telephone Data Entry (TDE) is a means by which contributors return prices by inputting prices via their telephones. This was pilot tested largely successfully with service sector prices and was extended to the main PPI during 1997 and 1998.

Imputation

The PPI computer programmes impute for non-response in the most recent few months.

The rules for the home PPI are:

- If response in the lowest level index is over 50 per cent, the computer imputes based on a simple average of the observed movements in the received returns within the relevant sub category.
- If response in the class is under 50 per cent, the computer imputes based on the simple average of movements at division level.

Imputation for EPI and IPI are similar, though if response at the first stage is below 50 per cent, imputation is based on movements for EC exports, non-EC exports or total imports as appropriate.

Treasury Targets

Targets are agreed with HM Treasury for response rates and revisions to ONS's key economic statistics.

The PPI is subject to two Treasury targets:

- Response in the all manufacturing output index at the first time of publication should exceed 82 per cent, with response weighted according to sales, and
- The revision in the estimate of the year to year all manufacturing output price index should not exceed 0.125 per cent between time of first publication and the first 'firm' estimate published two months later.

Allowances for Quality Changes

Care must be taken when a the specification of an item changes to ensure that only the 'pure' price change is recorded as such for PPI purposes. As well as changes of good, specification changes take place for alterations in terms of terms or units of sale. There are three types of specification changes in the PPI system:

Revisions Policy

The policy is to show significant revisions, but to suppress minor changes to avoid unnecessary inconvenience to users of the PPI. Indices for the most recent two months are shown as provisional and can be changed as later data are received the following month. Indices published for the third month are made firm as long as response is 95 per cent or more. Indices are always made firm after five months. Once an index is made firm it is only changed if there is a revision of 0.2 or more. Only the most recent five months indices are recalculated normally but earlier data will be revised if the revision in the first stage index is over 1 per cent or 5 per cent. Higher level indices are only changed if the revision is 0.2 per cent or more.

Linking between Base Years

The general policy for linking PPIs between different base years is as follows:

- To link earlier data onto the present base year, users may either link onto the earliest month published on the present base year—which is January 1991 for the 1995=100 database, or follow the national accounts practice of linking on at January 1994.
- To link later data onto an earlier base year—link later data onto the latest month published as firm—say July 1998 for the 1990 = 100 database.

Confidentiality

Under the Statistics of Trade Act 1947, criminal sanctions are in place to prevent the unauthorised release of company data by ONS staff. Depending on the circumstances either the Office or individual members of staff would be liable for fines and/or imprisonment for unauthorised release. In addition, because of the confidentiality of the data, company price information is not released outside the division responsible, apart from direct line managers.

An index is only published if it is felt it would not disclose company information either to a member of the public or another company in the industry, though confidential indices can be used by other parts of the Government Statistical Service for national accounts purposes or for the calculation of other inflation measures as long as the publication of these other outputs is at a sufficiently aggregated level not to disclose the levels of these confidential indices.

Ad hoc Indices

ONS offers the facility to produce *ad hoc* indices to customers specification. For instance, an oil company may supply the weighting details of the various components that go into making an oil rig. For a fee, the ONS will calculate an index with monthly updates.

COLLECTION MAINTENANCE

Collection maintenance refers to the daily care of collections: keeping the stacks/storage area neat and clean, performing general housekeeping tasks in the building, and periodically cleaning the collections themselves. These activities may differ somewhat from institution to institution. The staff of a public or academic library may need to straighten its shelves daily, while in archives, staff must ensure that collections are in the right order and returned to the proper storage area. A library with general collections may undertake a cleaning project using student assistants, while a special collections department may contract with a conservator to clean certain materials. The common element in all these activities, however, is the need to continually observe the condition of collections and ensure that they are properly cared for.

HOUSEKEEPING

The practice of good housekeeping is probably the simplest and least expensive method of preventive conservation for any type of collection. Housekeeping will keep particulates such as dust, dirt, smoke, ash, and mold spores from gathering on or around objects in your collection.

These particulates can cause abrasion of delicate objects such as photographs and will attract moisture from humid environments to form acids that cause chemical deterioration. Dust and dirt contain organic materials that serve as food for insects and mold, and therefore provide an ideal environment in which they can live and flourish. By keeping collections clean, you reduce the risk of these types of damage. Moreover, a building that is clean and neat engenders respect for the collections within it and makes for a healthier, more pleasant environment for staff and patrons. Housekeeping is thus an excellent method to help ensure the safe, long-term preservation of your holdings.

A Housekeeping Plan

Housekeeping for the building and for collections in storage or on exhibit should be discussed and defined in a written housekeeping plan. This plan should be part of a larger building maintenance plan that includes routine inspections and maintenance of key building elements and systems (*e.g.,* roof, drainage systems, pipes and plumbing, fire protection equipment, and HVAC equipment). The housekeeping plan should carefully delineate who will do the work, how often the work will be done, and with what tools and methods it will be completed.

The plan should detail weekly, monthly, quarterly, and yearly tasks, as well as special instructions for specific materials. Keep in mind that several different people will likely be performing the different housekeeping tasks (*e.g.,* custodians, paraprofessionals, students, librarians, collections curators), and written schedules for each person and/or task may be needed.

How Often Should You Clean?

Housekeeping work should be performed on a regular schedule based on need and circumstance. For example, spaces are usually very dusty in the fall, during the first few weeks after the heating system has been turned on. Dust in the ductwork is dried out by the heated air, becomes airborne, and is then circulated throughout the building. Therefore, dusting and vacuuming will be required more frequently in the early fall than in other seasons.

CLEANING COLLECTIONS

The cleaning of general book collections is typically recommended once a year. Special collections materials may require specialized cleaning procedures because of potential damage that may occur during cleaning. In some cases they will need to be cleaned by a conservator.

Cleaning General Book Collections

It is usually not practical to clean all collections at once in a large library unless an outside cleaning service is brought in. When cleaning is done in house, the job is often divided into specific projects, where one part of the larger collection is cleaned at a time. This prevents book cleaning from turning into a never ending (and discouraging!) project.

In most libraries, time and staffing limitations mean that collections are cleaned too infrequently rather than too often. But remember that overdusting and overcleaning of collections increases wear and the risk for damage from handling. Active cleaning of individual special collections items should be performed only when necessary. Storing collections inside boxes or furniture or under muslin dustcovers will reduce the amount of dirt and debris that settles on the collection itself, thereby lessening the need to clean.

Cleaning Individual Paper based Objects in Storage or on Display In general, cleaning of individual paper objects should not be a high priority for cultural institutions just beginning a preservation programme. Because of the potential for damage that may occur during cleaning, the cleaning of paper objects of any kind in a collection should not be undertaken lightly. A conservator should be consulted to assess all the issues relating to the care of the object(s) in question.

Objects exhibiting the following conditions should be cleaned only by a conservator:

- Pastel or charcoal media;
- Loose or friable materials of any kind;
- Loose or flaking gelatin or baryta layers;
- Active or wet mold;
- Extensive repairs; and/or
- Objects that have been rolled and will not stay flat without assistance.

In addition, if you are unable to positively identify the process by which a photographic object was made, do not attempt to clean it. Even light surface brushing can remove silver image particles from a degraded salted paper print.

STACK MAINTENANCE

The most basic function of stack maintenance in a public or academic library is to reshelve materials. The people doing this are often lower wage employees, student workers, even volunteers, and they must be carefully trained to understand the importance of their job.

Library collections must be treated with great care and the shelves must be kept orderly, because the condition of the stacks conveys a sense of the library's commitment to the well being of its collections.

Preservation Concerns in Stack Maintenance

When transporting collections, shelvers must use a sturdy and easily maneuverable book truck. Materials must be packed on the book truck in such a way that they cannot easily fall off.

There should be step stools and open shelves provided in the stacks so that patrons can safely access books and materials without damaging them.

Shelvers should pay attention to the following issues:

- Make sure books do not extend beyond the edge of the shelf.
- Shelve oversize books properly, usually flat in stacks of three or less.
- Straighten books that are leaning.
- Shelve books spine down; shelving spine up causes the text block to come loose from the covers.
- Use book supports (bookends) where needed.
- Do not pack books so tightly that removing them becomes difficult.
- Report overcrowded stack areas, and shift materials within the stacks when necessary to remedy this problem.

Fig. On the left, the Crowded Shelves show Books Leaning against each other, with some shelved Spine up; this will Cause Distortion. On the right, these Books are shelved Upright and Well supported by Bookends. Space is left on the shelves to allow for Easy Shelving and Removal.

Staff members who are reshelving books should also keep an eye out for damaged volumes that might need repair or cleaning, and they should report any storage areas that are particularly dirty and need to be cleaned by the custodial crew.

HANDLING OF COLLECTIONS

Artifacts are easily damaged by poor or improper handling. Researchers should be supplied with instructions and supervised at all times when using the collection. Staff, too, need to be made aware of proper handling techniques through regular training. This part will cover proper handling procedures for paper based collections and for film and electronic media collections. The latter are particularly vulnerable to damage from dirt and dust, as well as to damage from playback.

HANDLING PAPER COLLECTIONS

Using Collections

As a result of both use and shelving, certain types of damage to book collections are commonly seen: headcap damage from pulling books off the shelf; spine damage from forcing books open; tearing and creasing from folding of page corners; and abrasion from being dropped. Documents may be torn, folded, or accidentally marked, while photographs may be damaged by dirt and oils from fingers. Making reference photocopies of frequently consulted documents and photographs is one way to greatly reduce this sort of damage.

Every time you handle collection materials, ask yourself the following questions:

- Do I have a valid reason for picking this up?
- What is its condition?
- What is the safest way to hold it?
- Is it too fragile to lift without a secondary support?
- Do I need a second person to assist? Do I need a cart or trolley?
- After I have lifted the object, where will I set it down again?
- Are my hands clean? Should I wear gloves?

Processing Collections

It is also important to remember that collections processing techniques suitable for general collections should not be used on materials with value as artifacts. These procedures include painting call numbers on books; affixing pressure sensitive labels; and attaching pockets, bookplates, and bar codes (the adhesives may damage the materials and leave a sticky residue when they fail). Sometimes it may be difficult to know whether books with long term research value may eventually have value as artifacts. One strategy for processing such materials is to use a polyester book jacket fastened with 3M double sided tape no. 415 and to label the jacket. If bookplates or pockets are used in books of enduring value, they should be made of low lignin, alkaline paper and attached with a stable, reversible adhesive, preferably wheat starch paste or methyl cellulose.

Take a few moments to look at the pictures below. What dos and don'ts for handling paper collections are represented in each?

HANDLING MEDIA COLLECTIONS

Careful handling and use of film and electronic collections is extremely important, as audiovisual media are vulnerable to even the smallest amount of dirt and dust. Cotton gloves must be used for handling, and the storage and use areas must be kept as dust free as possible. The provision of service copies is an excellent strategy for reducing the handling of originals.

Motion Picture Film

Cotton gloves should be worn when handling motion picture film. Always hold film along its edges, being careful not to touch the sound track or the image. Do not project film to examine it, since this can further damage already deteriorated film. Special viewing equipment is available for inspecting film, or you can commission an outside service provider to do this.

Microfilm

Always wear gloves when handling master negatives, since oils and fingerprints can damage film. Always handle film by the edges or leaders. Pulling rolled film tight on the reel can cause abrasion of the film. Do not remove more than one microfilm or fiche from its enclosure at a time, and immediately resleeve or rebox items when you are done using them.

Sound Recordings and Video

As a general rule, never touch the playing surface of any recording. Always make sure your hands are clean before you handle recordings. Be sure that all playback equipment is cleaned often and maintained properly. Cylinder recordings should be handled by putting two fingers in the center hole. Wax cylinders must be at room temperature before you touch them, as the warmth of your hand can split cold wax cylinders. Do not touch the grooves of wax cylinders. Grooved discs (LPs, acetate discs, etc.) should be held by their edges and label areas only. Compact disc recordings should be handled by their outer edge and center hole. Reel to reel tapes should be handled only by the outer edge of the reel flanges and the center hub. Take care not to squeeze the flanges together, as this will damage the edges of the tape. Cassette recordings (audio and video) should be handled only by their outer plastic casing; never put fingers or other materials into the case openings. Take care not to drop tapes, and don't stack tapes on top of equipment.

CDs/DVDs

Always handle discs by the outer edges or the center hole; never touch the surface of the disc. Take care not to bend discs when handling them, and do not scratch the label side of a disc. When cleaning discs, wipe with a clean cotton fabric in a straight line from the center of the disc to the outer edge instead of wiping in a circular motion around the disc.

STORING PAPER COLLECTIONS

What are the proper storage practices for specific types of paper collections? How do you know whether your current storage is acceptable? In this part, you will review commonly recommended storage practices for paper based collections and use this knowledge to evaluate your own storage methods.

You will be looking for poor storage practices that are common in the collections (*e.g.,* rubber bands holding covers together, poorly supported books, overstuffed file folders, acidic inserts in books or files). Although this examination may locate individual objects that need repair or other treatment, its primary goal is to identify general needs and areas of the collection in need of remedial actions (*e.g.,* boxing, enclosing photographs, replacing manila folders with archival quality folders and boxes, and photocopying news clippings).

If important individual objects requiring conservation treatment are identified during this process, a conservator can evaluate whether emergency care is indicated.

This review of collection storage needs is organized by type of material, since for the purposes of preservation it is usually best to store like materials together. It is sometimes necessary, however, to consider mixed collections as a whole.

BOUND MATERIALS

Shelving

The non-knifing variety of bookend, which has a lip, is preferred to the knifing variety, which allows books to be jammed onto its sharp edge. A brick covered with book cloth fastened with PVA adhesive can be a good book support. Another alternative is a piece of acid free foam core covered with book cloth and slipped over the upright of a knifing bookend to shield the metal edge.

Boxing

Boxes constructed of preservation quality materials can be custom made to fit a book's measurements. They provide support for the volume and protection from dirt, dust, light, and mechanical damage. Volumes with artifactual value, where the fragile binding is to be retained in its present condition, should be boxed. Volumes that have low value or are rarely used and do not warrant treatment or repair of the binding may also be boxed.

Boxes can be made in house or contracted out. Drop spine boxes provide the most protection. Phase boxes are not as rigid or impervious to light or dust, but they are an acceptable cost efficient alternative. Ready made rare book boxes can be purchased from conservation suppliers, but if they are to provide proper protection, they must fit the books closely and the weight of the board or card stock must be appropriate for the size of the books. Many vendors make both drop spine and phase boxes. Deteriorated books of great value should have custom made drop spine boxes that fit the book exactly.

Alternatives to Boxing

Infrequently used deteriorated books can be wrapped in buffered paper or fitted with polyester book jackets. Both of these strategies will prevent dispersion of the "dust" from red rot and provide some protection from dust and abrasion. These strategies are cheaper than boxing, but they offer less protection. Among the disadvantages: a polyester book jacket does not cover the book completely; the paper and polyester film do not provide as much support as box board; and it can be difficult to replace a paper wrapping properly once it is removed for use.

If detached covers must be tied onto books as a temporary protection, ties should be undyed cotton or linen tape or undyed polyester ribbon. Any knots should be at the top or fore edge of the text block to prevent damage from pressure against other books. Never hold damaged bindings together with rubber bands; the rubber bands will deteriorate themselves and cause further damage.

PAMPHLETS

Pamphlets and small booklets can be stored in specially made enclosures, in folders and boxes, or in hanging folders in file cabinets. Pamphlets of the same cover size can be stored in drop spine or phase boxes. Pamphlets that differ in size may be stored according to guidelines given for manuscripts and documents. Pamphlets more than about a quarter inch thick should be stored spine down in individual folders. Pamphlets of very different size should not be stored in the same folder.

If individual pamphlets must be shelved between books, they should be individually boxed. Groups of pamphlets shelved between books can be boxed together if the guidelines above are followed. If pamphlet binders are used, they must be of preservation quality throughout, and they should never be glued directly to pamphlets. Where stitching is used to join pamphlet and binder, it should be done through the fold or, where possible, in original fastener holes.

DOCUMENTS/MANUSCRIPTS/EPHEMERA

General Recommendations

Documents should be stored in low lignin, buffered file folders, with a maximum of about 15 sheets per folder. The folders should then be placed in archival quality document storage boxes as close to the size of the folders as possible. All folders in each box should be the same size. Boxes should be full enough to prevent slumping of the contents; partially full boxes can be filled with spacer boards available from conservation suppliers. Do not stuff boxes. This can cause damage when sheets are removed and refiled.

An alternative to boxed storage is a standard baked enamel file cabinet equipped with hanging racks and hanging folders. Archival quality hanging folders are available, but the conventional kind are acceptable as long as the enclosures within them are buffered.

Store objects of the same size and category together whenever possible. Archivists habitually organize collections by subject group, but objects of differing bulk and weight can cause damage from uneven pressures in a drawer or box. It is not advisable to store single sheets in the same box with books or pamphlets unless there are separate enclosures and supports for each category of material. Generally speaking, heavy objects should be stored separately from lighter objects, as should bulky objects.

Parchment and Vellum

Parchment and vellum are highly susceptible to damage from fluctuations in relative humidity and thus require stringent humidity controls. Such documents should be enclosed for additional protection. Suitable enclosures include encapsulation, folders, matting and framing, boxing, or a combination of these techniques.

Ephemera

Ephemera may have raised surfaces or three dimensional decoration. Items should be grouped by size and type (*e.g.*, postcards, printed material, documents), enclosed to protect them from chemical migration and mechanical damage, and stored to support the structure of the artifact (encapsulated, boxed, stored flat or in hanging files). Some vendors of archival supplies offer custom size storage boxes and sleeves for common ephemera such as postcards and stereo views, or they can produce custom size boxes in large quantities to meet special needs.

NEWSPRINT

Because groundwood papers were commercially produced after about 1840, newsprint after that date is likely to be highly acidic. Long term preservation of this paper is difficult at best. It is possible to treat newsprint by deacidification to retard its deterioration, but this treatment is usually economically impractical. Once paper has already turned yellow and brittle, deacidification will not make the paper white and flexible again. Microfilming is usually the preferred preservation option for bound newspaper collections or large collections of clipping scrapbooks.

Most news clippings are important because of their information, not for the value of the clippings themselves. For this reason, photocopying or microfilming are considered the most practical preservation options. All photocopying should be done on archival quality paper; originals can then be deaccessioned at the discretion of the librarian or curator. News clippings with photographs that do not photocopy well may be physically separated from other papers in a folder by placing them inside an enclosure made of polyester. News clippings to be retained in their original form should be deacidified and stored in buffered enclosures.

OVERSIZED MATERIALS

Flat Storage

Prints, maps, broadsides, and other oversize objects are best stored flat in map drawers or in large covered boxes of preservation quality available from conservation suppliers. It is acceptable to store documents legal size or smaller in upright archival boxes, but anything larger than 15 by 9 inches should be stored flat. Sheets smaller than 30 by 40 inches will fit into archival boxes, which come in various sizes and are cheaper than map cases. Objects should be protected in neutral or buffered folders cut to fit the size of the drawer or box, since smaller folders tend to shift position as the drawers open and close and get jammed at the back of the drawers. Several objects may be placed in a folder. Items of special value should be interleaved with buffered or neutral tissue paper.

It was traditionally recommended that some items (such as blueprints) should not be stored in alkaline buffered folders because they are sensitive to alkaline materials and might be damaged by contact with the folders. Recent research, however, has indicated that as long as the relative humidity in the storage area is kept moderate (between 30 per cent and 55 per cent), alkaline folders should not cause damage.

Rolled Storage

If map drawers or boxes are not available, or if objects are too large to fit in map drawers, oversize objects can be rolled on tubes, as long as the paper is not too brittle to withstand unrolling. If rolling the object on a tube, use a tube longer than the rolled object and at least four inches in diameter (larger diameters are preferred).

If the tube is not archival quality, the object must be wrapped in neutral or buffered paper. Carefully roll the object onto the tube, and wrap the assembly with neutral or buffered paper to protect it from abrasion. This assembly can then be stored inside a larger tube for added protection. Tubes should be stored horizontally. Alternatively, oversize objects can be rolled within a polyester folder.

FRAMED MATERIALS

Any prints, drawings, or other objects that have been matted or backed with acidic materials or wood should be removed from those mounts. They may be matted using preservation quality materials and reframed in their original frames using museum quality materials. These objects may also be safely stored flat (unframed, matted, or unmatted) in folders inside boxes or drawers, like oversize items.

Frames should not use eye screws or other protruding hardware for hanging, because they can cause damage to other frames or glazing. Protruding hardware should be replaced with D rings on brackets, available from framers. Glazing should filter ultraviolet (UV) light and should never touch the artifact inside the frame.

An additional layer of preservation quality matboard should be used behind the board on which the object is mounted. The frame should be deep enough to accommodate all the layers, and it should be sealed so that it is as airtight as possible.

Framed items should not be exhibited permanently. When not on exhibit, they should be stored vertically. Usually a padded frame rack is most practical for smaller institutions, while custom sliding storage racks (where metal grill panels are suspended from tracks) may be appropriate for institutions with larger collections of framed objects. Frame racks are available ready made or can be constructed (be sure to use non-damaging materials). Each compartment in a frame rack should be cushioned at the bottom, and foamboard should be used between framed items within the compartments to prevent abrasion.

SCRAPBOOKS/ALBUMS

Scrapbooks pose challenging preservation problems because they frequently contain a variety of components and media. In addition, they are often unique, fragile, damaged, or of significant associational value. If they must be interfiled within archival collections, they must be well supported and separated from direct contact with other materials. Scrapbooks that have informational value alone (for instance, clippings scrapbooks) can be photocopied onto archival quality paper and/or microfilmed. The originals would then be retired from use and copies made available to researchers. Scrapbooks that have enduring value in their original form should be individually wrapped in archival quality paper and/or boxed in custom fitted boxes. Valuable scrapbooks may have a high priority for evaluation by a conservator.

PHOTOGRAPHIC PRINTS AND NEGATIVES

Enclosures

Photographic prints and negatives are best stored in individual enclosures.

This reduces damage by giving the photograph or negative physical support and protection. Enclosures can be made of paper or plastic.

Paper enclosures:

- Protect from light and buildup of moisture and gases inside the enclosure;
- Require more handling, as the object must be removed from the enclosure for examination; and,
- Are cheaper and easier to write on than plastic enclosures.

Plastic enclosures:

- Allow the user to view the image without handling it;
- Can abrade the photograph during insertion and removal from the enclosure;
- Can trap gases and moisture within the enclosure;
- Can be difficult to write on and sometimes flimsy; and,
- Usually have heat sealed seams, which eliminate potential damage from adhesive seams.

Suitable plastics have been discussed elsewhere in this part. There are several types of individual plastic enclosures, including L-Velopes (sealed on two adjacent sides); plastic folders that can be used within paper envelopes; and plastic sleeves that are open at two opposite ends, with a self locking fold on one of the remaining sides. There are also a number of styles of ring binder pages for prints and negatives.

When using paper enclosures for photographic storage, conservators used to recommend that photographs be housed in low lignin neutral paper enclosures rather than in alkaline enclosures, since it was thought that colour images, cyanotypes, and albumen prints would be damaged by the alkalinity in buffered enclosures. But recent research indicates that this is not the case. Rather than choosing enclosures according their pH level, paper enclosures should be chosen based on whether they pass the Photographic Activity Test (PAT), which determines whether the enclosures contain harmful chemicals that will cause image fading or staining.

If envelopes with adhesive seams are used, the adhesive must be stable, pH neutral, and it must not react with silver; the seams should be on the sides or the bottom of the envelope; and the emulsion of the photograph should face away from the seams.

Boxing

Once they have been individually enclosed in paper or plastic, photographs must be placed in archival quality boxes. Where possible, items of similar size should be stored together; the mixing of different sizes can cause abrasion and breakage and can increase the risk of misplacing smaller items. Horizontal storage of photographs is usually preferable to vertical storage, since it provides overall support and avoids mechanical damage such as bending or slumping. The photographs should be stored flat in drop front boxes of archival quality housed on shelves or in metal cabinets. All enclosures within a box should be the same size, fitting the size of the box. Neutral or buffered file folders may be used to organize photographs within the box.

Vertical Storage of Photographs

If necessary, vertical storage can be used. Small photographs of uniform size can be individually enclosed and placed vertically in boxes the same size as the photographs. Boxes of various sizes and types are available from conservation suppliers.

For vertical storage in a filing cabinet, protected photographs should be placed in archival folders that are themselves placed in hanging file folders. Several photographs may be stored in each folder, and several folders may be placed in each hanging file. Lightly filled hanging file folders will prevent photographs from sliding down under each other in the drawer and will facilitate their handling. Alternatively, folders can be placed in archival document boxes, but the folders should not slump, and the photographs must be well supported.

Oversized Photographs

Give special care to the storage of oversized photographic prints mounted on cardboard. This cardboard is often acidic, causing the mounts to become brittle with age. Embrittlement of the support can endanger the image itself if the cardboard breaks in storage or during handling. Such prints should be placed in individual folders in archival quality boxes of appropriate size and stored flat on shelves. They require careful handling.

Negatives

Negatives should be stored separately from prints. Larger negatives can be stored in individual enclosures and then boxed, while the smaller 35mm strips can be stored in plastic ring binder storage pages. Nitrate and acetate negatives must be stored in paper envelopes that pass the PAT. MicroChamber or other proactive storage enclosures that contain scavengers to remove pollutants should also be considered for acetate and nitrate negatives.

Each type of film base should be stored separately, in a well ventilated area, apart from other types of collections. This is particularly important for nitrate negatives.

Both nitrate and acetate negatives should be monitored on a regular basis so that any deterioration can be identified early. If deterioration is discovered, isolate the deteriorating materials from those that are still in good condition. Nitrate and acetate negatives should be duplicated onto polyester film whenever possible, as this will provide a stable copy.

COLLECTION MANAGEMENT

There are several basic collection management activities that play a crucial role in the preservation of collections. These include development of an institutional mission statement and collecting policy, as well as organization and cataloging of collections.

Preservation planning requires a manager to set priorities and make choices by looking at the resources available for preservation and weighing the condition, needs, and value of materials against them. When time and resources are limited, it makes most sense to concentrate preservation efforts on materials that serve the mission of an organization. To do this, a repository must have a detailed understanding of its goals and objectives for its collections—exactly what it wishes to document, who it wishes to serve, and what types of material it will collect to accomplish those goals.

Making effective preservation choices also requires good intellectual control of collections, since relative values and preservation priorities cannot be assigned unless staff is familiar with the content of collections. In addition, intellectual control is crucial to providing access to your collections. Your collections may be housed in archival boxes, stored in a moderate environment, and protected from disaster, but if they are not accessible to users, you have neglected a basic responsibility.

MISSION AND COLLECTING POLICY

While it is easy to jokingly dismiss the institutional mission statement as a gathering of buzzwords with little real meaning, in fact, the importance to preservation activities of a carefully thought out mission statement and collecting policy cannot be overstated.

In an ideal world, you would devise a basic statement of your repository's mission and collecting goals before actually identifying and acquiring collections. In reality, however, at least some collections may have been gathered haphazardly over time. Devising a mission statement and collecting policy will help you to look critically at all the materials you hold and decide whether they really belong in your collection.

Mission Statement

A mission statement should spell out your repository's overall goals. It may be short or extensive, depending on the size of your repository and the circumstances. In repositories such as public libraries, museums, or historical societies, where paper based historical collections are part of a larger institution, it may be helpful to prepare a separate mission statement and collecting policy for the historical paper based materials, because they need to be managed differently from general circulating books or museum objects. You must, however, ensure that these policies support the overall repository goals.

Your mission statement should articulate in general terms the purpose of the repository or collection's existence. What types of people, activities, and/or subjects do you wish to document? Will you focus on a specific time period or geographical area? Will you collect materials relating only to your institution, or will you collect materials from other sources as well? What users will you serve? If your repository is part of a larger institution, such as a university, how does your mission statement relate to that of the larger entity?

It is also very important to include a reference to the preservation of collections within your mission statement, along with references to collecting materials and making them available. For example, a historical society might be "dedicated to collecting, preserving, interpreting, and promoting interest in the history and culture of the local area." The presence of such a reference gives preservation equal status with other institutional activities, and demonstrates a commitment by the institution to long term maintenance of collections.

Collecting Policy

A collecting policy expands upon the mission statement, providing specifics about the current scope of the collection, the areas in which additional materials may be collected in future, and the audience to be served. A good collecting policy will take into consideration the holdings and collecting activities of other local repositories. It is also crucial for a repository to have a clear sense of what it will not collect, since collections must be limited to those items that serve the real needs and mission of the repository.

Subjects to be discussed in a collecting policy include:

- The type of programmes and activities that will be supported by the collection (*e.g.*, research, exhibits, publications, outreach to the community);
- Potential user groups to be served (*e.g.*, scholars, genealogists, undergraduate students, local schoolchildren, the general public);
- Specific materials to be collected (*e.g.*, subjects, geographic areas, time periods, formats, languages) and levels of collecting (*e.g.*, existing strengths and weaknesses, desired levels of collecting in different areas, materials that will not be collected); and
- Information about acquisition policy, cooperative collecting efforts with other institutions, deaccessioning/weeding policy, and procedures for periodic review of the overall collecting policy.

INTELLECTUAL CONTROL: LIBRARIES

Effective selection of collections for preservation requires good intellectual control, since relative values and priorities cannot be assigned unless staff is familiar with the collections' contents.

An inventory of collections using standard library and archival descriptive practices can also assist systematic comparison of an institution's holdings with those of other repositories, especially when cataloging has been automated using the standard MARC (*M*achine *R*eadable *C*ataloging) format. Whether or not materials are preserved elsewhere can be an important factor in determining your own priorities.

Organizing Library Collections

Most institutions with library collections will be familiar with standard procedures for cataloging and classification of library materials. Printed materials are cataloged and classified according to Library of Congress (LC) procedures that follow the *Anglo American Cataloguing Rules*, Second Edition, or *AACR2*. This cataloging system was originally used to create catalog cards, but now computer files that are searched directly by the user are created using the MARC format. Call numbers are assigned for books using Library of Congress classification numbers or Dewey Decimal System numbers. The Library of Congress provides cataloging records for most U.S. and international publications.

The MARC format was established by the Library of Congress in the 1960s, when it began to computerize its catalog records. Using numbers, letters, and symbols to mark the information within a cataloging record, the MARC format has become the standard for library computer cataloging. Having undergone many incarnations since its inception, the version currently in use is called MARC 21; the Library of Congress maintains it and all its associated documentation.

Computerized cataloging records are shared among libraries nationally and internationally through the Online Computer Library Center 's WorldCat database.

INTELLECTUAL CONTROL: ARCHIVES

This part will briefly review standard procedures for organizing and cataloging archival materials, which may be unfamiliar to some organizations, such as public libraries or historical museums, that hold archival materials in addition to other types of collections.

Archival materials are generally organized in groups, with related materials cataloged together as one unit instead of separately.

When arranging collections, archivists follow two primary principles:

- Provenance requires that records created or accumulated by the same source whether an organization or an individual be kept together, since as a whole they shed light on the activities of the records' creator. For institutional collections, maintaining provenance allows the researcher to discern where certain types of information might be found by determining what organization, department, or person would have produced that information.

- Original order requires that the archivist maintain the original organization of documents within a collection. This can provide useful information about the routine activities of an organization and also help date documents or attribute documents to an author. If, however, there is no discernible order to the collection, the archivist will impose as straight forward an order as possible.

Archival description enables the researcher to find both the collection he or she needs and the information within the collection by using various types of written guides. The availability of written guides prevents users' rummaging through large numbers of boxes and documents, which can cause handling damage and general disorder. Furthermore, the researcher is not solely dependent on the personal knowledge of the archivist or other staff member(s) present to access the materials.

If you are starting with a significant backlog of material that has never been organized at all, you should begin with a basic collection level inventory of all materials. This should provide information about the records' creator, the dates of the collection, the amount of material in it, and a general paragraph about its contents. Eventually you will arrange and describe all these materials in some detail, using standard archival practices.

Sharing Cataloging Data for Archival and Manuscript Materials

If possible, cataloging data for archival and manuscript materials should be automated at the local level using the MARC format. This might be done through an existing online library/museum catalog or through a stand alone system that runs on a PC. In addition, there are a number of state level databases of historical records that create automated cataloging records from information submitted by the repository.

For unique materials, cataloging records should be entered into the OCLC bibliographic databases. For smaller institutions without the ability to input records into these databases, cataloging information can be submitted to the National Union Catalog of Manuscript Collections, a cooperative cataloging programme operated by the Library of Congress.

Based on information submitted by the repository, NUCMC's catalogers create MARC records in the RLG database and establish pertinent name and subject authority headings. The submitting institution must then be prepared to make the cataloged materials available to researchers on a regular basis.

While the OCLC and RLG bibliographic databases are excellent resources, MARC records inherently provide limited detail. Access fees can also create a barrier to using these services. Archivists are now using the Web with greater frequency to provide comprehensive access to their collections by listing collections online.

Some have begun to put entire finding aids online, but this task requires an enormous amount of time and effort when done in a useful and standardized manner. Standards have been developed for encoding finding aids for the Web. The Encoded Archival Description (EAD) Standard is maintained by the Society of American Archivists in partnership with the Library of Congress Network Development/MARC Standards Office.

6

Accountability in Library Management

INTRODUCTION

Having defined the environment it is obvious that while in the internal environment there are more weaknesses than strengths, in the external environment there are more opportunities than threats. How then can libraries take advantage of the opportunities that the 21st century has to offer when library resources are inadequate and their role more peripheral than integral? The answer is to strategise – through well designed strategic plans, efficient organisation, capable leadership and effective control measures. It is only when these management tools and strategies are in place can libraries ensure the achievement of their goals and objectives. The onus therefore lies with the libraries to maximise their opportunities and be accountable for the success of their performance. Seen in this light, accountability therefore is the key factor to whether or not they can meet the demands and challenges of the 21st century

STRATEGIC PLAN

A well designed plan would provide direction, minimise uncertainty and impact of changes, reduce waste and establish standards for goal achievements.

The planning process incorporates the following steps:

- Setting of goals and objectives
- Formulating strategies
- Developing action plans
- Coordinating activities
- Monitoring accomplishment of goals
- Review/ revise plan

For the libraries, it is crucial that they understand what their core business is, which is SERVICES. Their core business must be integrated into the core business of their organisations

In designing the strategies, the library has to first determine a strategic focus which will be incorporated in its:

- Vision,

- Mission and
- Objectives statements.

Where does the issue of accountability arise in the formulation of the strategic plan? It is in the quantitative methods used to measure the accomplishment of goals and objectives, in the time frames given to accomplish each activity and in the quality measures used in the performance such as monitoring, setting standards (ISO) and benchmarking. But however brilliant the plan, unless implemented, it is useless.

ORGANISING

The organisation structure should facilitate the achievement of goals so it is important that the organisation structure is designed to facilitate work flow (whether via function, specialisation or process), define the chain of command (whether hierarchical, flat, etc.), define the span of control (the wider the less effective) and clarify issue such as centralisation vs. decentralisation.

The library management would have to structure the organization in such a way as to ensure that the organisation structure facilitates rather than hinder the achievement of goals. The library management is therefore accountable in this aspect.

LEADING

Leading is influencing others to carry out tasks towards the achievements of goals. There are different types of leaderships but there are certain traits or characteristics that reflect good leadership:

- Develop corp of excellent staff
  - Staff development plan
  - Motivation
  - Competency training
  - Leadership training
  - Performance measurement
- Monitor activities
- Monitor achievement of goals
- Flexible and adaptable leadership
- Establish value culture – leadership by example

Leadership is not confined to being the Chief Librarian or the Library Director but leadership is found at all levels. Leaders may be managers but not all managers are leaders. The quality of human resource in any organisation depends on the quality of leadership. In this way, the library manager should be held accountable if staff cannot perform and goals cannot be achieved.

CONTROL

Control measures must be in place to monitor activities and ensure that goals are achieved. The effectiveness of any control system depends on how effectively it can facilitate the achievement of goals. Why is a control system important?

- It is a means of measuring whether goals are met and if not why. You can have well formulated strategic plans, well designed organisation structure, highly motivated staff but without control there is no measure of goals achievement.
- It is a management tool that can be used to monitor and measure activities with greater objectivity.

There are basically three types of control measures that libraries can use:

- Monitoring
- ISO
- Benchmarking.

GOVERNMENTAL ACCOUNTING STANDARDS BOARD (GASB)

The GASB was established as an arm of the Financial Accounting Foundation in April 1984 to promulgate standards of financial accounting and reporting with respect to activities and transactions of state and local governmental entities. The GASB is the successor organization to the *National Council on Governmental Accounting* (NCGA). The GASB Concepts Statement 1 states: "Governmental financial" reporting should provide information to assist users in

- Assessing accountability and
- Making economic, social and political decisions."

In order to meet these overall objectives, GASB issued the following guidelines regarding financial reporting:

Accountability

Financial reporting should assist in fulfilling government's duty to be publicly accountable and should enable users to assess that accountability. To accomplish this goal, financial reporting should meet the following criteria:

- Provide information to determine whether current year revenue was sufficient to pay for current year services.
- Demonstrate whether resources were obtained and used in accordance with the entity's legally adopted budget; it should also demonstrate compliance with other finance related legal or contractual requirements.
- Provide information to assist users in assessing the service efforts, costs and accomplishments of the governmental entity.

Decision Making

Financial reporting should assist users in evaluating the operating results of the governmental entity for the year.

To accomplish this objective, financial reporting should also meet these criteria:

- Provide information about sources and uses of financial resources.
- Provide information about how the governmental entity financed its activities and met its cash requirements.
- Provide information necessary to determine whether the entity's financial position improved or deteriorated as a result of the year's operations.

MISCELLANEOUS ITEMS

Library Types

There are a variety of library types and sizes. State laws governing how a library is established, levies taxes, issues and pays for debt, qualifies for state funded revenue and performs other business functions vary depending on the type and size of a library. Refer to the Library Laws Handbook from the Library of Michigan, the State Laws Relating to Michigan Libraries, or consult legal counsel for detailed information concerning legal matters for the type and size of your library.

Users of Governmental Financial Statements

The public is vitally concerned with the cost of public services, the adequacy of revenue in meeting such costs and the stewardship and efficiency of both elected and appointed officials. Contributors and bankers are also interested in the financial status and operating results. With the development of extensive and complex intergovernmental fiscal relationships in the form of grants in aid, shared revenue and administrative supervision, governments must be provided with adequate financial data on the operations of other governmental jurisdictions with which these relations exist. In addition, educational and research organizations, statistical reporting agencies and such individuals as accountants, financial analysts and economists whose professional activities embrace the study and improvement of financial administration and, of course, public management whose responsibility it is to evaluate past performance in daily decision-making and in planning future operations are also users.

Grants

In recent years, many libraries have received grants and other revenue from various federal and state agencies. In connection with these, recipients agree to comply with various statutes and regulations that accompany the grants. The various statutes and regulations may vary among libraries, thus every library should follow its own agreement accordingly. Typically, most agreements are pass through monies.

These types of grants are usually reimbursement in nature and as expenditures are incurred, revenues are accrued. In addition, some statutes and regulations require that certified public accountants perform audits of libraries to test the compliance with these statutes and regulations in addition to performing financial audits.

Chart of Accounts

A chart of accounts is an organized listing of all accounts used by a library to record financial information in its general ledger. The chart of accounts is to the accounting function what the Dewey Decimal System is to a library. It provides a foundation for arranging financial data into useful information. To provide reliable and consistent financial information, it is imperative that the chart of accounts be simple and functional. Accordingly, a "Uniform Chart of Accounts" has been developed by the State of Michigan under Public Act 2 of 1968, as amended, for all Michigan units of government.

Record Retention

Under MCL 399.5 and 750.491, government agencies must keep official books, papers or records unless it has received approval by filing a MH-38, Certificate of Records Disposal, with the State Archives of Michigan. However, a library may adopt its own record retention and disposal plan.

Tax Exempt Status

The General Sales Tax Act and Michigan Sales and Use Tax Administrative Rule, generally provides that governmental and not for profit library purchases are not subject to sales and use tax. Michigan Department of Treasury Revenue Administrative Bulletin 1996 6 illustrates the recommended sales and use tax exemption claim formats. Typically, a library will provide its vendors with a blanket certificate of exemption at the time of purchase.

Selection of Accounting Software

There are a number of factors to consider when selecting accounting software. This is true for both large and small library organizations.

Key steps involved in selecting accounting software include the following:

- *Assess Existing Resources*: Determine current resources in terms of software, hardware and funding.
- *Assess User Requirements*: Survey individuals that will be using the software to determine needs/desires over the near , medium and long term, volumes of transactions in the near and long term and expectations concerning the potential benefits to be gained from use of the software.
- *Identify Available Software*: Identify available software by surveying similar organizations, reading articles and software directories, attending trade shows or contacting consultants. Make an initial determination of potential vendors.

- *Evaluate Vendors*: For entry or mid level "off the shelf" software packages, evaluation of vendors may be accomplished by identifying the perceived strengths and weaknesses of the different packages based on research conducted before making a final determination. For other software packages, a more formal selection process may be undertaken. This could include developing detailed software specifications, soliciting bids from potential qualified bidders, evaluating bid responses and attending vendor demonstrations prior to making a final determination. Factors to evaluate include, but are not limited to the following: ease of use; vendor knowledge, stability and support; flexibility; expandability; security; ability to track needed information and ability to access needed information.
- *Implementation*: Once software has been selected and purchased, a strategy should be developed for how to implement the software. Establish dates for accomplishing specific tasks. Regularly review progress of implementation. A rule of thumb is to run both the old and new systems for a month or two to ensure that a back up exists if problems occur with the new system. This is typically time consuming and, therefore, should be taken into account when planning the implementation.

LIBRARY FUND ACCOUNTING

PURPOSE

The purpose of a library accounting system is:

- To show that all applicable legal provisions have been complied with; and
- To represent fairly and accurately the financial position and results of financial operations of the library's funds and account groups.

Definition of a Fund

A fund is defined as an independent fiscal and accounting entity with a self balancing set of accounts recording cash and/or other resources together with all related liabilities, obligations, reserves and equities that are segregated for the purpose of carrying on specific activities or attaining certain objectives in accordance with specific regulations, restrictions or limitations. Each fund is a completely separate accounting entity in itself, with its own accounts to record various transactions. Funds with similar characteristics are grouped together in fund groups.

Comment

While a private business enterprise can be viewed as a single economic entity with one group of assets, liabilities and equity accounts that are normally reflected in a single set of financial statements, a library may have several funds, each of which has its own assets, liabilities and fund equities. A library may be a combination of several distinctly different operations, each of which functions, and must be reported on, independently from any other fund. The implementation of GASB Statement 34 will add a layer of financial reporting in addition to the distinct fund reporting. This new layer will consolidate the activity of governmental units into a single financial report, similar to the way private enterprise prepares financial reports. This new layer of financial reporting will be on the "full accrual" basis of accounting. It is important to realise that the day to day recordkeeping will not change substantially. The recording of receipts and disbursements and the preparation of budgets for most libraries will continue to be maintained on the "modified accrual" basis of accounting.

Users of Library Financial Information

- Taxpayers.
- State Treasurer/Oversight Bodies.
- Administrative/Finance.
- Bond Rating Agencies.
- Intergovernmental Grantors).
- Contributors/Creditors.
- Employees.

BASIS OF ACCOUNTING

There are two basic methods of accounting for funds: the modified accrual basis and the accrual basis. Under the modified accrual basis of accounting, revenue and expenditures are recorded. Under the accrual basis of accounting, revenue is recorded when earned and expenses are recorded when incurred. In general, governmental libraries will utilize the modified accrual basis of accounting in the day to day accounting records and budgets. When preparing the year end financial report, they will also prepare government wide financial statements on the full accrual basis of accounting.

Characteristics of Modified Accrual Basis of Accounting are as Follows

- Expenditures are recorded when incurred, not when cash is paid or when an invoice is received. Special rules are provided for the following:
  - Prepaid expenses: Purchases that benefit more than one period may be prorated between periods.
  - Interest on long term debt should be counted on the due date of the debt.
  - Employee compensated absences should be counted when the amount comes due for payment, *i.e.* time is taken off, or the employment is terminated.

  - Contingent liabilities should also be recorded at the time they come due for payment.
  - Capital assets should be counted as expenditures when purchased rather than capitalized and recognized over its useful life.
- Revenue is recorded when collected or collectible soon enough to be used to pay current liabilities. "Available" generally means collectible within 30 to 60 days. Special rules are provided for the following:
  - Property taxes should be recorded in the fiscal period for which they were levied, provided the "available" criterion is met.
  - Grants receivables for reimbursement of expenditures should be counted at the same time that the expenditure is recorded, however, GASB Statement number 33 requires that the corresponding revenue be recorded using the "measurable and available" rules. When a grant receivable will not be collected until a date beyond the "available" criterion, a deferred revenue should be recorded.
  - Miscellaneous revenue such as fines and fees etc., are generally recognized when the cash is received.
  - Proceeds of long term debt are recorded as an "other financing source", rather than as liabilities of the fund.

Characteristics of Full Accrual Basis of Accounting are as Follows:

The full accrual basis is used to report the government wide financial information. After the accounting records of the individual funds have been completed on the modified accrual basis, then each government will also create government wide financial statements on the full accrual basis. This basis of accounting measures total economic resources, rather than just the current financial resources.

As a result:

- Revenue is recorded when earned, regardless of when it is received.
- Expenses are recorded as soon as a liability is incurred, and are allocated to the periods benefited.

Some of the more significant differences from modified accrual includes:

- Property tax revenue is recorded in the period levied, less an allowance for uncollectible amounts
- Unused vacation time is recorded as an expense when it is earned
- Capital purchases are not recorded as an expense at the time of purchase; instead, depreciation expense is recorded over the estimated useful life of capital assets. This means that purchases of library books would be capitalized as an asset and depreciated over an appropriate time period.

TYPES OF FUNDS

Following is a list of the typical funds which may be found in accounting for governmental libraries.

General Fund

The General Fund accounts for all revenue and expenditures that are not required to be accounted for elsewhere. This fund typically accounts for the daily revenue and expenditures necessary to operate and provide service of a library. Most revenue and expenses are recorded in this fund. In many cases, this may be the only fund the library maintains.

Special Revenue Funds

Special Revenue Funds are used to account for the proceeds of earmarked revenue or financing activities requiring separate accounting because of legal or regulatory provisions. In many cases, the use of the separate fund is mandatory. Typical special revenue activity might include accrued employee benefits and LSTA grants. This could potentially include endowment type situations, where the principle of the gift may be spent to support the Library's programmes.

Debt Service Funds

Debt Service Funds are used to account for the annual payment of principal, interest and expenses in connection with certain long term debt. The proceeds from bond issues or other types of debt are typically recorded in the General or Capital Project Funds, depending on the stipulations of the debt instrument.

Debt service fund resources are typically received via special voted property tax levies or transfers from other funds. In many cases, the use of Debt Service Funds is optional.

Capital Projects Funds

Capital Projects Funds are used to account for the development of capital facilities, such as an addition to a building. Typically, this fund is established to account for the construction of fixed assets or to set aside money for future capital needs. In many cases, the use of Capital Projects Funds is optional.

Endowment Funds/Permanent Funds

Prior to GASB (Government Accouting Standards Board) Statement number 34, Endowment Funds were established to account for gifts and bequests that may be either expendable or nonexpendable, depending on legal restrictions that apply. While recording activity under a separate fund is common, it is not mandatory.

In many instances, gifts and bequests may be accounted for under the General Fund. GASB Statement number 34 created a new fund type called Permanent Funds that are used to report resources that are legally restricted to the extent that only earnings, and not principal, may be used for purposes that support the reporting government's programmes. Permanent funds report trust arrangements in which the reporting government is the beneficiary, including public purpose funds previously classified as non-expendable trust funds.

Account Groups

Prior to the implementation of GASB Statement number 34, there are also two self balancing account groups:

- *General Fixed Assets Account Group*: The General Fixed Assets Account Group is set up to account for long lived assets. The assets are always acquired through a fund, usually the general fund or a capital project fund. The acquisition is accounted for as an expenditure and, therefore, no depreciation is applied against the asset. However, beyond the date of acquisition, the assets are accounted for in the general fixed assets account group. Essentially, the account group is a summary of all the long lived assets. When recording assets in this account group, consideration should be given to materiality and useful life of the item. Only material items need to be accounted for as fixed assets. Libraries should establish a dollar threshold for items to be capitalized. The objective is to establish a limit high enough to avoid too much detailed record keeping yet low enough to record material fixed assets. In the event the items are sold or retired, the cost of the item should be deleted from the account group. Prior to GASB Statement number 34, books, periodicals, recordings and film were often recorded at one dollar per item. When GASB Statement 34 is implemented, assets including books, periodicals, recordings, etc should be reported at their historical cost, net of accumulated depreciation. Replacement value is often estimated based on trade publication average costs adjusted for discounts and processing costs applicable to a library's purchases. Periodically, a library should compare its insurance coverage to replacement value.
- *General Long term Debt Account Group*: The General Long term Debt Account Group is set up to account for the unmatured principal of bonds, warrants, notes and other forms of long term indebtedness that is secured by the full faith and credit of the library. The proceeds from issuing general long term debt are recorded as revenue, typically in a capital projects fund or the general fund as "other financing sources." The debt service fund typically records the expenditure of the debt payments. However, beyond the date of issue, the outstanding principal amounts are accounted for in the general long term debt account group. Essentially, the account group is a summary of all long term debt owed by the library. As debt is retired, the account group is reduced.

Effective with the implementation of GASB Statement 34, reporting of the account groups will no longer be required, however, fixed assets and long term liabilities will be reported on the Statement of Net Assets. It will be necessary for each governmental unit to maintain the records regarding the historical cost of assets, along with the related accumulated depreciation expense and the long term debt. Although there are several alternatives to maintaining this information, libraries should consider continuing to track the information in a manner equivalent to the current techniques used for the General Fixed Asset Account Group and the General Long tem Debt Account Group, with the added emphasis on recognizing annual depreciation expense and accumulated depreciation.

COMPARISON OF GOVERNMENTAL FUNDS AND COMMERCIAL ACCOUNTING

Similarities

- Periodic balance sheets or statements of net assets, income statements and statements of changes in equity balances are prepared by both The double entry system of accounts is utilized by both.
- The historical cost principle, consistency principle and, for the most part, generally accepted accounting principles are used by both.
- Fund accounting and commercial accounting use the same accounting terminology. However, fund accounting has some terminology unique to it.

Differences

- A profit motive is absent from all the funds. Libraries are service and responsibility oriented.
- Most libraries use a "modified accrual" basis of accounting, where commercial accounting uses accrual basis. Under the requirements of GASB Statement number 34, the day to day recordkeeping will continue to be done on a modified accrual basis. The new statement will, however, add a layer of financial reporting to the current modified accrual basis of reporting. The new layer will bring together the financial information of the Library as a complete entity using the full accrual basis of reporting in a manner similar to most commercial accounting.
- The fund accounting emphasis is on "budgetary accounting."
- In the fund level "modified accrual basis" of accounting, capital expenditures are treated the same as operating expenses. Accordingly, governmental libraries typically do not compute depreciation expense at the fund level of financial reporting. This practice differs from commercial accounting where capital purchases are accounted for in

asset accounts and charged to expense over time through the depreciation account.

- Some accounting systems record purchase orders on the books as encumbrances in the library funds. Generally accepted accounting principles do not record these as expenditures, however the accounting rules do allow encumbrances to be included in the comparison of actual results of operations to budget. Although not a common practice, encumbrance accounting may provide a superior form of budget control during the year.
- A library may be a combination of several distinctly different financial operations, each having its own set of accounts or funds.
- Governmental accounting is concerned more with a comparison of actual results to budgeted amounts, rather than a maximization of net income or working capital, as in commercial accounting.

LIBRARIES READY FOR THE 21ST CENTURY

To fight, one has to recognise the enemy – so it is with libraries. Unless libraries understand what is demanded of them by the 21st Century, it would be difficult for them to face the onslaught of the changes that the century will bring. To prepare themselves for the onslaught, they would need to not only assess their current "strengths" and "weaknesses" but to also recognise the "opportunities" or "threats" presented by the 21st century.

A SWOT analysis of libraries is important because it provides libraries with a more 'clinical' approach to library development, minimising trial and error in the process.

The SWOT analysis is not based on research data but based on the perception and certain assumptions on the part of the authors, resulting from their reading of the relevant information literature as well as their experiences as Chief Librarians.

The SWOT analysis is used merely to illustrate the need for librarians to be introspective and understand their capabilities as well as to be aware of developments taking place in their surrounding environment.

Internal Environment:

- *Strength*:
  - Collection
  - Reputation
  - User Education
- *Weakneses*:
  - Collection
  - Staff
  - Funds
  - Usage

- Peripheral role
- Non integrated Strategic Plan

External Environment:

- Opportunity:
  - Lifelong education
  - Innovative technology
  - Knowledge management
  - Globalisation
  - National policies and Objectives
- *Threat*:
  - Proliferation of information providers
  - Globalisation

DEFINING THE LIBRARY'S ENVIRONMENT

INTERNAL ENVIRONMENT

Any assessment of the library's strengths and weaknesses must be based on user feedback in the form of complaints or user studies or benchmarking. In the absence of such feedback however and purely for the purpose of this chapter, the authors have drawn on their own experiences as Chief Librarian and Consultant Librarian to identify the strengths and weaknesses of the library.

Strengths

Three areas can be identified as the library's strength, notably:

- Collections
- Reputation
- User Education

Collections

Collections are the library's greatest strength because without collections, there can be no library. The strength of the collections however depends on its size and uniqueness. In the 1950s and 1960s, the size of the collection is the measure of the library's worth. As such weeding exercises were seldom undertaken for fear that large libraries will lose their competitive edge. Today, the issue of size is not the main criteria to assess the library's stature because with the advent of digital libraries, the world's collections are easily accessible. The uniqueness of collections however has became a more important criteria for assessing the library's strength because of their heritage value and their potential as a national asset.

In the case of Malaysia, the various Malaysiana collections at the National Library of Malaysia, at the 17 public university libraries, at government research agencies in the form of research collections, at the State Public Libraries in the form of the state collections, are examples of unique collections that are found in the country. Collectively, the collections found in all types of libraries in any country can be deemed to be the country's national asset. The fact that they are professionally organised for easy retrieval makes library collections indispensable for national development. However, while the monetary value of these collections may be easy to quantify by totalling the annual budgets of each library, their academic and cultural value are priceless. But the main issue in question is: Are the collections used? However priceless the collections, their value will come to naught unless used.

Reputation

Libraries exist today because people believe in the traditional concept of the libraries as being at the heart of learning. Since the education system provides the nation's manpower and serves as the catalyst for national development and advancement, libraries are accorded the same value. They believe that a literate population is the country's foremost asset and critical for national advancement. This belief has prevailed till today but it is a perception that has not been substantiated by library usage. It is obvious that while libraries are still regarded as an important tool for education and a mechanism for development of manpower for the country, reputation alone is not sufficient. The perception that libraries are important must be replaced by a more realistic view of the library's worth.

User Education

Teaching users how to retrieve materials via the library systems, whether manual or electronic, has long been undertaken by libraries. However, user education programmes have become more urgent in recent years when library systems became ICT based. The underlying premise of all user education programmes is that however excellent the library's collections and systems are, if not used they serve no purpose.

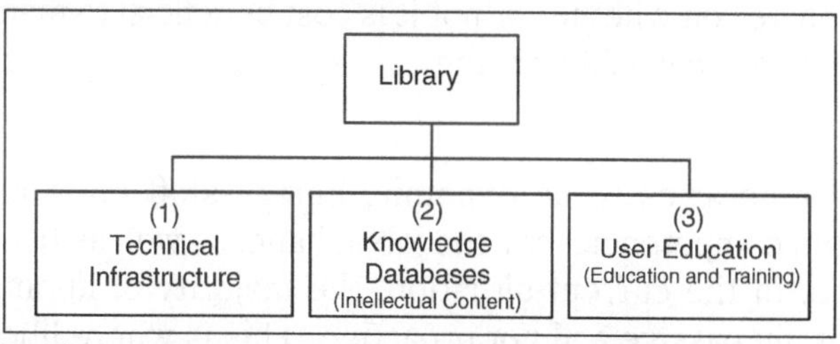

User education programmes are now offered by most libraries, both formally or informally. It is the best way to promote libraries and library use because not only do these programmes enable librarians to come into direct contact with the clients, demonstrate to the clients the proficiency of librarians in both the academic aspect of library work as well as the technical aspect, it also provides libraries with the opportunity to.

- Be integrated into the teaching and learning process in the case of university libraries or

- Develop literacy skills among members of society in the case of public libraries.

Weaknesses

Unfortunately, there are more weaknesses than strengths in our analysis of the internal environment:

Collections

Generally, notwithstanding the size of their collections, libraries have in their collections, materials that contain data more archival than current. They are excellent for scholars and researchers from the academia but users of the 21st century are weaned on ICT and expect information at a press of the button.

Library collections are mainly passive collections, sitting on library shelves for years, unused. Consisting mainly of printed secondary and tertiary sources, they stand the risk of being replaced by e-books, e-journals and internet. It has become very common for libraries to have e-books, e-journals and internet services provided by commercial vendors at a very high cost. It would not be a surprise however that later in the 21st century, access to Internet and electronic databases will themselves become passé and by the end of the 21st century, materials would be more readily available in palmtops and accessible while showering in the bathroom or driving in cars. Will libraries have the funds to update and upgrade their collections will be the main issue facing libraries in the 21st century.

Unless libraries have collections that are relevant and can meet the demands of the 21st century, library collections comprising of secondary and tertiary data, will be rendered obsolete. The main weakness of library collections however lies in the fact that they are not used to the optimum, giving rise to management debates on whether or not it is cost beneficial to maintain libraries when alternatives are available on line.

Staff

In order for libraries to be dynamic, library staff must have the right qualifications and competencies for the job in hand, as well as the right attitude towards service. In the current situation, the majority of library staff can be said to be generally passive and not proactive. This is where library education plays a part.

Librarians of the 21st century must be multi skilled, have sound subject knowledge and good leadership. Library schools would have to be more responsive to these needs and take into account that librarians of the future will not be sitting at a desk in a library but will work in a virtual environment with PC(s) as colleagues. Multi skilled, she will need to communicate well, preferably in several languages, be knowledgeable in specialised subject areas, innovative in the use of ICT, personable and independent.

Funds

Lack of funds is a perennial problem faced by all libraries. Notwithstanding the fact there are libraries that are well endowed funds are never adequate to fulfill all objectives. This has resulted in libraries undertaking resource sharing of collections and services to reduce expenditure and optimise usage. In some countries, libraries have embraced the concept of 'corporatisation' through which libraries have imposed membership fees and service charges. Other libraries depend on sponsors and donors for funds. The issue is: will libraries in the 21st century have to be self funding?

Usage

The most important issue in library usage is the need to provide evidence of usage. Much of the professional literature has alluded to the fact that despite their importance, libraries are not used to the optimum. Also, with the establishment of digital libraries, which makes remote access easy, library visits will soon be more for pleasure than for information gathering.

In a recent survey of undergraduates at the University of Malaya Library only a small percentage visit the library every day (17.2 per cent), with the majority (54 per cent) visiting a few times a week. The survey also shows that the majority of students do not use the electronic databases preferring the printed books instead. There is a need to market library services to increase usage, whether on site or remote.

At the OUM Library, statistics obtained from logins of e-books and e-journals show that:

- Remote access is greater than on site access and
- Usage of e-books higher than e-journals.

Peripheral Role of Libraries

Is the role of library passive or proactive? There is no real evidence to show that libraries are integrated into the core business of their institutions, especially academic libraries and special libraries. In the case of University libraries, while there is no evidence of a correlation between usage of library resources and academic achievement evidence of Faculty library integration can be discerned by asking the following questions:.

- *Teaching*: Is there resourcebased teaching? Are library resources integrated into teaching activities?
- *Learning*: Is there resource based learning? Are library resources integrated into learning activities?
- *Research*: Is there evidence that the more specialised the research, the less need there is for library resources?

With regard to the library's role in learning, in a survey undertaken at the University of Malaya, to determine whether the user education programme is useful for their learning, the majority of students surveyed replied in the affirmative.

EXTERNAL ENVIRONMENT

To be prepared for the 21st century, libraries would have to be aware not only of developments taking place in the world outside library walls but to interpret these developments into "opportunities" or "threats" for libraries. Those that can be considered as "opportunities" must be taken advantage of while taking steps to be prepared for those that are considered as "threats". These "opportunities" and "threats" found beyond library walls must however be seen in the right perspective, against the background of the library's capabilities or its "strengths" and "weaknesses".

Weaknesses

What can be interpreted as 'opportunities' can be subjective, depending on how the librarians perceive them to be.

For the purpose of this chapter, the authors have identified five areas:

- Innovative Technology.
- Globalisation.
- Lifelong Learning.
- Knowledge Management.
- National Policies and Objectives.

Innovative Technology

The phrase "innovative technology" is deliberately used here to denote the innovative aspects of technology because not since the wheel has there been a development so global that it has not touched every aspect of life and every level of society – *e.g.* e-learning, e-government, e-business. From the Parliament to shopping, technology has become part of life. Reaching the moon, artificial intelligence, cloning of genes have become mundane news – innovative technology has made them possible.

The advantages provided by innovative technology can be summarised as:

- More efficient work processes, with less mistakes and greater output
- Provides global access to information
- Encourages independent learning

But the issue that confronts libraries in the 21st century is: To what level should librarians be trained in technology?

In the case of libraries, innovative technology has been identified to facilitate:

- Day to day tasks such as acquisitions, cataloguing, loans etc.
- Interaction with users via the use of portals. The development of information gateways or portals has made it possible for library and information professionals to upgrade their services. Information portal

can offer users one stop work stations where they can search across a multitude of resources and retrieve electronic and book resources in one station. Information portals can provide integration of sources for searching and for location and delivery of materials – in whatever format they exist. Portal brings the opportunity to develop elibrary services – to meet the growing expectations of the student population.

- Enables user education programmes to be conducted in large groups with hands on sessions. Undertaking user education programmes provides libraries with the opportunity to optimise usage because users are taught lifelong learning skills such as information–retrieval skill and ICT skills. Implementing a portal can change the environment in which users discover information and get better access to the wealth of contents.

Globalisation

The term "globalisation" is associated mainly with business – giving rise to concepts such as 'global economy', 'global markets', 'global competition' or hyper competition', etc. A global economy is one in which goods, services, people, skills and ideas move freely across geographic borders.

Relatively unfettered by artificial constraints, such as tariffs, the global economy significantly expands and complicates a firm's competitive environment". Is globalisation relevant for libraries? The authors are of the opinion that since 'information delivery' is a business and globalisation is basically a business concept than globalisation will have an impact on libraries. Innovative technology has made it possible for business to be conducted in a global environment but how does globalisation affect librarians?

Self Efficiency vs. Outsourcing

Concept of self sufficiency has given way to global outsourcing by cutting out the role of the middle man, including the librarian. This has implications for the library in matters relating to human resource and organisation structure.

Examples:

- *Acquisitions*: Librarians do not need to go though local agents. There are many more companies on Internet who can acquire anything for libraries, ranging from equipment to books.
- *Cataloguing*: OCLC is a case in point although it does not contain records for non-English items.
- *Information Services*: It is a matter of time before information services are conducted on a global basis replacing libraries and librarians except for the provision of local information which however may be taken over by local companies with enough entrepreneurial acumen to take over the information market.

Demand for Wide ranging Information

Imagine providing information services for the whole world, when most libraries cannot even satisfy the information needs of their own clientele. Theoretically, however, this is what globalisation could generate. Do librarians have the potential for it? In reality, no. Working on the premise that no one person can provide all information on everything, it will be a massive task but if libraries do not do it other more enterprising professionals would. It is worth a thought. For example, libraries in Malaysia need not confine themselves to providing information merely about Malaysia but through databases subscribed and information networks established via the universities and ministries, librarians can play a role. This will have implications for the library in terms of collections, human resource and job expertise and skills. The question that begs to be asked at this juncture is: Do we still need libraries and librarians in the face of globalisation?

Lifelong Learning

The move towards a more democratic form of education in the 1960s and 1970s resulted in a shift in the concept of education from one that was authoritarian and elitist to one that advocated 'equal opportunity in education'. 'Equal opportunity in education' was seen as the democratic right of all individuals–irrespective of race, status, age or ability but at the same time 'equal opportunity' does not mean the same treatment for everyone. For equal opportunity to be meaningful, however, education must be extended on a continuous lifelong basis with opportunities for success provided at every stage of the continuum.

Any attempt at early elimination would render the democratisation process ineffective and make a mockery of the principle of 'equal opportunity' Conceptualising education as a lifelong process was an effort at translating democratic principles into educational practice. Democratising education on the principles of equal opportunity meant a re-appraisal of traditional aims and methods.

Unlike the traditional concept, the modern concept of education believes that education should produce a learning society, not a learning minority. In simple language, higher education should be catering to the masses. The change in emphasis in educational aims and objectives has made it necessary for teaching and learning methods to be reviewed, giving rise to a productive learning environment with the focus on learning and the learner rather than teaching and the teachers, in greater emphasis given to differentiation in needs, abilities and personalities in the development of independent and active learning the democratisation of higher education has given the concept 'equal opportunity' a new meaning, encompassing a wider scope of educational aims and objectives. It has given modern education certain characteristics.

Greater and More Flexible Access to Higher Education

Greater access does not mean mainly increasing the number of people enrolled in mainstream university programmes but also to provide opportunities for those previously "excluded" for various reasons. Propagating lifelong education would ensure that any one who wishes to acquire qualifications at any stage of his life would be able to do so because there are alternative means by which the opportunity is provided

Learner centred Approach to Learning

The importance given to the learner in the modern approach to education ensures that learner needs are given priority. In lifelong learning, the focus is on teaching the learner how to learn, not what to learn. In modern terms, it would mean "empowering" the learner such that he can be independent and resourceful throughout his lifetime of learning experiences. This also means that the learner is given the opportunity to learn at his own pace and according to his own style.

He can undertake his learning anywhere, anytime, anyhow. Learning therefore becomes flexible, at a pace dictated by the learner and in accordance with negotiated objectives.

Variety of Teaching Strategies

With the learner's interest at the heart of the teaching learning process, the method and strategy of instruction need to adapt. Instruction has now to be skills based, not subject based, consistent with the need to prepare learners for lifelong learning, so as to teach them how to learn rather than what to learn. Instruction is individualised to cater to individual differences of the learners making it necessary for small group teaching rather than the whole class approach which assumes that learners learn at the same pace.

A greater variety of teaching strategies have been devised in recent years to cope with the learner centric pedagogy such as interdisciplinary team teaching, project work, problem based teaching and with greater ICT capability, web based teaching, e-teaching, etc. What implications does lifelong learning have for libraries?.

Bearing in mind that lifelong 'students' are now not confined to the 5-14 age cohort but more likely 5-65 years age cohort as the learning population moves from primary schools to universities, libraries will have to reassess its collections, services and delivery systems to accommodate this learning continuum.

There will be traditional as well as non-traditional universities. In the case of the non-traditional universities offering open and distance learning programmes, libraries will need to focus more on digital collections, services to be more flexible providing for remote access and delivery systems need to be efficient. The issue is: When libraries move from providing library centred to usercentred services, the library can no longer be a building but a system.

Knowledge Management

The concept of Knowledge Management (KM) is basically one that advocates sharing of knowledge within a company or agency such that with the sharing of knowledge it will help the company or agency to combat competition and provide it with the competitive edge.

It is a process that involves:

- *Knowledge creation*: Recording information from top management downwards and vice versa. It includes documenting unwritten knowledge or in other words, documenting experiences of people relevant to the company operations. This is not an easy task because the information may not be current and people are not forthcoming, preferring to be secretive.
- *Knowledge organisation*: Documenting and using retrieval systems to store and make accessible the necessary information. What to document, how detailed and for whom are issues related to KM. In certain agencies, there will be a committee or jury of specialists to decide which information to document and store.
- *Knowledge dissemination/sharing*: KM was introduced to reduce barriers in information/knowledge sharing in companies to facilitate decision-making and prevent unnecessary duplication of effort. Knowing what others are doing in other department will help departmental heads to make more informed decisions. Knowledge sharing is more effective if it involves all levels of staff – from top management downwards and vice versa. The logic of sharing strategic and operational knowledge is to make processes more efficient and intradepartmental communication more effective. As for its role in ensuring the company's monetary gains it has been reported in the professional literature to be 'successful'. KM has also been described as "organisational learning" because in sharing the information or knowledge the whole organisation goes through a learning process. The success of KM is difficult to quantify because it is difficult to measure the success of knowledge sharing or to ascertain to what extent organisational learning takes place.

But what does KM mean to libraries?

- The library can become the Centre for Knowledge Management in the institution by being involved in documenting, organising and disseminating the information or knowledge gathered from within the organisation This is particularly viable for all libraries *e.g.* in the case of university libraries information about teaching, learning and research activities can not only be documented via published reports but also by interviewing the VC, Deputy VC's, Deans, lecturers, students, Ministry of Education officials, etc. In special libraries at government agencies or private companies, there may be problems with access to confidential information like pricing of commodities, marketing policies, marketing research results, etc. In Malaysia, these are a few successful agencies undertaking KM. From their experience, it can be said that the success of KM depends on the support of the management of the organization while the main problem is that colleagues are not cooperative and not forthcoming with information, especially tacit information.

- The library can create primary "live" information, instead of dealing with "passive information" which is often secondhand, outdated, irrelevant and insignificant.
- Staff must be trained or retrained in certain areas in order to function effectively. The ability to interview effectively, the ability to relate to people without either intimidating them or being intimidated by them, knowledgeable in relevant subject areas, proficient at handling ICT information delivery systems, etc.
- Allows library to be creative because there is neither universal approach to KM, nor one or best way of implementing it.
- Recognition that information is an important commodity but like any other product needs good marketing strategies. If the library wants to function as an information centre it has to convince its own market and society at large of the importance of its role as information provider.

National Policies and Objectives

All countries have long term strategic plans. In Malaysia, it is a 25-year plan which forms the basis for national development till 2020. Briefly, the V2020s aim is to make Malaysia an industrialised nation by the year 2020. In order to achieve this aim, nine thrust areas were identified to drive the V2020. One of the thrust areas is to make the Malaysian society a knowledge based society. In this case of Malaysia, not only is the public sector committed to achieving the strategic objectives of V2020 but the private sector as well. Knowing where the nation is heading towards and the role played by each sector of society is important to the library and although the role of libraries is more indirect than direct, libraries do have in their custody the nation's intellectual wealth which should be optimized in the development of the knowledge society. Considering the wealth of information resources located at libraries throughout Malaysia, if they had been read and used, Malaysia does not need to wait till the year 2020 to have an information rich society.

Threats

Proliferation of Information Providers

A potential threat is the proliferation of non-library information providing companies and agencies that provide information via Internet. They may impose charges for the information but the information is usually current. How can libraries compete when the collections available at libraries are mainly secondary information found in print and electronic media?

There are three areas that the new breed of information providers has found foothold:

- Delivery systems
- Content development
- Content management

At the International Conferences of Asian Digital Libraries, held in Kuala Lumpur in December 2003, it was remarkable to listen to ICT specialists who have devised systems for information delivery. The focus was systems rather than content but it gave a good indication of what is imminent in the near future. Much as librarians were awed by the current developments, it also gave the impression that unless libraries take on a more pro-active approach, libraries will be by passed as information centres. So the issue is: Can libraries compete?

Globalisation

There are two aspects in globalisation – the positive and the negative, depending on how one views it.

There are two potentials:

- Ability to outsource certain aspects of library functions such as acquisitions, cataloguing and information sources.
- Provide information services beyond home shores. It will be a daunting task as there will be a need to upgrade staff expertise but notwithstanding this, we need to explore the possibility.

From the negative point of view, it will spell the end of library services as we know it now, specifically with regard to information delivery. The library will remain the centre for loans and reference, using print and electronic resources. These materials can be accessed on site or from the home or office. But the critical issue is currency and variety of information that cannot be supplied by libraries. Globalisation will then take away from the library its information delivery function because in speed and variety libraries will not be able to compete with information centres worldwide despite the cost.

7

Financial Management and Resource in Library

BUDGET

DEFINITION

A budget is a plan of financial operations embodying an estimate of proposed expenditures for a given period and the proposed means of financing them. In the State of Michigan, all general and special revenue funds are required by law to be budgeted annually. Revisions to the Uniform Budgeting and Accounting Act in 2000 removed Debt Service Funds from the type of funds required to adopt a budget.

PURPOSE

Under Michigan Public Act 621 of 1978, a budget appropriation must be in place before a governmental unit may commit to spending money in their General Fund or Special Revenue Funds. However, there are other reasons for developing a budget. An important reason is to ensure that libraries establish a plan on how to allocate resources in order to meet the goals and service expectations of the library. For that reason, although an official budget is not required for debt service or capital project funds, it is prudent to develop a financial plan for those activities. The plan could be prepared on an annual basis, or on a project basis. A budget also allows for easy evaluation of whether the goals and service expectations are being met.

BUDGET PROCESS

Regardless of the type of library, the annual budgetary process involves the following three generic phases.

Preparation

The preparation phase is usually the responsibility of the library director.

It is accomplished by analysing past financial data and allocating the anticipated library resources to provide the various services and activities for library patrons.

Adoption

Once the budget has been prepared, it is presented to the library's legislative body for consideration, possible modification and final approval. Typically, the public is invited to participate in this phase via public hearings on proposed budgets.

Execution

Budgetary accounts are set up to record the estimated revenue and expenditures for the appropriate funds. As economic conditions and circumstances change, budget amounts can be amended by a process determined by the library's legislative body. Typically, the process is very similar to that of the original budget. The budgetary amounts are then compared with actual amounts periodically. This allows the library's management team to effectively operate the library. The comparison of budget to actual results can be accomplished using a variety of formats.

TYPES OF BUDGETS

Types of budgets available to libraries are:

- *Line Item*: A line item budget shows a library's budget by account type
- *Cost Centre*: A cost center budget shows a library's budget by groupings
- *Fund Total*: A fund total budget shows a library's budget in fund totals

All of the above budget types are acceptable methods of budgeting. Typically, the line item or cost center budgets are used. The use of either of these not only meets legal requirements but also provides management and the board with an effective tool to help operate and manage the library.

BUDGET REQUIREMENTS

Budget Questionnaire	Yes/No
1. Has a budget been adopted (General and Special Revenue Funds)?	_______
2. Was a public hearing held on the budget?	_______
3. Was all the necessary information included in the budget document for the budgetary funds:	
A. Actual prior year (both revenue and expenditures)?	_______
B. Estimate of current year (both revenue and expenditures)?	_______
C. Proposed budget (both revenue and expenditures)?	_______

	D. Amounts for contingencies if appropriate?	______
	E. Amount of fund balance (deficit) accumulated from prior years and the estimated surplus or deficit expected in the current year?	______
4.	Is the budget balanced (budgeted fund balance is zero or positive)?	______
5.	Has the budget been amended when necessary if actual revenue is less than the budget estimated?	______
6.	Has the budget been amended to allow expenditures in excess of the original appropriation?	______
7.	Are expenditures equal to or less than amounts appropriated?	______
8.	Are all expenditures authorized in the budget?	______

In order to comply with the Michigan Public Act 621 of 1978, certain requirements must be met. The following questionnaire is a general guide to the specific requirements. All questions should be answered "yes" to comply with the Budget Act.

BUDGET CALENDAR

The following is an example of a budget calendar for a library with a fiscal year of January 1 through December 31.

Timeline	Process
July	Library director begins process – concludes on format, sets management team's workshop sessions and submits data request to management team
August	Data request forms collected and summarized in workshop sessions – initial budget is formed
September	Proposed budget submitted for board review
October	Board reviews and provides input on proposed budget
November	Public hearing and budget adoption

BUDGETING AND BUDGETARY CONTROL

INTRODUCTION

Budgets can be prepared for and used by anyone and anything. That is, we can prepare and use personal budgets and organisations, ministries and non profit making organisations can all use them.

Budgets, by definition, have to be prepared in advance; and for this reason, they are often referred to in terms of their being part of a feedforward system.

Feedback is a term frequently heard both in accounting and ordinary use. Feedforward, on the other hand tends to be less frequently heard, yet this word incorporates the most important aspect of budgeting: looking at situations in advance, thinking about the impact and implications of things in advance, attempting to take control of situations in advance.

BUDGETS

A budget is a plan expressed in quantitative and money terms. Budgets need to be prepared and approved in advance of the period in which they are to be used. Budgets can include some or all of income, expenditure, and the capital to be employed.

Moreover, a budget can be drawn up for an entire organization, any segment of the organization such as a department or sales territory or division, or for a significant activity such as the production and sale of a specific product.

We should also add that a budget can include non- monetary as well as monetary information in it.

BUDGETARY CONTROL

Budgets are simply exercises in calculation unless they are used. When we use a budget, we do so as part of a system of budgetary control. That is, we have some basic ideas of what we want to do, we prepare budgets to help us achieve those ideas; and then once we have done whatever it is that we wanted to do, we check to see if we kept to our budget. Budgetary control relates to the establishment of budgets relating the responsibilities of budget holders the needs of a policy. Budgetary control also relates to the continuous comparison of actual with budgeted results: it does this to try to ensure that the objectives of that policy are achieved; or to provide a basis for the change of those objectives. In summary, a budget is a statement setting out the monetary, numerical or non- quantitative aspects of an organisation's plans for the coming week or month or year. Budgetary control is the analysis of what happened when those plans came to be put into practice, and what the organisation did or did not do to correct for any variations from these plans.

THE BENEFITS OF BUDGETING

Many of us prepare budgets on a personal level: how much is my income for the month?; how much am I going to spend?; and, most importantly, is there anything left over? It seems true, however, that many businessmen do not prepare budgets for their businesses. Thus, even though managers prepare budgets for their relatively simple lives, when it comes to the much more complex situation of their business, they prefer to let cash inflows and outflows look after themselves. The purpose of this part of the chapter is to demonstrate that budgets are useful, informative and communicative. We will see that a budget is a necessity not a luxury.

We will also see some of the problems underlying organisations: the nature of the organisation and the interactions of the people working in them. By considering these problems, we will be considering ways in which your budgeting system, or the organisation itself, can be changed, if necessary, to overcome them.

APPLICABILITY OF BUDGETING AND BUDGETARY CONTROL

Budgeting can be applied to virtually every situation. It does not matter whether we work in the Public or Private Sector of the Economy. We may work for a profit making business or a non- profit making business. Your company may be engaged in trading, manufacturing, or providing a service. In all of these situations, budgeting and budgetary control is of use to you.

As we will see, there are many issues underlying the use of a budgeting system that need careful consideration. For example, we will see that budgeting systems cannot just be imposed on an organisation nor do they run themselves. Managers at all levels often resent budgets and budget targets for a variety of reasons.

THE BUDGETING PROCESS

It would be easy to dismiss the budgeting process as beginning when the first budget is prepared, and as being complete when the master budget is finalised. In reality, the budgeting process begins for many organisations a long time before the budget period begins; and the process ends once the budget period has ended. This means the budgeting process is a very lengthy process: typically, for a large organisation, the pre budgeting phase can begin up to a year before the budget period starts.

Jones and Pendlebury (1984), pp62-63, give us some insight into the beginning of the budgeting cycle when they present a "Timetable for preparation of detailed revenue budget and capital programme" for a Local Authority. They show that the process starts in June in the year preceding the budget period with the draft budget manual being sent to Finance Officers, who will discuss this draft with their departmental staff (with a view to adoption or amendment). The budgetary planning phase is completed in March (ready for an April start) when the printed budget book is published and the approved estimates are put into the financial control system. (Colville (1989) presents a similar view, but this time of the budgeting for a Police Authority in the UK).

THE BUDGET PERIOD

The budget period is the period for which a set of budgets is prepared: typically the budget period is of one year's duration, and will be designed to coincide with an organisation's financial, or fiscal, year. There is no reason why a budget period has to be one year, but typically it is.

On the other hand, if we are dealing with a project, then the budget will clearly be linked to that project. A three month project will have a budget covering the whole project and will thus be a three months budget.

Most organisations will divide their budget period into calendar months (or periods); whereas others have thirteen period years (all of an equal four week period). In certain situations, the budget period will be analysed according some particular feature of the work in that situation: for example, stockbrokers have their year divided into "accounts" of two and three weeks' duration. These divisions of a budget period are control periods.

BUDGET CENTRES

In a similar way to the way in which the financial year is divided, the organisation will be divided up into budget centres. A budget centre is one part of an organisation for which budgets are prepared. That is, a budget centre, like a cost or profit centre, is a section of an organisation (division, department, building, individual) for which a separate budget is prepared.

Whilst there is a lot of organisational work that is put into budgeting and budgetary control, this page is concerned mainly with an outline and understanding of the preparation aspects of budgets. A later page may deal with the organisational and strategic aspects of budgetary control.

INTERRELATIONSHIPS OF BUDGETS

One of the key reasons why management accountants and other planners are using spreadsheets more and more for budgeting purposes is because of the many inter relationships that exist in budgeting and budgetary control. If we are preparing budgets for our organisation we will quickly find that the sales budget has strong links with the stock budget and it has strong links with the cash budget.

When, then, the sales budget is changed, the stock and cash budgets will also have to change. Similarly, if the stock levels are changed, as a result of a revision of managerial policy during the budgeting process, say, then that could impact on both the sales and cash budgets.

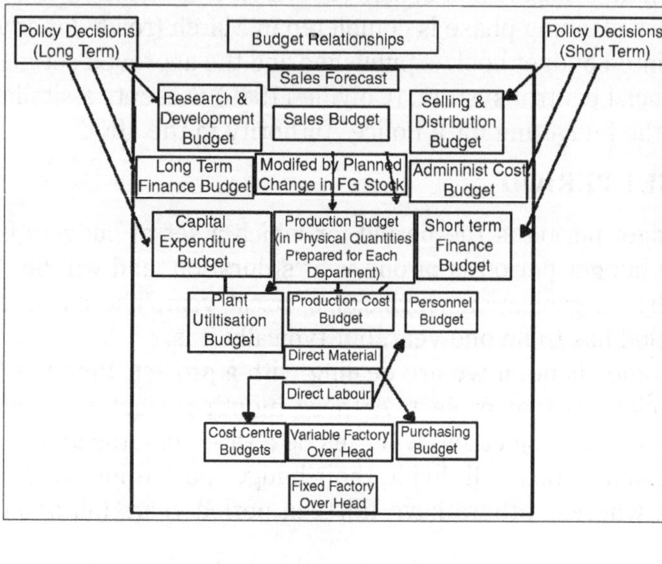

The more complex the organisation and the more complex the processes within that organisation, the greater the number and variety of interrelationships that any budget for that organisation is bound to contain. The following diagram takes a general view of some of the interrelationships found in organisation. The diagram is relatively complex but we will find that a study of it helps us to understand the examples that follow.

Not all organisations have all of these interrelationships; and, as we saw above, some organisations prepare budgets only for part of the organisation so some aspects of the above diagram will apply to them and others will not.

Whenever you come across a budgeting and budgetary control situation, try to fit that situation to this diagram: make and not any changes you feel are necessary to the diagram following on from what you have found. We can see that this diagram begins with the sales forecast and then the sales budget. This is not an accident; and it doesn't always have to be this way. The reason that sales are the starting point of the diagram is because the organisation on which the diagram is based must believe that sales are its limiting factor.

LIMITING FACTOR

In the example that follows, we will find: "As far as sales are concerned, they are fixed anyway: everything else depends on them." In the examples we are working through this will be true: everything the Andy's wholesaling organisation was does centres around its sales levels: both purchases and stock levels depended upon the level of sales for any given month. In this situation, Sales is considered to be the limiting factor (which is also known as the principal budget factor, and the key factor).

The limiting factor is anything that limits the activity of an entity. Examples of limiting factors are shortages of supply of a resource and a restriction on sales at a particular price. That is, the limiting factor is the one factor that dominates all other factors: the limiting factor can be any factor that is important to the carrying out of the organisation's activities can be the limiting factor.

EXAMPLES OF THE LIMITING FACTOR

Each of the following can be, depending on the circumstances of the case, the limiting factor:

- Cash
- Raw materials
- Skilled labour
- Land
- Equipment

CRUCIAL ELEMENT CONCERNING

The most important point about the limiting factor, then, is that this must be the budget that is prepared before all others. There is no point in preparing every budget except the raw materials budget only to find that the assumptions built into all other budgets means that the amount of raw materials needed just cannot be acquired. Similarly, if cash is the limiting factor, preparing any budgets that take no account of the cash position may lead to a lot of unnecessary work having to be carried out. The following section uses an example to demonstrate the full impact of the inter relationships of budgets: it does so in a wholesaling environment.

WORKED EXAMPLE

Andy is a wholesaler of cricketing equipment: he trades in cricket bats, pads, gloves, sweaters and so on. Andy's territory covers much of the South and East of England and his business is sufficiently large that he needs to consider each product line as its own revenue centre. To this end, he prepares detailed budgets line by line. Consider the following details for his purchases and sales of cricket bats. Andy's assessment of the coming season is that the weather will be hot and dry, and the demand for cricket bats will be high from June and for the rest of the season (until early September). After September, Andy will concentrate on his overseas business (selling to agents in India, Australia, New Zealand and South Africa).

Andy's 1994							
	J	J	A	S	O	N	D
Sales (units)	950	950	750	600	600	500	600

Stocks at the end of any month is to be set at the level of 100 bats plus 20 per cent of the number of bats scheduled to be sold in the following month.

REQUIRED

For the seven month period June to December 1994, prepare the stock and purchases budget and the sales budget: the selling price per bat is œ20 and the purchase price per bat is œ15. The first part of the solution to this example is the purchases budget, expressed in terms of units. The format is that we start the schedule with the opening stock, add purchases and subtract the closing stock to leave us with the sales amounts.

Purchases Budget (Units). Cricket bats 1994							
	J	J	A	S	O	N	D
Balance b/d	290	290	250	220	220	200	220
Purchases	950	910	720	600	580	520	640
	1,240	1,200	970	820	800	720	860
Balance c/d	290	250	220	220	200	220	260
Sales	950	950	750	600	600	500	600

Once we have the units situation sorted out, it is a straight forward matter to multiply the relevant parts of the stock and purchases budget by the relevant cost and sales values, so that we obtain the stock, purchases and sales budgets expressed in terms of monetary amounts.

Stock Budget (£). Cricket bats

	J	J	A	S	O	N	D
Opening stock	4,350	4,350	3,750	3,300	3,300	3,000	3,300
Closing stock	4,350	3,750	3,300	3,300	3,000	3,300	3,900

Purchases budget (£). Cricket bats

	J	J	A	S	O	N	D
Purchases	14,250	13,650	10,800	9,000	8,700	7,800	9,600

Sales budget (£). Cricket bats

	J	J	A	S	O	N	D
Sales	19,000	19,000	15,000	12,000	12,000	10,000	12,000

INTERRELATIONSHIP ASPECTS

The interrelationship aspects of this example have probably not bothered us so far: the nature of interrelationships is that they often pass by unnoticed! In order to arrive at the purchases in units, we have had to determine the opening and closing stock amounts, and we were given the sales units.

Thus, if we have calculated the stock budgets incorrectly, the purchase amounts will be wrong, and the purchases budget will be misleading. Similarly, an error in the sales budget guarantees an error in the purchase and stock budgets.

We can assess the extent of the interrelationships between the various budgets we are preparing by, for example, changing one of the variables involved in this example. Assume the stock levels are to be set at 50 bats plus 20 per cent of the sales units for the following month: what effect does that have on the purchases, opening and closing stock budgets?

Stock and Purchase REVISED budget (Units). Cricket bats 1994

	J	J	A	S	O	N	D
Balance b/d	240	240	200	170	170	150	170
Purchases	950	910	720	600	580	520	640
	1190	1150	920	770	750	670	810
Balance c/d	240	200	170	170	150	170	210
Sales	950	950	750	600	600	500	600

Stock REVISED Budget (£). Cricket bats

	J	J	A	S	O	N	D
Openingstock	3,600	3,600	3,000	2,550	2,550	2,250	2,550

	J	J	A	S	O	N	D
Closingstock 3,150		3,600	3,000	2,550	2,550	2,250	2,550

Purchases REVISED budget (£). Cricket bats

	J	J	A	S	O	N	D
Purchases	14,250	13,650	10,800	9,000	8,700	7,800	9,600

The workings for these revised schedules are identical to the workings for the original budgets.

The effects of what we have done are that the opening and closing stock units and values have changed, but the effect on purchases and sales has been nil. As far as sales are concerned, they are fixed anyway: everything else depends on them. Purchases can change with stock levels, but since the change to stock levels is constant between opening and closing stock, there is no overall change to purchases.

This page has introduced the basic ideas and theory underlying budgeting and budgetary control. We have explored the ideas underlying budgets: what they are and what they contain, whether that be monetary, qualitative or non-quantitative aspects. We have also seen that budgeting needs to be used as part of a budgetary control system, otherwise budgets are merely arithmetical exercises that mean little. We have also seen the basic elements of the budgeting process, the budget period and budget centres. Finally, this page has also shown the interrelationships that exist between the various parts of a budget and the nature and meaning of the limiting factor.

A budget is a plan expressed in quantitative, usually monetary term, covering a specific period of time, usually one year. In other words a budget is a systematic plan for the utilization of manpower and material resources.

In a business organization, a budget represents an estimate of future costs and revenues. Budgets may be divided into two basic classes: Capital Budgets and Operating Budgets. Capital budgets are directed towards proposed expenditures for new projects and often require special financing. The operating budgets are directed towards achieving short term operational goals of the organization, for instance, production or profit goals in a business firm. Operating budgets may be sub divided into various departmental of functional budgets.

CHARACTERISTICS OF A BUDGET

- It is prepared in advance and is derived from the long term strategy of the organization.
- It relates to future period for which objectives or goals have already been laid down.
- It is expressed in quantitative form, physical or monetary units, or both.

Different types of budgets are prepared for different purposed *e.g.* Sales Budget, Production Budget, Administrative Expense Budget, Raw material Budget etc. All these sectional budgets are afterwards integrated into a master budget, which represents an overall plan of the organization.

NEED FOR BUDGETING IN LIBRARIES

A budget is a guide or directive for fiscal management. Libraries need funds for services, and these services must be budgeted for. Fletcher gives two definitions of a budget, calling it "the overall picture of ... allocations and ... income," as well as 'the financial allocation for specific purpose or purposes during a given period.'

Although libraries are service oriented and have little or no revenue generating motives or objectives, they still obviously require a budget. Technical services are not a significant source of income in the library system. Very small amounts of income are made from reprography and binding, but the amount is infinitesimal compared to the funds expended on technical services. The need for budgets in libraries is increasingly important.

In public institutions, government funding continues to dwindle. The literature that must be managed continues to grow. There is an increasing demand for online resources and services. Libraries must effectively divide funds between staff and materials, which include acquisitions, services, and equipment. Library fiscal management is becoming more decentralised. Current trends give a measure of financial control to divisional, sectional, and unit librarians. It is within this framework that budgeting for library technical services is approached.

TECHNICAL SERVICES BUDGET CONSIDERATIONS

A number of studies have been carried out on budgets and financing of library services; however, budgeting for technical services has received little attention. Most discussions of budgeting for technical services use a line item budget as a focus. A line budget itemises elements of the budget, which add up to the totality of what the library hopes to spend in any fiscal year.

Perhaps the most important item to budget for in technical services is personnel.Personnel, for these services can be broken into three: Professional staff, technical staff, and auxiliaries. Tools, equipment, and supplies are also important, and services and functions are also included in the technical services budget, as is equipment maintenance.

Those include cataloguing and catalogue maintenance, labeling, binding, serials control, and reprography, as well as others, depending on the type of library and its goals. Especially when libraries are automated, there should be guaranteed sources of funding. Automation is more expensive than manual systems. When libraries are planning for automation, not enough may be allocated and some costs are either underestimated or overlooked.

Smallen and McCredie prescribe solutions that go beyond 'budget dust,', *i.e.,* using funds that come as windfalls, that come occasionally, and that cannot be relied on to be available on an ongoing basis.

TECHNICAL SERVICES WITHIN CONSORTIA

Consortia are a form of cooperation or resource sharing among groups of libraries and information centers. In technical services, cooperative acquisition, joint cataloguing and classification, and shared union catalogues are aspects that are shared. Library consortia encourage participating libraries to digitise collections, create online catalogues, and improve information technology.

For this to happen, technical services must be up to date in skills, equipment, and technology. Ekpenyong calls for renewed consortial efforts among university libraries while identifying constraints that can militate against such projects, including funds, infrastructure for networking, uninterrupted power supply, and training for technical services personnel. Budgeting is most necessary in an emerging ICT environment. The cost of ICT hardware and software is also very high.

There are automated tools and databases for ordering and cataloging, including OCLC's WorldCat, the public catalogs of the Library of Congress, and vendor databases such as Blackwell's Online. The use of these tools has led to the creation of union catalogues. At the University of Botswana Library (UBL) for example, the selection, ordering, receipt, cataloging and routing of materials are done online.

UBL is a member of SABINET, a library consortium in South Africa, and any materials not available in UBL are obtained from other members of SABINET or other document delivery services through the Inter Library Loan Service. Generally, consortia eliminate replicating processing of the same materials over and over again, thereby cutting costs, time and energy among consortia members.

METHODOLOGY

A questionnaire was used to elicit responses from technical services librarians in the libraries. An Internet search was also conducted, to examine the Web sites of the university and research libraries.

This was to compare them with libraries abroad that were used as models in this research. The research was carried out over a period of three months by research assistants who traveled to the libraries in different parts of Nigeria. One hundred questionnaires were prepared and some were posted to the respondents with self addressed envelopes for the responses to be mailed back.

The mailing method was not quite successful as many did not respond. Thirty two University libraries, ten Research libraries, and ten public libraries were eventually surveyed, totaling fifty two in all, giving a 52percent response.

The questionnaires were administered to the technical services librarians or the chief librarian as applicable. The questions concerned the date of establishment, size of the collection, and budget for the current year. It also asked if they budgeted for technical services, and, if so, how much. Those who did not have budgets were asked if they planned to create one. Their general opinion on budgeting for technical services was also sought.

FINDINGS

The response rate shows that budgeting is not given much priority in Nigerian libraries. In many libraries, expenditures are controlled by the chief librarian. Of those questioned, 45 (86.5 per cent) technical services librarians had little or nothing to do with the budget; they simply took what was given them. For 39 (75 per cent), their interpersonal relationship with the chief librarian determined whether they got what they needed for their departments.

Almost all, 51 (98 per cent) said their libraries had no budget for technical services. In the one library (2 per cent) that claimed to have a separate budget had it contained within the general library budget and it was not clearly demarcated. Twenty one (40.38 per cent) of the technical services librarians surveyed have plans to draw up budgets, 18 (34.6 per cent) have no intention of doing so as it is not part of their responsibilities, and 13 (25 per cent) are undecided.

The Internet search was carried out from May 20 th to June 20 th 2007. It took this long due to electrical power problems. Searches had to be abandoned and resumed when there were power outages Since, there is no alternative power supply for the facility used. Twenty one Web sites were searched using google. Results showed that some Nigerian University libraries (70 per cent of the 21studied) do not have links on their Web sites to the library. None of the Web sites examined included information on the funding of their libraries.

This may be due to the fact that libraries in this part of the world are not run like those in the West, where libraries are given priority and publicity. The public library system in Nigeria also is quite different in terms of administration and financing.

BEST PRACTICES

Libraries are storehouses of knowledge. It is unfortunate, however, that 'libraries rarely feature in the top ten priorities of institutional administrators'. This is one of the reasons why even library administrators sometimes treat budgets for libraries lightly.

Whether out of frustration or a lack of grounding in fiscal management, budgets are often ignored in libraries. This is not a good trend, as pointed out by Oyelude, in discussing the state of the art in academic libraries. This Non chalant attitude may also be due to the 'invisibility' of libraries in the community.

A library must be highly visible to get adequate funding and recognition. User support is very important in this regard. If the users feel the library's impact, they will make demands on the library's behalf. Ubogu asserts that university librarians should be signatories to their library's account(s). He also recommends that the libraries should budget adequately for personnel, so that trained staff do not migrate to greener pastures; budget for maintenance with a fixed percentage. He further advises that software vendors should have a concrete budget and agreement with the library they are serving and funds for staff development should be part of the technical services budget.

It is also good practice for librarians in technical services to become 'lobbyists' to get their budgets approved and implemented. In a situation where so many things are competing for limited resources, one cannot afford to be politically lethargic. Library administrators should lobby for funds maintaining high standards, compiling statistics, and using the statistics to advantage. By implication, the technical services librarian should lobby the chief librarian who should in turn lobby the head of the institution. Library friends and the community are good tools in advocacy. Understanding the workplace climate and politics involved are also important. It is also best to set priorities in asking for what is reasonable. It is essential to establish a good relationship with the chief librarian, the library accountant, members of the library committee, and others who may be involved with the technical services budget. The best method is to get other people to argue your case with little or no prompting from you. For example, certain services that should be included in the budget should be asked for directly by library users. Technical services should be showcased at every opportunity, including when the library creates exhibits. Technical services should see itself as part of an integrated system and should speak up for other areas of the library when necessary. This will bring about reciprocity when issues concerning technical services are discussed. Most importantly, funds should be judiciously used and wisely disbursed.

MODELS OF LIBRARY BUDGETS

There are a number of useful models for library budgeting. The Sno Isle Libraries are a large public library system that provides library service to residents of Island and Snohomish counties in Washington State. Each annual budget includes an increase over the previous year, basing the figures on percentages. For example, technical services had 25.2 per cent of the total budget in 2005, which was increased to 25.6 per cent in 2006. The technical services budget has an appropriate prominence, receiving a quarter of the total library budget. The University of Alberta Library budgets by committing itself to digital collection research, content creation, and access services. They identify staffing for the digital environment as critical for the next few years. They have also planned extensively for technology replacement through 'lifecycle budgeting.' These budgets can serve as models for Nigerian libraries who are trailing behind in the electronic age.

FINANCIAL ACCOUNTING

WHAT IS FINANCIAL ACCOUNTING

Financial accounting is focused on providing accounting reports and analysis to other areas of the business. Financial accountants are responsible for the creation and issuing of the company's financial statements, providing accurate and timely information to management and ensuring that all regulatory reporting requirements are met. In financial accounting, the goal is to consistently provide the valuable, accurate and reliable information.

The issuing of the financial statements is the responsibility of the financial accounting department. These statements summarize the business's activities for the year and are used by shareholders, banks, employee bargaining units, and the general public to evaluate the financial worth of the company. The statements are audited by independent accountants to validate the information and provide assurance to readers.

The financial statements are comprised of five documents; balance sheet, income statement; cash flow and owners or shareholders equity and notes. Notes to the financial statement are written explanations of items in the financial statements. Any unusual items or change in procedure that has impact on the financial statements are detailed here. The balance sheet is a summary of all the assets and liabilities at year's end. The accounts reflect the total amount of cash and liquid assets on hand, the amount of debt the company is carrying, and how much money was spend in various categories. Financial accounting firms perform analysis of these values using ratios and other calculations to determine the financial health of the company.

An income statement is a critical component in financial accounting. It provides a clear list of all the sales for the year, the expenses and the net profit or loss of the firm. This statement provides insight into the sales performance for the year and the overall profitability of the firm.

A cash flow report provides details on funds received and disbursed. This section provides insight into the revenue values listed in the income statement. Funds received or lost from interest bearing investments are detailed here.

The statement of owners' or shareholders' equity shows the total net income from the year and how it will be distributed among the shareholders or reinvested in the business. Publicly traded companies must provide the number of shares issues, the type of share and the amount of divided to be paid on the shares, based on the articles of incorporation and the shareholder agreement.All certified public accountants have complete intermediate and advanced courses in financial accounting. There is no additional designation for a financial accounting specialty. The skill set for a financial accountant must focus on analysis and data manipulation software and tools.

DESCRIPTION OF THE EXAMINATION

The Financial Accounting examination covers skills and concepts that are generally taught in a first semester undergraduate financial accounting course. Colleges may award credit for a one semester course in financial accounting.

The exam contains approximately 75 questions to be answered in 90 minutes. Some of these are pretest questions that will not be scored. Any time candidates spend on tutorials or providing personal information is in addition to the actual testing time.

KNOWLEDGE AND SKILLS REQUIRED

Questions on the Financial Accounting examination require candidates to demonstrate one or more of the following abilities.

- Familiarity with accounting concepts and terminology
- Preparation, use, and analysis of accounting data and financial reports issued for both internal and external purposes
- Application of accounting techniques to simple problem situations involving computations
- Understanding the rationale for generally accepted accounting principles and procedures

DEVELOPMENT AND MANAGEMENT OF A RESOURCE MOBILIZATION PROGRAMME

This part discusses the major steps in resource mobilization planning:

- Reviewing the organizational strategic plan
- Determining resource mobilization targets
- Identifying constituencies and broadening stakeholders
- Developing key messages
- Reviewing and selecting resource mobilization strategies
- Gearing up for resource mobilization

Ideally, these steps are to be performed in successive order, and you will notice that they build upon each other to create a full understanding and appreciation of the resource mobilization planning process. Throughout the succeeding chapters, we have provided case stories, studies, tools and exercises you can use in your own planning exercise.

Reviewing the Organizational Strategic Plan

This part starts with the importance of revisiting your Organization's Vision, Mission and Goal statements, accompanied with an exercise that can be used in reviewing or refining existing statements. The part on Situational Analysis discusses the merits of going through this exercise, and how this can be used to determine the strengths and weaknesses of your resource mobilization capacity, as well as the opportunities and threats to the organization. Accompanying this part are guidelines to Planning for a Situational Analysis, and an excerpt from the SWOT analysis of eHomemakers. Also included are case stories of FRLHT, ANSAB and KADO, as well as excerpts from a Donor Scoping Study commissioned by the IDRC.

Bringing the Future into the Present

Linking Resource Mobilization with the Vision and Mission

Most established non-profit organizations possess an articulated Vision and Mission and engage in a regular strategic planning exercise. Ideally, at the end of each Strategic Plan cycle, the members of the organization engage in a review of its collective achievements, challenges faced, and current realities *vis à vis* its Vision, Mission and goals, in order to plan for the next cycle. A similar process is employed when developing a Resource Mobilization Plan, since your organization's Vision, Mission and Strategic Plan are the bases for its formulation.

The nature of a non-profit is to fill its funding gaps from sources other than its beneficiaries. In an organization's constant quest for resources, it can be tempting to develop a project just to match a donor's requirements and criteria. In some cases, an organization's good intentions can lead it to decide to serve this or that beneficiary, without taking into consideration its financial limitations and available resources. Many non-profits are born out of the fiery goodwill and intentions of an individual or a group of individuals who identify social needs that are unmet and seek to find solutions to those needs.

In the early years of the non-profit, operations run informally, almost intuitively, and the initiator or prime advocate sets the direction of the organization. However, as your organization grows, more complex programmes will require more formal systems, and stakeholders would like to have greater influence in the running of your organization, it is easy to lose sight of why the organization was formed in the first place. The vision and mission statements are what keep an organization on track. A non-profit without a vision statement is like being on a boat with no compass, flailing at the changing winds of a funder's, or a founder's, preferences.

The Vision

There are as many definitions of a "Vision" as there are organizational development consultants, but in the simplest of words, an organization's vision is the "shared hopes, dreams and images of the future." Much more than a statement of identity, your vision is a proactive, public declaration of how your organization sees the ideal future in the area in which it works.

The forward motion of your organization depends on the clarity of your vision. Your vision statement is your prescription for pointing you in the right direction. All other documents and tools – your mission statement, strategic plan, marketing plan, business plan, and even your fundraising campaigns–are the means to reach your destination. When your vision is internalized by all the members of your organization, all of your work leads you towards accomplishing this. Because you know your vision, you believe in it, and you all live it. As you begin to plan for resource mobilization, it is time to put on a resource mobilization lens and analyse your existing vision statement using the following criteria:

- Is your vision powerful?
- Does it capture the organization's image of the future?
- Can members of the organization relate to it and be motivated to achieve it?
- Do they live the vision in their daily lives and passionately share this vision with others — with potential donors and with the community?

The International Center for Integrated Mountain Development (ICIMOD) has a clear, to the point vision statement:

- ... ICIMOD is committed to a shared vision of prosperous and secure mountain communities committed to peace, equity, and environmental sustainability.

The Foundation for Revitalization of Local Health Traditions (FRLHT) has an even shorter one:

- ... to revitalize Indian medical heritage.

When clearly crafted, an organization's vision is unchanging, and timeless. A well thought out vision statement attracts donors that share common aspirations.

It discourages your organization from force fitting programme elements that have nothing to do with your vision, which may have only been created to meet the requirements of a particular donor. Staying focused on vision driven vs. donor driven programmes will address real, and not perceived needs within beneficiary communities. Conversely, it helps your organization determine the prospective donors to approach and as a result, moves you forward to its achievement.

The Mission

An organization's mission statement is a brief expression of why it exists– its reason for being. It states your organization's purpose, with and for whom your organization works, how your organization will go about fulfilling its vision, and the values that your organization adheres to.

A mission statement:

- Is clear, concise and understandable
- Expresses why the organization does its work or the organization's ultimate purpose
- Is broad enough for flexibility but not too broad to lack focus
- States with and for whom the organization works
- States the organization's distinctive competence or the difference the organization will make for those it serves
- Serves as an energy source and a rallying point for the organization

The following example of the mission statement of FRLHT captures the organization's focus.

To demonstrate the contemporary relevance of Indian Medical Heritage by designing and implementing innovative programmes related to:

- Exposition of the theory and practice of traditional systems of medicine;
- Conservation of the natural resources used by Indian systems of medicine; and
- Revitalization of social processes for transmission of the heritage on a size and scale that will have societal impact.

The mission statement of the Indian Institute of Forest Management clearly states its intended outcome, as well as its particular area of focus:

- To provide leadership in professional forestry management aimed at environmental conservation and sustainable development of ecosystems.

Such mission statements provide a guiding star to help an organization stay on track and keep its activities well focused. When applied to resource mobilization planning, your organization's mission becomes the anchor by which you will communicate your cause to your potential donors, why you are deserving of support, and how you will prioritize your limited resources. As a result, your mission statement also gives you a sense of your organization's resource gaps.Which, ultimately becomes a major component of your resource mobilization plan.

Goals

When the vision or dreams for the future have been defined, those who will benefit from that vision have been identified, and how to go about making that a reality has been fleshed out through a mission, your organization's goals now shape the targets towards which plans and actions are directed.

A framework that is most useful for setting goals is the S-M-A-R-T goal framework:

- Specific – what is required is clearly stated
- Measurable – results are quantifiable
- Attainable – targets are realistic but challenging
- Relevant – goals have an impact on intended communities
- Time bound – a clear timeframe is defined

SMART goals ground the vision and mission, and help your organization carve out a niche for the services you render. The goals distinguish your organization from others within the sector. Vision, mission and goal statements have the power to hold your organization together, and thus, present a consistent image to your publics. These keep your organization on track with what you would like to accomplish, and provide a yardstick to measure your present performance against your future plans. The example illustrates the link between ANSAB's Vision, mission and goals, and how these direct its resource mobilization efforts. Resource mobilization for a Clear Purpose:

The ANSAB Story:

- The *Asia Network for Sustainable Agriculture and Bioresources* (ANSAB) was founded in 1992 by Enterprise Works, the Government of Nepal — Ministry of Agriculture and Asian country representatives to help improve peoples' livelihoods. According to Bhishma Subedi, Executive Director, ANSAB is committed to enterprise oriented solutions to biodiversity conservation and economic development. ANSAB has a vision of rich and productive biodiversity for prosperous communities. Rich, healthy, and productive ecosystems are actively managed and used by local communities who are capable of addressing threats to biodiversity and advancing sustainable resource management. Focusing its services at the grassroots, national, and regional levels and collaborating with key stakeholders and clients, ANSAB integrates and builds on local and scientific knowledge systems, innovations, perspectives, and opportunities for ground level tangible impacts and wider replications. The organization started with a US$200,000 project budget with three staff members, and now has grown to over 60 staff members and 200 partner organizations implementing seven to eight projects per year. Dr. Subedi cites the following strengths of ANSAB–the capacity to design projects well, credibility, having unique tools, and persistence, which he further explained to mean not always following what the donor wants. "We always want to stay in the practical level, and what want us to do may not always be in the general direction." He adds, "ANSAB has various types of donors, those who support environmental conservation and those interested in livelihood improvements and community development. This twin focus helps to increase the pool of interested donors. However, it is still a challenge to find donors who are interested in both." In ANSAB, the Executive Director leads the resource mobilization. Board members, a loose committee and programme managers are also involved in identifying project opportunities and proposal writing.When asked about what others can learn from ANSAB's experience, Dr. Subedi says, "My tips to other organizations are:
  - To choose a focus and to stay focused; and
  - To choose good programmes first before looking for funding opportunities."

Your vision and mission statements are your organization's guides in creating programmes. In the process of identifying possible funding for your programmes, you will come across those that fund activities in your area of work, but do not match your existing programmes. This does not mean that your organization develops a programme because there is available funding.

Rather, you need to look at how your project can be modified to meet the donor's requirements. If there really is no fit, there is no need to force the issue!

Crafting Vision Mission Goal Statements

How do you go about crafting your vision mission goal statements?

There are a number of ways:

- Choose representatives from all the units of your organization to form the Vision Mission team. They then draft the statements, which are then presented to the general body for feedback.
- Have an individual draft the statement, then present to general body for feedback.
- Contract an organizational development consultant to facilitate the process within a workshop setting.

The key is to use a participatory process involving all the stakeholders of your organization, including your beneficiaries. Especially for non-profit organizations, the days for top down dictation of vision, mission and goal statements are long gone.

Developing Your Organization's Vision and Mission Statements: Vision Statement Exercise

In a vision mission planning process:

- Individually, have each participant list ideas of the ideal future vision for the organization five years from now:
- Have each participant share their individual list with either a subgroup, or directly with the entire planning team.
- After all have shared their statements, have each group create a bullet list of common concepts from all the statements.
- Have each sub group share common concepts with the larger group. On behalf of the entire group, one person writes down the list of common concepts.
- As a unified group, create a short, positive, and inspiring vision statement that has the consensus of all.

Mission Statement Exercise

Individually, answer each question below:

- Why does our organization exist? What is our purpose?
- Whom do we serve?
- How do we achieve our purpose?

Procedure for Revising Your Vision and Mission Statements

When board, staff and volunteer leaders take the time to regularly examine and measure organizational achievements and its current challenges and realities in relation to its vision, long lasting benefits can be realised. The organization's Vision and Mission electrifies and directs its efforts. On some occasions, there will be a need to revise the organization's Vision and Mission statements, in light of major shifts in its environment, a need to change the organizations programmes due to increased demand for specific services which fall within its expertise, or decreased support for existing programmes.

There is one crucial question that will spur the need to revisit your Vision Mission statements:

- Are the current vision and mission statements clear and on target in today's operating environment?

If the answer to this question is a "No", the following procedure can be adopted:

- Define your organization. What is the end result of your efforts? Of what value is this end result to your stakeholders?
- Solicit the opinions and impressions of your external stakeholders on why your organization exists, what it has achieved, the quality of your programmes and what are the emerging needs, if any, of these external stakeholders. These inputs can be used to help define your organization's reason for being.

Knowing Where you are before Getting to Where you are Going: Situational Analysis

Development organizations come up with methodologies and technologies that contribute to the viability and sustainability of the communities with which they work. But does your organization "walk the talk" of sustainability? Do you have enough funding to see your own projects through? Is there a strategic plan in place that allows you to see resource gaps, and create action plans to close the gap? Who decides on funding targets and priority projects? What are the targets and timelines? Is there a participatory system in place to elicit from various programme units their resource mobilization needs and concerns? In short, what are the prevailing factors affecting your organization's ability to raise resources? The answers to these and many more questions stem from situational analysis tools. This chapter discusses the rationale of going through a situational analysis using a resource mobilization focus, and introduces a method often used in both for profit and not-for profit settings.

Why do a Situational Analysis?

A situational analysis is conducted for many different reasons, including assessing organizational performance, capacity in various skills and knowledge areas, motivation and environmental influences on its performance. This process can likewise be utilized to assess the resource mobilization capacity of your organization.

It is all very well to have high hopes and dreams for long mid and even short term programmes, but if passion is not matched with the infrastructure to make dreams a reality, then at the end of the fiscal day, your organization will be staring at many unfunded proposals in the face. The process involves the undertaking of a SWOT Analysis to determine your organization's strengths and weaknesses to your resource mobilization capacity, as well as opportunities and threats to your resource mobilization efforts.

Revisiting this process while using a resource mobilization lens presents a clearer, realistic view of what particular programmes to generate resources for, the particular constituency groups you wish to target, what resource mobilization strategies will appeal to this targeted group, and what systems and structures must be present within your organization to be able to generate resources efficiently and effectively, and ultimately, fulfil your vision and mission.

What Information Can you Get From a Situational Analysis?

A situational analysis report has the potential to determine what are the internal factors, or factors within the control of your organization that contribute or hinder resource mobilization efforts. In addition, a situational analysis report can also identify the responses of your organization to external factors, those that are beyond your control, that similarly contribute to or hinder your resource mobilization efforts.

For the following internal factors, a situational analysis may:

- Affirm resource mobilization successes to date
- Provide a sense of history and present the organization's evolution in its responses to changes in the funding environment
- Present a "reality check" on where the organization is at currently *vis a vis* the achievement of its vision, mission and existing strategic plan goals
- Validate funding targets over a set period of time, identify available funding and resource gaps
- Indicate gaps in administrative systems such as Finance and Accounting
- Indicate gaps specific to resource mobilization skills and systems such as proposal writing, implementation of other strategies, donor acquisition and upgrade
- Establish ownership of resource mobilization functions
- Open new doors or widen perspectives on prospective resource providers

- Determine buy in, or lack thereof, of various stakeholders to organization's funding priorities and resource mobilization strategies
- Establish resource mobilization policies and code of ethics anchored to the organization's core values
- Review the relevance of the organization's existing key messages
- Determine the organization's capacity to invest in a resource mobilization programme

A situational analysis may also reflect your organization's response to the following external factors:

- Funders' priorities and changing trends
- Demand for your organization's services
- Technological innovations related to your area of work
- Legislative and regulatory changes
- Competing grantees
- Prevailing political, social and economic conditions

The situational analysis therefore, is a powerful process that keeps you grounded in the current realities existing for your organization. When you are able to see things as they are, and have increased awareness about what is going on within and outside your organization, you are then able to set realistic resource mobilization targets.

Knowing where you are in the present maps out a clearer direction for where you are going in the future.

How do you do a Situational Analysis?

One of the most popular frameworks used by organizational development consultants in conducting situational analysis is to determine the *Strengths, Weaknesses, Opportunities and Strengths* (SWOT) in the achievement of an organization's mission. Each area is defined as follows:

- *Strengths* – attributes/factors internal to the organization, which it can manage or control, that support or aid in the fulfillment of its mission
- *Weaknesses* – attributes/factors internal to the organization, which it can manage or control, that act as hindrances to the fulfillment of its mission
- *Opportunities* – conditions external to the organization, which it cannot control, that may contribute to the achievement of the organization's mission
- *Threats* – conditions external to the organization, which it cannot control, that may hinder the achievement of the organization's mission

During resource mobilization planning, these areas are examined once more in the context of their impact on the organization's resource mobilization performance, as well as its potential.

Some Things To Remember About SWOT:

- The SWOT tool does not exist in a vacuum or in the abstract. The tool is used towards achieving a holistic view of a current situation, with the intention of deciding what the next appropriate step is. A desired end result must first be determined. For example, your organization can use the tool to determine if it has the capacity to generate a total of US$50,000 from a minimum of four sources within the next three years.
- SWOT questions must be able to draw out answers that point to factors relevant to the desired end result, and not count aspects that do not have any connection to the desired end result.
- Opportunities are sometimes interpreted as strategies. However, opportunities are conditions, and strategies are actions.
- One organization's opportunity may be another's threat, and vice versa. This also applies to its strengths and weaknesses. A SWOT map is very specific to an organization: one size DOESN'T fit all!

Answers are then placed on a matrix like this:

<table>
<tr><td rowspan="2">INTERNAL</td><td>Strengths</td><td>Opportunities</td><td rowspan="2">EXTERNAL</td></tr>
<tr><td>Weaknesses</td><td>Threats</td></tr>
</table>

Once the matrix has been filled out, you can then formulate resource mobilization goals, and choose strategies that match your organizations resources and targeted constituency groups. It would be ideal if you consciously take into account your organizational Strengths to ward off or reduce vulnerability to Threats, or use Strengths to generate strategies to take advantage of Opportunities. Conversely, you see the Weaknesses that need to be overcome to pursue Opportunities and parry Threats. The SWOT is constructed primarily through a series of questions specifically formulated to draw out answers that cover the four areas. There are various methodologies to conduct SWOT interviews, and once a methodology is decided, a list of interviewees or participants is drawn up, making sure that there is a mix of respondents to provide a multidimensional view of the organization.

Planning for Situational Analysis

Data Gathering Steps

- Determine the focus, goals and overview of the *Situational Analysis* (SA) Process.

  - *Focus*: Desired end result as determined by the organization
  - *Goals*: To assess systems, skills, personnel, resources in place in terms of effectiveness, relevance and usefulness in support of the desired end result
  - *SA Process Overview*: Determine appropriate methodology for information gathering
- Identify who will be the sources of information or who will be interviewed.
- Decide whether the situational analysis is to be done by external reviewers or internal reviewers.
- Work on a common definition of terms to be used by all reviewers.
- Review existing relevant publications, documents, web sites, etc.
- Handle logistics: set time, date, venue of interviews.
- Prepare interview guide questions.
- During interview process, present objective of interview to participants.
- Conduct interviews.
- Review notes between interviews and check for accuracy.
- Transcribe interviews.

Determining Resource Mobilization Targets

This part focuses on the importance of Setting Realistic Targets as a part of a well grounded resource mobilization plan. It starts off with key Considerations in Determining Targets. The part ends with a Resource Timeline tool, a grid that can be used to identify current resources, gaps, prospective funding sources, and projections.

Finding out how Much you Really Need

After assessing your organization's capabilities and peripheral factors affecting performance, it is time to find out how much money you really need to raise and what are the resources you need to mobilize in order to continue the work you do. Setting goals is one of the most essential factors in the success of your resource mobilization undertaking.

It cannot be overemphasized how crucial this step is as it requires that you:

- Make an inventory of your current resources, both financial and in kind; and
- Project the needs that your activities may still require to achieve fundamental results.

Not only do determining resource mobilization targets allow you to plan for the future of your programmes, *i.e.*, where you want to be and what you want to accomplish given a specific timeframe, but it also gives you a clearer picture of what you can do here and now.

Advantages of Setting Resource Mobilization Targets

There are some scenarios common to development research non profits. In some cases, an organization may seek resources only when the need arises, or when the end of the grant period draws nearer. In this scenario, there's a tendency to fall into the trap of being fund driven: a programme exists only when there's funding. It often is the case that funding targets are set without consideration to real needs. For example, a non profit may set a target of US$50,000 just because it is their 50th anniversary. They dream of building a training center to have a space of their own, without considering the costs of building maintenance. By determining realistic resource mobilization targets, you are able to check if the goals are actually linked with or rooted in your organization's strategic plan and your current programmes, and see if the time and effort you exert are well worth it.

Key Considerations in Planning

- A review of the organization's current resource situation is important to be able to plan resource mobilization activities realistically.
- The resource target should be based on the programmes you are implementing at present and the activities you are planning to execute. It is pragmatic to always go back to the organization's strategic plan to determine which programmes or activities must be pursued that would make possible the realization of your organization's mission.
- Financial management and strategic budgeting are of high importance in planning your resource mobilization programme. These contribute to getting the most accurate and updated budgetary figures, as well as in helping determine the best strategy for closing the resource gaps.
- A Resource Timeline becomes a very important tool in determining targets as it provides you with sufficient lead time to ensure the sustainability of your programmes. If carefully laid out, it helps you visualize what your current resource situation is and enables you to see how long your resources can sustain your programmes.

Identifying Resource Needs Using the Resource Timeline

The resource timeline is a tool used to identify the existing resources, both financial and in kind, that are currently available with your organization, as well as to project the programme requirements for the immediate future. This tool will help you identify the total amount of funds and resources that need to be mobilized in order to sustain the programmes of your organization. Essentially, information on funding targets and resource needs puts your resource mobilization programme in a proper perspective as it guides you in determining which strategies will work best in filling resource gaps.

Objectives

- Review current resource situation
- Determine programme areas in need of funding and resources throughout a three year period by using a resource timeline
- Identify the funding gaps or resource needs

Mechanics

1.Activity/ Progam	2. Resources		3.Resource Gaps/Needs	4.Resources Providers	5.Timeline			6.Resources Classification
	2.a. Requirement	2.b. Available			Yr1	Yr2	Yr3	
			Total RM Target					

- In column 1, list down programmes that your organization is implementing at present and the activities you intend to pursue over the next three years.
- In column 2a, indicate the funding and resource needs of your activities/ programmes. This should reflect the sum of monies and the equipment your organization ought to have in order to achieve the programs' key results over a three year period. It is best to consult with your finance unit so as to show the most realistic projections.
- Among the requirements presented in column 2a, specify the amount of funds and in kind resources that already exist with your organization. Again, confer with your finance unit to get the most updated figures.
- Column 3 should be able to show the variance between column 2a and 2b in terms of funds needed, as well as present a listing of items and equipment. These are the resource gaps, which would be the resource mobilization targets and the basis of developing your resource mobilization programme.
- In column 4, indicate the sources of your available funds and resources. Include individual contributors, donor agencies and funding partners, other non-profit organizations, resource mobilization strategies, etc.
- Draw an arrow in column 5 to show until when the money and resources will be available.
- The last column must indicate if the available funds in column 2b are restricted, *i.e.* to be used only as proposed or how you have committed it to be spent/utilized, or unrestricted, *i.e.* to be utilized freely, when you want to or whenever it's necessary.

Identifying and Broadening the Stakeholder Group

Building relationships with your community is at the core of resource mobilization planning. This part discusses how to Identify and Define your

Community Using the Constituency or Stakeholder Map, and how you can use the 3Cs – Connection, Capability, Concern — in qualifying prospective donors and partners.

Also featured are insights from SEARICE as it engages its stakeholders. The Case Stories of the Govi Gnana Seva Project and GREEN Foundation show the wide network these organizations have used to implement their initiatives. Then you'll find a summary of the findings of the seven country research project, *Investing in Ourselves: Giving and Fund Raising in Asia*. The study affirms the belief that philanthropy is alive and well in Asia, and explores the giving attitudes of individual givers across Asia. The part closes with an exercise on Identifying your Stakeholders using the Stakeholder Map.

Looking Beyond the Usual Sources

Stakeholder Development in Resource Mobilization

While the tendency to pursue grants still prevails among non-profits, more organizations are realizing the need to broaden their base of support beyond the usual sources of funds. Nearly every door in the global donor community now puts out a welcome mat only for organizations with selfsustainability and long term viability of programmes and projects.

For several years now, counterpart funding and exit strategies have become necessary components in grant proposals. Exit strategies include activities and programmes that ensure a non-profit organization's sustainability beyond the grant period. A few grant giving institutions have included resource mobilization training as part of their exit strategy. Donors want to ensure that their grantees know how to raise resources after the donors have pulled out of a country or programme. They need assurance that the organization they have funded will work to raise resources and not just be dependent on funds provided by them or by other funding institutions.

What Stakeholders Give:

- Money.
- Technical Assistance.
- Volunteer time.
- Seconded Staff.
- Goods/Products.
- Sponsorships.
- Assets.
- Joint promotions/ cause related marketing.
- Equipment.

Golden Lessons on Broadening Stakeholders

The first golden rule, then is that development research organizations need to move on from dependence on grants to diversifying funding sources. The second is that this can happen only when your organization seeks to build its own constituency by mobilizing local support through other strategies. Raising resources from a local base implies that an organization has the mandate from the community to continue its programmes.

Assuming that your organization has elected to work on a valid cause, what you do benefit more people than just the direct beneficiaries. Defining your "community", also known as constituents or stakeholders, helps you determine whether what you are doing is relevant or not, and helps you identify possible linkages and partnerships beyond the obvious. It makes sense then to begin by identifying who are the individuals or groups that are directly served or influenced by your organization's mission, and whose needs shape the strategies your organization undertakes.

These people have an intrinsic connection to your organization, and have a stake and interest in the continuing existence of your organization. Stakeholders could consist of members of your general assembly, past and present consultants and contributors, past and present participants of trainings or seminars or other projects that you've run, institutional donors, corporate donors, local NGOs, cooperatives, community leaders, local government units, academic institutions, your staff, their families, beneficiaries, and volunteers as well as other similarlyinclined people and institutions who have been involved with your work in various capacities.

The rationale behind focusing on these groups, as opposed to the more typical route of going after grantmaking foundations and large benefactors, is that if you're able to inspire people that are closest to you to give or give of themselves, then it may become that much easier to get those remotely connected at least interested in knowing more about your organization.

Developing a Stakeholder Map

To visualize the environment your organization finds itself in, you can use a tool called a constituency or stakeholder map. The map is a simple diagram made up of a series of concentric hexagons containing the people most connected to your organization. Each level indicates their degree of participation, with those at the core having the most involvement, and those in the outer levels with the least. People with similar interests and general donors are placed on the outer layer, while major donors, the board, staff, and loyal supporters, regarded as key movers, are in the inner circle.

As you go through the exercise of drawing your own constituency map and filling it with the names of individuals, organizations and other groups that matter most to your work, you will find that you can create a picture of the mix and degrees of commitment represented by your current set of constituents. The map not only provides baseline information from which you can assess the health of your organization, it more importantly allows you to qualitatively measure the impact of your work as it requires you to deliberately identify your constituency.

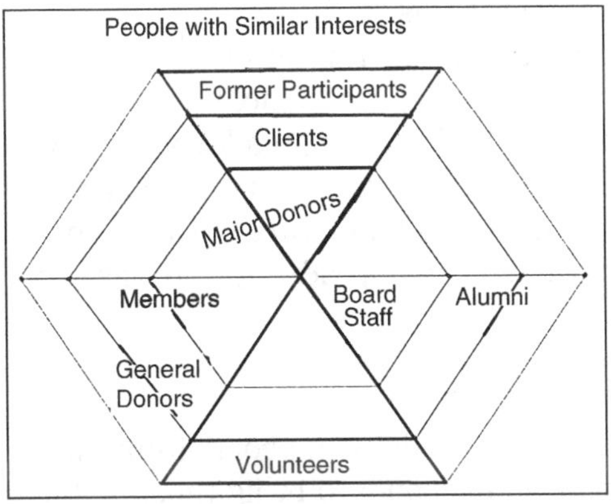

Fig. Stakeholder Map for a Training Organization.

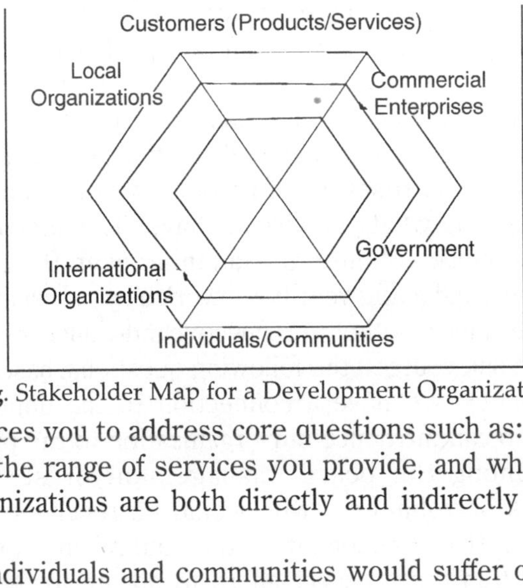

Fig. Stakeholder Map for a Development Organization.

The map forces you to address core questions such as:

- What is the range of services you provide, and what types of people and organizations are both directly and indirectly serviced by what you do?
- Which individuals and communities would suffer or have their lives disrupted if you were to cease operations or pull out of a geographic area?
- What are the possible confluences of interest that could induce greater participation among those situated on the fringes of your map?
- Is your work inadvertently imposed upon by a small core that has failed to establish genuine ties with those at the grassroots, who in turn feel that there is no place for them within your mandate?

Looking into these concerns allows you to determine who may be receptive to your overtures for either fresh or higher degrees of support, who among your constituents you need to woo and which openings or leads you can explore as you seek to harness resources waiting to be tapped and mobilized. Over and above this, the stakeholder map helps you determine if you already have the right mix of supporters or if you need to bring in new people with other competencies.

The stakeholder map is a graphic device that not only serves as a barometer of your relationships but also helps you define your sphere of work in resource mobilization.While the map allows you to identify the types of individuals and organizations that you should target as you broaden your reach as an organization, it also helps you figure out how you can deepen the level of participation of those who are already close to the core, but not as close as they could, or should be.

Fund Raising is Friend Raising

The goals are then first, to draw in people from the larger universe to the periphery of your map; and second, to bring those at the outer levels of your map closer to the center, where a greater level of participation and commitment, financial and non-financial, can be expected. This is the primary objective of "friend raising", as opposed to mere fund raising. Friend raising emphasizes the development and nurturing of relationships both within and outside your immediate spheres of influence. Fund raising, on the other hand, may tend to be more like one shot, take themoney and see you around approach.

While drawing on old reserves of resources, you need to be constantly enriching and enhancing what you already have. This may entail your board members, staff and close volunteers examining even the most mundane of personal connections, and doing your homework as you research for prospects.

In order to determine whether a prospective individual or organization would make a good donor, ask yourself the following questions, based on the 3Cs:

- *Connection*: Do we have a connection to the donor? Do we know anyone who can introduce our organization to the prospect? Is there anyone among the board, management or staff, contributors, consultants or volunteers who would be received more warmly by the prospect than someone from the fund raising staff?
- *Capability*: Can the prospect afford to donate to the organization? If not, can the donor still be able to contribute to the organization in other ways? How small or large are the amounts that this prospect has contributed in the past? Is this a good time to ask, or has she just had a major expense recently? How's he doing at his job or business?
- *Concern*: Are the prospect's values and interests aligned with those of your organization? Is this donor someone who will genuinely care about the welfare of the organization and its beneficiaries, and not only worry about its impact on his personal reputation or standing in society? What are her pet causes? Who have been his beneficiaries in the past? Does she have roots in the community you serve?

Bringing stakeholders closer to your organization: What's in it for them?

- Personal sense of satisfaction
- Result/impact to which they are contributing
- Information, contacts, public recognition to enable them to maintain or expand their interests
- Economic returns on their social investment

Once you have satisfactorily answered the questions posed by the 3Cs, move on to learning more facts about the prospective donor, his donation pattern, and specific interests. This will help you see how your own programmes can match the prospect's needs, and vice versa. A good prospect is one who meets the criteria of all 3Cs. As the goal of resource mobilization is to cultivate lifelong relationships, you must ascertain that this relationship starts out on the right foot, and with both parties clearly understanding the responsibilities involved in a partnership.

Identifying Stakeholders Using the Stakeholder Map

The stakeholder map is a tool used to identify current and potential supporters and partners. These stakeholders are classified into six categories: customers, commercial enterprises, local organizations, international organizations, the government, and individuals and communities.

Activity Mechanics

Identify the different stakeholders, both current and potential, for your organization. Plot them on the map according to the three Cs — Connection, Capability and Concern. The higher their CCCs, the closer they should be to the center of the map.

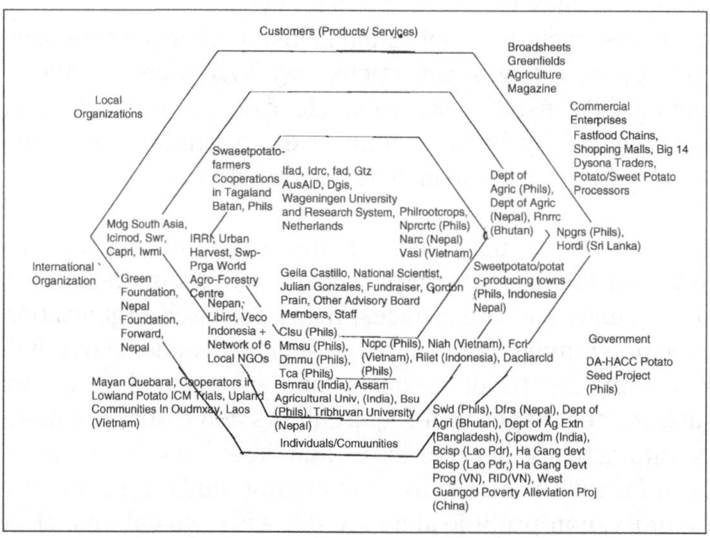

Fig. User's Perspectives with Agricultural Research and Development (UPWARD)

For example, if the prospects that you have identified have 3 of the 3 Cs, then they should be put in the core of the map. Create a pattern so that prospects with 2 Cs are placed in the outer layer next to the core of the map while those with just 1 C are placed in the outer layer of the stakeholder map.

The UPWARD is an Asian network of scientists and development specialists working to increase participation by farmers and other users of agricultural technology in research and development.

The UPWARD used the stakeholder map to identify and plot their various stakeholders in the map based on the level of resource support and programme influence that they provide. Stakeholders with the highest involvement and contribution to UPWARD are placed in the core or inner part of the map while those in the outer layers of the map were perceived to have the least involvement with UPWARD.

UNDERSTANDING RESOURCE MOBILIZATION

LOOKING BEYOND JUST RAISING FUNDS

Most development research organizations have had, up until recently, a comfortable, sheltered life. In order to access funding for an applied research project, a board member, executive director, programme officer or some other staff member would write up a grant application addressed to one, two, or a handful of institutional donors. They would get part or all of the funding required; implement the research; then submit midterm and final reports to the donor, documenting results, and meeting financial reporting requirements. Projects would have to meet donor requirements, and their successful implementation could mean more money for another project cycle.

In some cases, the grant application is just a token gesture because funds are assured anyway. A few organizations may have other, smaller sources of income: training and consulting services, sale of organic products and traditional medicines produced by local communities, a random rummage sale or participation in a bazaar. But the income generated from such activities is rarely substantial.

The bulk of the organization's funding would still be from one or two funders. Now that funding from aid agencies has become less reliable due to shifting donor trends and preferences, many research organizations are left with unfunded programmes, and may even begin to wonder about their survival. More grant making institutions require counterpart funding, and token grant proposals just to meet paper trail requirements don't work anymore.

Non-profits actually have to earn their keep! As the non-profit sector comes face to face with the reality of declining funds from the international donor community, non-profit leaders are left with two options: close shop, or aggressively and creatively look for alternative funding sources to fill the gap. The latter poses as a challenge for non-profits that have been used to writing up grant proposals to secure funding. Board members, executive directors and non-profit managers must now learn to diversify funding sources and come up with creative resource mobilization strategies to ensure survival.

The Importance of Diversifying Funding Sources

A diversity of funding sources provides protection against fickle donor trends. Other than grants, income sources include gifts and earned income.

The characteristics of each are found in Table:

Table. Different Funding Sources.

Sources	Characteristics	Examples
Grants	Usually restricted, project based, time bound, short to medium term funding	Governments, foundations, associations, multilateral and bilateral agreements
Gifts	Unrestricted, can lead to endowments, medium to long term funding	Individuals, groups
Earned Income	Unrestricted, short to long term funding, for profit operation, needing different management skills	Sale of products, fee for service, interest income

Rather than focusing all energies towards bagging large grant amounts from big funders, there is value to develop a following made up of individual donors, corporations and groups with various degrees of affinity for the organization's programmes. Their support may come in the form of large or small gifts, could be unrestricted, could be one time donations, or could lead to long term funding.

An organization in search of unrestricted funding would do well to expand their base of individual givers. There is also value in professionalizing existing earned income activities to the point where they could significantly impact an organization's financial viability. This alternative approach encourages a healthy mix of funding sources, thereby spreading the risk in the event that one source dries up.

Building Constituents

The call now for development research organizations is to make the shift from dependence on grants to building their own constituencies and mobilizing local support through other strategies. Raising resources from a local base has direct implications on the relevance of an organization's reason for being. A community willing to support the organization's research efforts, financially or otherwise, suggests that it shares the objectives of the programme, understands them, and aspires to see them realised. This becomes an endorsement of the organization's mission, and serves as an indicator of how wide and deep the organization's impact is on its constituents. In addition, more grant giving institutions, foundations and corporations are using the level of community support as a criterion for funding. Developing a base of support should thus be a part of an organization's resource development plan. The task then falls on the organization to identify who these people are in the community, find a way of talking to these people, offer them opportunities for support, and have systems in place that assure these supporters, or donors, that their donations are directed towards the projects for which they were intended. To accomplish the above requires more than just the technical skills of resource mobilization. It involves the complex and delicate task of building relationships with other people who share similar values and goals, and upon whom the organization can rely for support.

Defining Resource Mobilisation

Thus resource mobilisation may be defined as:

- A management process that involves identifying people who share the same values as your organi sation, and taking steps to manage that relationship.

Looking closely at this definition, one can see that resource mobilization is actually a process that involves three integrated concepts:

- Organizational management and development,
- Communicating and prospecting, and
- Relationship building.

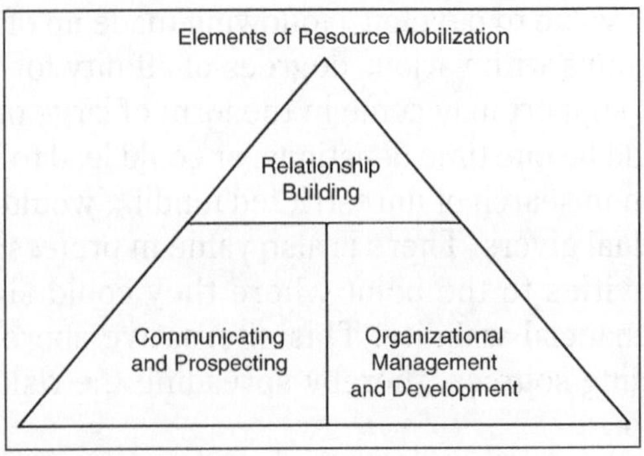

The key concepts are:

Organizational Management and Development

Organizational management and development involves establishing and strengthening organizations for the resource mobilization process. It involves identifying the organization's vision, mission, and goals, and putting in place internal systems and processes that enable the resource mobilization efforts, such as: identifying the roles of board and staff; effectively and efficiently managing human, material, and financial resources; creating and implementing a strategic plan that addresses the proper stewardship and use of existing funds on the one hand, and identifies and seeks out diversified sources of future funding on the other.

This concept covers the following principles, elaborated throughout the practical guidebook:

- Resource mobilization is just a means to the end, the end being the fulfillment of the organization's vision
- Resource mobilization is a team effort, and involves the institution's commitment to resource mobilization; acceptance for the need to raise resources; and institutionalizing resource mobilization priorities, policies and budget allocation
- The responsibility for the resource mobilization effort is shared by the board, the president or the executive director, and the resource mobilization unit
- An organization needs money in order to raise money
- There are no quick fixes in resource mobilization

Communicating and Prospecting

Once an organization has achieved a certain readiness for resource mobilization, it must then take on another challenge: ensuring its longterm sustainability by acquiring new donors and maintaining a sizeable constituency base. The art of resource mobilization entails learning how to connect with prospective donors in a manner and language they understand, and finding common ground through shared values and interests. It also entails discerning the right prospect to approach, and matching the appropriate resource mobilization strategy to the prospect.

This concept is governed by two principles:

- Resource mobilization is really FRIEND raising. Financial support comes as a result of a relationship, and not as the goal in and of itself.
- People don't give money to causes, they give to PEOPLE with causes. People give to organizations to which they have personal affiliation, in some shape or form.

Relationship Building

And thus the courtship begins: once you identify your donors, the objective then is to get closer to them, get to know them better, very much the same way as developing a casual acquaintance into a trusted friend and confidante. As the relationship deepens, this increases the chance of donors giving higher levels of support over time, intensifying commitment and enlarging investment.

As cultivation techniques become more targeted and personal, a donor may become more involved in the organization. Initiating new relationships, nurturing existing ones, and building an everexpanding network of committed partners is an ongoing activity, embedded as a core function of the organization. This requires the dedication of board members, staff and volunteers, and in order to build enduring relationships, the following principles should be remembered:

- Donor cultivation means bringing the prospect to a closer relationship with the organization, increasing interest and involvement
- Start at the bottom of the resource mobilization pyramid to get to the top

The Resource Mobilization Pyramid and the 80–20 Rule

The resource mobilization pyramid is a graphic depiction of the proportion of an organization's supporters *vis a vis* their level of involvement in its activities:

- Major Donors make up only 10 per cent of an organization's support base, but contribute 70 per cent of total donations received.
- Repeat Donors make up 20 per cent of an organization's support base, and contribute 20 per cent of total donations received.
- First time Donors make up 70 per cent of an organization's support base, but contribute only 10 per cent of total donations received.

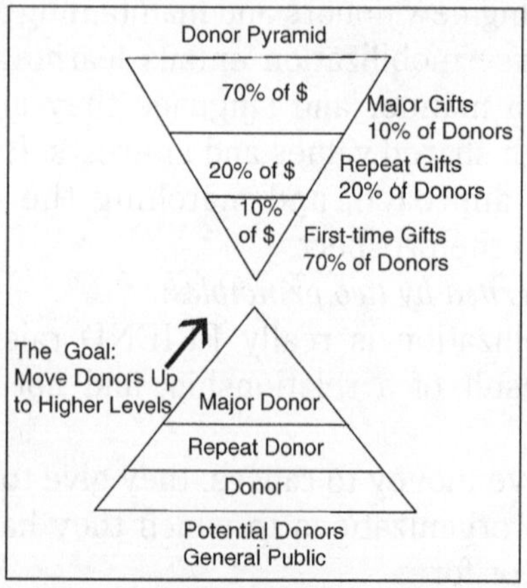

The pyramid reflects a concept called the Pareto Principle, also known as the 80-20 Rule, which states that a small number of causes is responsible for a large percentage of the effect. In one business application, it can mean that 20 per cent of the customers generate 80 per cent of the sales, or that 80 per cent of merchandise comes from 20 per cent of the vendors. In the non-profit application of the Pareto Principle, it can mean that 20 per cent of an organization's funding comes from 80 per cent of its donors, forming the base of the pyramid.

Majority of the supporters are involved in a smaller capacity. Further up the pyramid, individuals with greater involvement become fewer, and the apex is the smallest group of supporters who contribute the most. The percentages per se are not as important as understanding that the higher the gift or donation, the smaller the number of donors who have the capacity or interest to give it.

The donor pyramid serves as a model to envision the resource mobilization strategies that are appropriate for each level. An entry level strategy such as a special event or a direct mail campaign can be used to draw in donors to an organization.

As a donor's capacity to give increases over time, other strategies, such as face to face solicitation, are then implemented to draw them up the pyramid, providing them with successive giving opportunities that may cultivate a deeper commitment and interest in the organization. Generally, only a few from the larger pool of donors move up into the next level. There are of course exceptions, and a major donor can surface at any level.

What Donors Look for

It would seem then that advocating for a good cause is not enough to attract local funding. In a seminal study conducted by the Asia Pacific Philanthropy Consortium, *Investing in Ourselves: Giving and Resource mobilization in Asia,* which covered case studies of how various non-profits and NGOs mobilized funds for financial sustainability, it was observed that in rallying for support, the nurturing of personal and community relationships was more critical than the espoused cause itself.

It further stated that these relationships were based on three major characteristics that an organization needed to have in order to attract support: legitimacy, transparency, and accountability.

Legitimacy

Different countries have different terms and requirements for recognizing the legal existence of organizations. But however diverse these requirements are across the region, each state still exercises a degree of control over the incorporation of non-profit organizations.

Only those that have been established according to their country's civil laws and traditions are considered to be legitimate. Such organizations are more likely to gain donor support because they have achieved some level of compliance with government standards, and are less likely to be suspected of being fronts for underground political movements or "fly by night" operations.

Transparency

This refers to open communication with internal and external stakeholders regarding an organization's financial and management health, and is a characteristic of organizations that disclose information ab0ut their programmes, activities, and even financial transactions and investments to stakeholders and anyone who wishes to know more about the organization. It is a criterion that is highly regarded by prospective donors and partners, as transparency assures them of an organization's trustworthiness and commitment to its constituents.

Accountability

This refers to an organization's ability to stand up for its mission, and to be guided by sound management and financial principles. An accountable organization is one that responsibly services its community, properly manages its resources, and is able to report back to donors regarding the use of donated funds. Such organizations are also likely to gain public support, as quite a number of donors now expect to be updated on how their funds have been used by their beneficiary organizations.

Moreover, it is not uncommon for donors to request visits to project sites to be sure that their monies are being used in the best way possible. If there is only one message to take home from this chapter it is this: In building a base of donors, the focus is less on resource mobilization, more on friend raising. The funds come as a by product of the relationship, and not so much as an end in itself.

POLICY MANAGEMENT LIBRARY

The *Policy Management Library* (PML) implements key components of a well known policy management architecture, and provides a generalized policy model able to support arbitrary policy languages. The library fully supports the Java binding for CIM SPL policies, a recently approved standard from the Distributed Management Task Force. PML provides conflict, coverage, and dominance analysis building on the Apache Imperius project, which provides the parser, Java binding, and policy evaluation engine. Finally, policies written in Groovy are also supported, although without the policy analysis feature that is available for those written in CIM-SPL.

HOW DOES IT WORK

The Policy Management Library builds on a common model for policy run times and includes the following components and capabilities:

- *Managed Environment*: A platform that requires the dynamic configuration and deployment of decision making. This might include the ability to change how a network fire wall is configured, who has access to a file system, or to downgrade information for a specific user. This is the application into which this library is deployed.
- *Policy*: A condition specification and an optional action to execute when the condition evaluates to true. The condition is defined over a set of run time data provided to the policy at evaluation time by the managed environment. The decision is defined over a set of run time data also provide at evaluation time.
- *Policy Enforcement Point* (PEP): A point in the Managed Environment that needs to have a decision made, for example, to decide whether access to a secured resource should be granted. It requests the

answer to this decision from the Policy Decision Point. One implements such points tin the Managed Environment as PEP instead of a hard coded decision so that the decisions can be configured with policy. There may be any number of PEP in the Managed Environment.

- *Policy Decision Point* (PDP): Provides for the execution of policies and provides results of the execution are returned to the PEP for action based on the decision. It decides which policies in the Policy Repository apply to the decision request.
- *Policy Repository*: Holds the policies that are available for execution by the PDP. Policies may be activated or deactivated within the repository.
- *Policy Analysis*: Provides a set of specialized algorithms that supports policy authors in assessing the interaction between policies. The operations supported by the policy analysis component are dominance checks, coverage checks, simultaneous applicability check and conflict detection/resolution.
- *Policy Transformation*: Enables rule based transformation of abstract policies to concrete managed environment resource models.

In addition to the base library and architecture a number of key components are provided and described here:

- The *Policy Authoring and Management Tool* (PAMNT) is a Web based tool used to author, negotiate, analyse and manage policies within the management environment. The policies are authored in a controlled natural language format based on templates. The templates are defined by an administrator prior to authoring of the policies. The analysis operations check whether there are any conflicts, uncovered regions or dominated policies among the set of authored policies. Once authored and analysed, policies can be deployed or removed from the managed environment. Policies may also be deactivated and left deployed within the environment.
- The Policy Negotiation Tool is part of the PAMNT tool and enables two or more parties to negotiate a single agreed upon set of policies. Each party brings their own polices to the negotiation and each party alternates making proposals. Goal based negotiation to remove conflicts between the policies is provided.
- The *Policy Enabled Network Gateway* (PENG) enables policy controls over MQTT messages flowing between two or more networks.
- *Distributed Policy Repository* (DPR) provides redundancy and resilience of policies storage within an unreliable, distributed network of Policy Decision Points. Support for policy supercession and rollback in support of network topology changes is provided.

8

Role of Library Information in Contemporary Economy

INTRODUCTION

In the information economy, many private sector firms and government agencies have become consolidated around a framework of telecommunication networks and related information technologies. However, integrating communications and information technologies into their organisations have affected organisational processes, including production, distribution, and administration of products and services.

Researchers have noted that organisational processes in both the public and private sectors have become characterised by applications, such as electronic data exchange, distributed databases, computer based communication, and client server computing. Other researchers have indicated that geographic concepts, such as space and location, are significant factors in the distribution of data as it flows between individuals and organisations across communication networks, therefore, the use of geographic information systems in the facilitating and analysis of data has also increased greatly. The development and integration of geospatial information in a variety of administrative, production, and service functions within organisations in both the public and private sectors can have an effect on the role that libraries play in the information economy. The geospatial information that is used by individuals and organisations in the information economy is often produced by a mix of private developers and government agencies.

The data used by geographers and geographic information systems analysts in their operations is diverse and distributed across a wide network of server locations, over a complex series of information nodes. Libraries can provide a unique entry point to this multitude of sources. Economic activities during the past few decades have increasingly been characterised by different functional uses of information. The establishment and growth of diverse information industries, such as statistical bureaus, marketing associations, trade journals, and consulting agencies, have integrated information in their operations.

The development builds on early studies of how information not only impacted, but helped define, different economic processes. During the decades following World War II, individuals in the banking and accounting sectors began defining information as having value and affecting production. Statements, such as the 'Statement of Basic Accounting Theory,' asserted that accounting systems could be conceptualised as an 'application of general theories of information to the problem of efficient economic operations'. The National Science Foundation began to fund research about the economics of information.

Other organisations, such as the Organisation for Economic Co-operation and Development (OECD) and the United Nations Economic, Scientific, and Cultural Organisation (UNESCO), were also debating policy issues about the economics of information. However, to develop an information policy, one must first understand that policy is '... the generic name of any formulation, simple or complex, vague or exact, general or special, discretionary or detailed, of guidance for action in the face of circumstances which, lying necessarily in the future, can be approached only by conjecture and imagination'. The first bibliography of information economics was published in 1971.

By the mid 1970s, developments in the literature illustrated how the general theories of information were being investigated by economists and other researchers in the sciences and social sciences. Clearly, "... the existence of learning processes and likely variation in policy criteria in a business organisation imply that the decision-making unit is undergoing continual change".

Further, "those responsible for shaping information policy must determine the appropriate mix of information inputs to achieve social objectives, while at the same time they must have regard for equity considerations". By 1976, the American Economic Association officially recognised information as an economic topic and incorporated it into core ideas. By the 1980s, research into this area was generating much debate among researchers about what comprised information economics. Among the ideas being debated was the emergent issue of how to incorporate information into modes of production and thereby study its effects in different sectors of the economy.

Early economists described three factors of production that included land, Labour, and capital. The competing theories on defining just how these three factors relate, especially capital, in a system is contentious and open to debate. Economists differ on how to define capital. It can be described concretely as something of value as in money or more abstractly as an association with Labour and consumption.

In examining the value of transformative functions of an economic activity, the definition of capital can be more broadly interpreted, in some cases to include information. For example, the definition of human capital is the "sum total of skills embodied within an individual: education, intelligence, charisma, creativity, work experience, entrepreneurial Vigour, ... it is what you would be left with if someone stripped away all of your assets your job, your money, your possessions". A number of articles and other publications that were produced in the 1990s discussed different forms of intangible capital including information, cultural capital, linguistic capital, and social capital.

Social capital would involve "networks of communication and communication based institutions and their rules, norms of social practice, and relationships of trust". Networks themselves would be considered as facilitating a sum of knowledge that would have value as a factor in production. Another perspective on integrating information into economic theory was in examining how change in the economy is affected by information.

Braman suggests that "the production of knowledge and its transformation into technologies and other applied mechanisms such as competition can alter the order of different sectors of the economy and thus its equilibrium". Since, the "defining trend of the modern economy is the shift to the intangible. The economic landscape is ...moulded by intangible streams of data, images and symbols.

The source of economic value and wealth is ... the creation and manipulation of dematerialised content ...Non-linear and Non-deterministic, the intangible economy raises a whole series of measurement issues. More fundamentally, it changes the role, the function, and the perception of economic measurement data. Because information is its key resource and output, the intangible economy is highly data sensitive and intrinsically self reflective".

However, as Goldfinger suggests, the effects of the applications of information and technology are only apparent over a period of time when it is possible to perform analysis with systematic data. Recent studies have focused on defining the role of technology in causing economic growth. Some researchers consider economic change as being influenced by aspects of the innovation process, aspects that are characterised as being 'information intense' or more developed technologically than what had currently existed. There has been much speculation on the correlation between technological development and economic growth and the social consequences of economic activities. In Marshallian neo-classical economics, externalities refer to by products of activities that affect the well being of people, where those impacts are not reflected in market prices; the costs (or benefits) associated with externalities do not enter standard cost accounting schemes.

The backbone of the information economy is in the linkages that combine to form a network. If the network is a combination of technology and human activities that processes information as they traverse the network, then the uneven flow of information across the network can cause externalities to manifest themselves. These externalities can be caused by incomplete information that can result in the fluctuating prices of a commodity.

The effect of content of information on the economy is up to debate. Are the contextual aspects of information processed in the economy irrelevant or do the contextual aspects of information in the economy have distinct sociopolitical value? For those who argue the latter, the contextual aspects of information do shape the perception and understanding of economic processes themselves. The cultural variability of information creates difficulties in determining the locational aspects of data.

Data may be associated with a physical carrier, but it is not bound by the location of that carrier. This aspect of information has created challenges to economists who have attempted to illustrate Braman's concept that would "distinguish between the costs of information at different stages of an information production chain". Further, the value of the information chain hinges upon relevance that "is a subjective question of mapping an utterance on the conceptual map of a given user seeking information for a particular purpose defined by that individual" and the "utility of a piece of information will depend on a combined valuation of its credibility and relevance". Most of the economic models that attempt to illustrate an information production chain have the elements of information creating, processing, flows, and use incorporated into their structure.

A number of organisations have created models that have the elements of information acquisition, production, assembly, storage, monitoring, interpretation, and exchange. United States federal documents describe an information cycle that includes information creation, collection, processing, and distribution as do international organisations. Creators, or individuals who are involved in the innovation of new concepts and new industries, are highly valued.

However, the idea of an information sector is not new. In 1962, over 50 industries were identified that comprised an information sector. Other economists preferred to identify information sector industries by using existing industry classifications, as identified by Standard Industrial Classification (SIC) codes. However, critics of the approach questioned the validity of defining information on so specific a criteria, fearing that existing industrial classifications "ignore a major part of the processes of investment in information in the economy" and that "most significant information activities do not produce goods in tangible form and thus not included in the SIC system". The debate over how to classify industries in the information sector illustrates the variability of trying to define information for econometric purposes.

The debate is further magnified when trying to define the economic aspects of information in an international sense. Cultural context is a factor in defining what comprises the information sector, with definitions varying between countries and methods that describe material and information related production. Even though legal negotiations about the nature of information and production between countries, such as with the General Agreements on Tariffs and Trade (GATT), have attempted to arrive at some definitional parameters for information, the process of trying to understand how information works in an international trade environment is problematic due to the great variability production across different countries. For example, the North American Industry Classification System (NAICS) was adopted in 1997, replacing the old Standard Industrial Classification (SIC) system. Developed jointly by the U.S., Canada, and Mexico to provide new comparability in statistics about business activity across North America, the NAICS also better distinguishes between manufacturing and information sectors. Although imperfect, the NAICS is an essential tool to determine service and product providers in the information sector, to remain current on industry analyses, statistics, and leading companies. The international economic environment is indeed a complex one, and in defining how information operates within economic systems, one can examine the redefining of economic components such as the agent, the firm, and the market.

As discussed in classical economic theory, agents tend to act in ways that put themselves in a better position than previously held. Braman questions the decision-making processes of economic agents as they improve their position according to economic theory. Processes including 'rationality, perfect information, and individualistic independence' are subject to myriad influences and the amount of information available. Further, there are limits to the amount of information that an individual agent can have access to or even process in order to maximise his position.

Research in the fields of psychology, that is, cognitive miserliness has indicated that there are cognitive and neurological limitations that affect how information is perceived and understood. Technology limitations can also affect the capture, recording, and transmission of information, thereby, affecting its cognition by an agent or organisation.

The cultural context of information, as well, can have an affect on how information is understood. The social organisation of society can have an significant impact on the flow of information creating barriers that can slow or impede the finding of information by individual agents. The concept of social organisation and community is also important in understanding how information is processed in regards to economic function. In classical economic theory, economic agents act purposively.

Since, they have an end in mind and find means to attain those ends, the actions of individual agents bear a causal relationship to overall market outcomes. Further, an economic agent uses information in order to "obtain satisfaction or benefits gained from consuming a particular good or service according to a hierarchical ranking of preferences". The social context of how information can be pursued and utilised also affects the actions of an individual economic agent.

An individual may use information and acquire goods and services beyond what is necessary for the maximising of their position and thus, may not make the best use of information in a classical economic sense. Cultural processes can affect preferences for a particular commodity adding or detracting from its value. The decision-making process is interconnected among various individuals in society, which can affect the utility factor in economic activities.

Societies and communities can be conceptualised as components of a larger structure or market in which economic activities are performed. The larger structure can operate as an "informational mechanism" with different types of information arrayed spatially across it. How economic agents operate within markets is subject to much debate as economists advocate different operational models about the functioning of markets.

One model centers on the prices of commodities and services that are distributed across a market. Economic agents enter the market with a certain knowledge level and assumptions about prices that influence their interaction with the market. The search for further price information for an eventual outcome process frames their activities in the market. Social aspects and cultural ties that are part of the market structure affect how information interacts with markets. The distribution of information across markets has an impact on the economic decision process of the firm as well as the individual. If a market is a social arrangement that allows buyers and sellers to discover information and carry out a voluntary exchange of goods or services, the firm is an alternative system of allocation to the market that exists to organise production in a Non-price environment. Although there is a distinction between a market and a firm, most economists admit that the two shade into each other.

A business model describes the elements and relationships that express the business logic of a firm. Just as NAICS classes businesses into sectors, firms are often classed into 'internally consistent sets of firms," referred to as strategic groups or configurations, allowing typologies and taxonomies to explore the determinants of performance. Early studies of information flow within existing business entities usually focused on individual managers. In a market environment in which reliable information was at a premium, business managers made decisions based on an individualised perspective that made use of personal social networks as well as market information.

The growth of larger business enterprises with extensive production and distribution linkages increased the need for accurate market information, which led to the eventual progression Towards extensive record keeping overseen by professional managers. The availability of accurate market information and information on other firms in related enterprises began to affect business decisions.

An increased efficiency in record management usually decreases what some economists have labeled transaction costs, or the searching for information needed for a particular type of economic activity. Early studies in the nature of transaction costs within business processes determined that firms usually invested in those transaction costs that were more expensive, while leaving the more inexpensive transaction costs to the marketplace. The application of advanced telecommunication technology by firms has encouraged commercial enterprises to distribute their transaction costs on an even wider basis for more efficiency. Contemporary studies in the nature of firms and different economic sectors have expanded the focus of study beyond the single firm to a hierarchy of firms or even larger social constructs, such as networks.

Research into the role of information and economic theory bridges the mathematical boundaries of idealised econometric models to account for information sector variability and the irrationality of human Behaviour. Research in the social dynamics of industries that comprise the information sector should take a wider, holistic approach. Studies on the information sector should integrate concepts and analytical methods from other disciplines.

One such discipline is political science, which has often focused on the effect of uneven flows of information and of the impact of imperfect information on decisions. In expanding their descriptive scope of the components of the information sector, economists expanded their idea of the firm and the market by including variables with wider spatial structures. Such structures include telecommunication networks and social communication networks.

It is with the physical network of the telecommunications sector that some researchers, especially in the field of geography, have sought to combine spatial concepts of space, place, and landscape to provide a rigorous and quantifiable platform in which to measure the complex socioeconomic phenomena that comprises the information sector.

ROLE OF LIBRARIES IN THE INFORMATION ECONOMY

The emergence of the new information economy comprised of computer networks that link users to one another or to larger organisations is creating a class of singular information users. To aid users in participating in the information economy, libraries designed a virtual presence to deliver information services, usually in the form of a 'digital library.' Digital libraries can offer a more varied informational experience to the community of online users. Libraries, with their traditional strengths of information collection, description, organisation, and dissemination, can provide a more holistic learning experience for these new user communities.

In commenting on the structure and environment of digital libraries, the DLF (Digital Library Federation) has offered the following definition: "Digital libraries are organisations that provide the resources, including specialised staff, to select, structure, offer intellectual access to, distribute, interpret, preserve the integrity of, and ensure the persistence over time of collections of digital works".

In elaborating on the concept, Hanani and Frank define six major characteristics that should be integral to digital libraries:

- "Collection of data objects: A library holds together a collection of data objects, items and resources. The items can be books, journals and documents, multimedia objects. The library objects can be available locally, or indirectly, by using a network to access them.
- "Collection of metadata structures: A library contains a collection of metadata structures, such as catalogs, guides, dictionaries, thesauri, indices, summaries, annotations, glossaries, and so forth.
- "Collection of services: A library provides a collection of services, such as various access methods for as well as consultation for. different users; management of the library (purchase, shelf arranging, computerisation, communication); logging/statistics and performance measurement evaluation (PME); selective dissemination of information (SDI) or push mode, as it is called on the Internet.
- "Domain focus: A library has a domain focus and its collection has a domain focus; purpose. For example, art, science, or literature. Also, it is usually created to serve a community of users and therefore, is finely grained.
- "Quality control: A library uses quality control in the sense that all its material is verified and consistent with the profile of the library. The material is filtered and its metadata is usually enriched.
- "Preservation: The purpose of preservation is to ensure protection of information of enduring value for access by present and future generations. Preservation includes the allocation of resources for preservation, preventive measures, and remedial measures to restore the usability of selected materials."

As librarians compile digital collections of materials, the networked environment of which they are a part offers access to many more information resources. In describing libraries and the new online environment in which they operate, libraries are placing lesser emphasis on the materials they collect and house, and more emphasis on the kind of material they are able to obtain in response to user requests.

The trend includes libraries forming partnerships to deliver material from elsewhere in time to answer a user's information needs. The shift to on demand delivery of material from elsewhere is an effect of recent growth in digital networking in an environment where standards for description were established and refined over the past 35 years.

Librarians are also moving primarily away from being caretakers of physical collections to people who identify resources that exist. The earlier survey of the information economy has illustrated a variety of information sector industries and organisations that utilise information, such as geographic data, in their varied production and distribution functions. The flexibility of spatially referenced information, and its applicability to a variety of research techniques and spatially referenced applications, create a powerful tool in which librarians can raise the profile of their institution's involvement in the information sector.

In defining the parameters of geographic information librarianship, the varied applications of geographic information in government functions, community initiatives, and private sector development can offer strategies in dealing with the social effects of trends like the digital divide and information marginalisation. The following section provides an overview of the development of geographic information systems and related applications.

THE LAM IN THE KNOWLEDGE ECONOMY

The LAM are arguably the oldest examples of knowledge organizations. Societies have built and sustained institutions to collect, organize, preserve, and provide access to knowledge bearing objects for more than two millennia. It would seem that these quintessentially knowledge based organizations would serve as models for other organizations making the transition to a knowledge driven economy.

In fact, the LAM are facing a period of deep uncertainty at the dawn of the new era due to economic pressures, competition from alternative service providers, changing expectations from consumers of their services, and a fundamental shift in their material base from tangible objects to digital representations. These factors are difficult to distinguish from one another, and as suggested, attempt to do a point by point assessment of them.

Instead, as suggested, raise a number of emerging conditions that illustrate the interwoven nature of the challenges, and that raise central questions about the missions and continuing relevance of the LAM and their core functions. The challenges facing the LAM are not new; they have been evolving as part of a larger constellation of changes for some time. However, some contemporary conditions bring the challenge facing the LAM into sharp focus. The advent of the World Wide Web has amplified the long standing role of radio and television in the competition for attention, and has extended it into competition for information access in ways heretofore impossible.

Through the Web, the LAM are facing serious competition from alternative service providers, possibly for the first time in their history. The Web can be thought of as a global substitute for the LAM because it allows a globally distributed population to publish and access information easily. Of course, the Web is weak on some traditional strengths of the LAM, such as legitimation and authentication of information, and in the persistence and structure provided for information access.

Nevertheless, there are some striking stories to tell about the Web's competition with the traditional LAM. For example, the on line bookseller,

Amazon.com, has an extensive on line database, not unlike a library catalog, listing several million book titles, 250,000 CD titles, and data about 250,000 motion pictures and entertainment programmes from 1891 to the present. Amazon probably compares well in the ranking of research libraries conducted by the Association for Research Libraries. For some kinds of information, the Amazon databases are more comprehensive and more current than the on line catalogs of large libraries.

Moreover, Amazon competes with other on line book sellers by adding services that mimic some of the selection and legitimating functions that libraries traditionally performed, such as alerts and recommendations based on user profiles and past purchases, and opportunities for readers to post and read book reviews. It seems reasonable to ask whether Amazon represents a first step in the migration of traditional LAN functions into a new model based on a commercialized Web infrastructure.

The advent of commercial services such as Amazon causes a subtle but important shift in the political and economic ecology of the LAM. For most of the last two centuries the LAM have operated as a kind of public good in which a patronage structure of universities, governments, and non-profit philanthropies provided funds, and the LAM carried out their missions as best they could. This arrangement never required a very robust means for judging the economic value of the LAM. To the extent that the measurement of value added was attempted at all, it tended to be built around a crude input/output model in which the raw materials of the LAM were considered inputs and the outputs were the number of patrons served or the number of reference questions answered.

Several important factors were missing from the middle of this model. For one thing, there was very little cost accounting to show how the LAM functions of selection, organization, curation, content delivery, and so on contributed economically to the services delivered. For another, the model provided no way to determine the value of the actual work being done by the users of the LAM's materials. It was therefore not possible to determine how any particular input led to any changes in a user's welfare. This was fine as long as the patrons accepted the idea that the LAM were an important public good and they had to be funded at the appropriate level.

The rise of examples such as Amazon call that idea into question, and the LAM have no useful measures of costs and benefits to fall back on. Amazon provides proof that something like a library can be built and provided on a commercial basis. This proof can refocus the discussion of the social welfare provided by the LAM in a critical way. The welfare model of the traditional LAM started with the aggregate welfare of society and worked backward. As Webster's suggests, the benefits of the "vast commerce in ideas" was the society at large — mankind, to use his term. Of course, the specific contributions that create these benefits were individual in origin, but the appropriate focus was not on the individual.

In the traditional LAM, especially as they evolved in the 19th century, individual contributions arose through the provision of socially organized affordances. The society provided the LAM for use by individuals, and at least some individual users leveraged those affordances into important new discoveries or creations that benefited society. Prosperous societies had robust LAM infrastructure, and any society that wanted to be prosperous should create such infrastructure through collective action. Amazon offers a fundamentally different economic model in which the starting point is individual welfare.

Individuals perceive a need for LAM-like services, and individual investors put up the resources and create the capacity to meet that demand. The individual users pay for the services, and presumably receive the welfare they paid for. As the welfare of individuals rises from use of the services, social welfare rises as well. In the realm of knowledge such as provided by Amazon, society might also benefit from the discoveries or creations of individuals who were able to leverage the knowledge they gained from the services. Amazon, simply by its existence, raises the question of why the society should support the LAM when the services provided by the LAM might be had through private enterprise using the Web as infrastructure. Fortunately for the traditional LAM, such questions are not yet challenging the heart of the enterprise.

But the questions suggest that the LAM cannot depend indefinitely on the rationales that have held their patronage structures together for the past two centuries. While some strict traditionalists within the LAM world might try to hold back the tide of changing arising from the Web, many are beginning to follow their user community into the Web world in order to leverage the power of the Web in ways constructive to the traditional LAM.

A study of the online habits of 2,000 American college students conducted by netLibrary found that:

- 82 per cent of the students surveyed own a computer and virtually all of them use the Internet.
- 93 per cent claimed that finding information on line makes more sense than going to the library.
- 83 per cent said they were frequently unable to get the materials they need for the library because of limited library opening hours.
- 75 per cent said they do not have enough time to go to the library.
- 75 per cent liked the convenience and 71 per cent liked the time saved by finding information on line any hour of the day.

Another recent study amplifies on the importance of these data:

"[b]ecause of easy access to the Web, undergraduates are using library collections and services less than in the past and, in the absence of quality information and tools on the surface, they may imperil the quality of student learning". A transformation is already under way among users of the LAM, but it is not yet clear how social welfare will be affected by the trasnformation. Those who care for the traditional LAM are challenged to decide whether and how they will try to shape that transformation. That challenge should begin in recognizing that the LAM and the Web cannot substitute for one another. They are complementary, and must be developed in a complementary manner. We see four areas in which key complementarities appear: access, information quality, social memory, and information property.

Access

An important complementary role of the Web and the LAM is in improving effective access to information for all strata of the population. The "digital divide" usually refers to disparities in access to Information and Communications Technologies (ICTs). People without access to ICTs have few opportunities to participate in on line discussions and debates, to use e-mail to communicate with friends and family, or to post their own content on the web. ICTs alone are only part of the problem, however.

Equally important is the development of the information and skills infrastructure necessary to exploit the availability of ICTs. Libraries have long served as equalizers in disparities of access to information by providing free access to materials that individuals cannot afford to purchase, and most have extended their efforts to providing computers with Internet access and licensing access to databases on behalf of their users. Libraries are still relatively new at this, and they are finding that their service provision models based on circulating physical items such as books do not map neatly to the demands of a the digital environment. Users can take a book home and use it at their leisure, but those who do not have a computer and an Internet connection can gain access at a library facility only during its opening hours.

Nevertheless, libraries are providing a vital complementary role in leveraging the Web among those who would otherwise not have access at all. An equally vital complementarity of the Web and the LAM is in the co-location of physical collections and the information necessary to learn from them. Museums can be used to illustrate this in two ways. The consolidated physical location of a museum's collections is beneficial for those who can visit the museum in person, especially for an extended period of time. Unfortunately, the same consolidation makes the museum's collections inaccessible by anyone unable to visit.

Using the Web a museum can make significant portions of its collections available to distant users through images of objects and text information about the objects. Of course, there is much lost in the experience of seeing a photograph of a dinosaur skeleton compared to actually being there to walk around and look at the skeleton. Still, even limited access can be far better than none, especially for scholars who have intimate knowledge of the class of objects being studied and who have need to review items spread across a large number of collections.

Even if some on site investigation is required, preliminary reviews of on line collections and commentary can dramatically narrow the search space and provide structure to the study. Another way the co-location of objects and information becomes valuable is in the provision of information at varying levels of depth at the location of the physical object itself. For many museum visitors the information contained on a plaque next to the exhibit is sufficient. But for many visitors, the ability to gain deep access into the records on a given object can be essential for study.

Such access is usually provided for scholars by museum staff allowing entry into areas of the museum not permitted to regular visitors. With Web based technology, the entire holdings of information on each object could be made available at will to any visitor using a hand held wireless device like a PDA. In this example of a museum it is possible to see that the LAM are a source of the authenticated information available to a distributed audience over the Web, and the Web provides unparalleled access to information about museum collections for visitors on site at the museum.

Information Quality Assurance

Taken together, the LAM and the Web permit easy access to authenticated information. The Web is easy to use and provides fast access to a vast amount of information. Unfortunately, it is inadequate for teaching and research where definitive and high quality information resources are instrumental for critical analysis, innovation, and new knowledge generation. A great deal of the information in the Web is not accessible through the large search engines, and thus is not available to most Web users. Recent studies of the architecture of the Web distinguish between the surface Web and the deep Web, or what is also called the dark or hidden Web.

Search engines index mainly the surface Web of unrestricted, static Web pages, and no single search engine indexes more than 16 per cent of the surface Web. All of the search engines combined are estimated to index less than half of the surface Web. The "deep" Web is estimated to be 500 times larger than the size of the surface Web, and it is growing faster. There is no question that the Web makes huge amounts of information accessible, and for many applications this is a genuine boon.

However, the Web and search engine package currently available falls short of the infrastructure required by knowledge communities now provided by the LAM. A more serious quality assurance problem with search engine dependence on the surface Web is the comparatively substandard quality of the information there. The deep Web's resources are typically superior in quality, organization, and structure to surface Web resources. Deep Web resources tend to be curated, meaning they have been selected, indexed, and controlled for quality and authoritativeness by subject experts or editors.

Deep Web resources tend to be narrower and richer in content than surface Web sites, and oriented towards specific domains or disciplines. Scholars who rely on Internet search engines might locate substantial information in the surface Web while remaining completely unaware of the better content in the deep Web. Even if their search skills and their ability to judge the comparative quality of resources available are highly developed, they will miss much of the best information. At the very least, this constitutes a major opportunity loss. The co-evolution of the objects, data, and metadata of the LAM was not accidental. It was an integral and necessary part of the knowledge communities that evolved with and were sustained by the LAM.

The full utility of collections of objects and documents was unattainable until the full set of complementary assets was available. Those complementary assets were the experts on the content in the collections–the librarians, archivists, and curators–and the tools they developed over time in the form of metadata tools such as indices, catalogs, and reference works. The vital need for those assets was made strikingly evident shortly after the heroic success of the expansion of the US public library base with the Carnegie library endowments.

Most of the... Carnegie libraries had been built by 1920, but the benefits were as yet elusive. The Carnegie foundation commissioned a report by... Williamson to investigate the matter. In 1923 Williamson's report argued that the investments in bricks and mortar and collections would never pay off until many more professional librarians were deployed to manage the collections and help the public use them. Most US schools of librarianship were established in the decade thereafter, and their graduates made the public library an essential part of the nation's epistemic infrastructure.

In a similar vein, the Web and associated tools such as search engines will not be adequate by themselves to achieving the full potential of the emerging epistemic infrastructure. Librarians and other professionals of the LAM provide essential expertise in information management quality assurance that is badly needed in the world of the Web. The complementary nature of the traditional LAM and the emerging Web is illustrated by the LAM-like services increasingly available on the Web.

These services are tied to large LAM collections, and the services are managed by LAM experts who know the collections intimately. The public's interaction with the collections is intermediated by LAM professionals, providing substantially greater benefits than non-expert users could hope to gain on their own. A good example of this is seen in the experimental on line library services such as the Internet Public Library. The IPL began in 1996 as a student experiment to create an on line service providing features of a public library. Since that time the IPL has demonstrated that essential library services such as reference can be provided on line to a globally distributed user base from a globally distributed set of reference specialists. The primary user base of the IPL is now students in elementary and secondary school who use the collections and reference services to do assist with their schoolwork.

The IPL infrastructure and concept has been extended to the American Indian Higher Education Council Virtual Library that has made it possible for a number of tribal community colleges to achieve accreditation for programmes that was previously denied due to lack of library resources.

The key to such services is their information quality: the content is authenticated by experts who know both the subject matter and the patterns of user demand for the content. The IPL and the AIHEC Virtual Library marry the traditional strengths of the LAM with the distributed access benefits of the Web to create a cost-effective form of epistemic infrastructure not possible before. These examples can be augmented by many others, and suggest that the future of the Web intersects with rather than departs from the traditional LAM.

Social Memory

The LAM provide socially vital core functions that are largely invisible and that cannot be provided by existing Web based collecting and dissemination mechanisms. A key function in the knowledge driven economy is the integration of widely distributed objects and collections. This requires a rich set of knowledge and skills in organization and classification, as well as a critical eye towards the epistemic regimes that systems of knowledge organization impose on the worlds they describe. That skill has been built up over two centuries, and is a key part of the role of the LAM in the global epistemic infrastructure. The Web in its current form cannot provide this infrastructure.

The Web provides access to a global user base, but custodianship of information in the world of the Web is largely in local communities, specific disciplines, and private content providers. This is good in the sense that the most intimate expertise resides at such levels, but over dependence at this level reinforces parochialism and limits the potential for knowledge integration across space and over time. The LAM are not free from such parochialism: the institutional distinctions between libraries as sources of published works, archives as repositories of unpublished documents, and museums as storehouses for three dimensional objects is artificial and inhibits knowledge generation. But at least across the subdivisions of the LAM a rich ecology for maintaining integrative knowledge has evolved.

Libraries cooperate closely with one another through shared cataloging and other mechanisms, and similar cooperative arrangements reinforce the shared missions of archives and museums. Effective knowledge integration requires a careful balance between local, subject, and domain knowledge as well as broader principles for rich representation. This remains a challenge for both the LAM and the world of the Web, but the LAM are much farther along than the Web in developing the means to achieve the right balance. An essential function of the LAM is the accumulation and preservation of knowledge that might someday be of vital importance.

Libraries, archives, and museums maintain collections over the course of centuries. The LAM are the most important form of longterm social memory. Preservation experts in the LAM fight a constant battle to maintain documents and objects from destruction and deterioration in the belief that losses inhibit future potential. This tradition is well established, and has found a respected place in all advanced societies. The Web reveals another side, in which loss of information is massive and routine. No social institutions equivalent to the LAM currently take responsibility for collecting and preserving digital objects.

Many of these objects are generated without much consideration beyond their first order uses, and in complete disregard for their long term potential for manipulation and repurposing. They are seldom collected and organized the way paper documents have been for the past centuries, and in some cases it is not clear whether anyone is going to keep them at all. This represents a major departure from the past, in which the physical and economic realities of publication made it more likely that knowledge would be collected and preserved. And even in the print world, the idea of "comprehensive collection" has largely disappeared.

No single library on Earth collects everything that is published, and it is virtually impossible to ascertain the fraction of total global titles held in all the libraries taken together.

It is almost certain that a large amount of material disappears forever each year, even as librarians and archivists presume that other libraries are preserving those items. There is no way to tell whether the material being lost is of long term value. The situation in digital information is much more problematic because there are almost no reliable standards or technologies for long term preservation.

A number of publishers provide full text digital databases made from content they physically own and manage. Libraries purchase access to this content, but they do not actually store or preserve it. Even if copyright laws and license agreements permitted such replication, most libraries would not do so because they figure the publishers will preserve their digital content in perpetuity. But publishers are not in the business of archiving and preserving they content they produce, and there is no reason to assume they will assume this responsibility. Libraries and publishers have not come to sustainable agreements regarding digital archiving responsibilities.

Some publishers pledge to preserve their digital into the foreseeable future; others do not. In any case, it seems that libraries, and especially legal deposit libraries, would be better equipped to perform this function over the long run. In most countries, laws covering mandatory deposit of published work ensure that the majority of published material at least has a chance of preservation. Legislation regarding mandatory deposit of published digital works varies widely from country to country, and the deposit libraries are not yet ready to accept and manage such works. Many Web documents are critical sources of information and important cultural artifacts, but there are few tools to capture and preserve these documents and almost no market incentives for Web archiving even in the surface Web. Long term preservation is one of the important areas in which the traditional LAM and the Web must depend on each other.

Information Property

One of the most challenging but important areas of complementarity between the traditional LAM and the Web is information property management. The LAM are expert on copyright laws and conventions that have evolved over the past two centuries. Copyright was designed originally to provide authors with a limited monopoly as an inducement to creativity, but it has expanded in scope and duration and placed constraints on alternatives to purchasing items or leasing access. The digital realm provides many new challenges for copyright.

Laws and licensing agreements usually permit libraries to provide access to authenticated or on site users, but they strictly prohibit wholesale downloading of entire databases. They also limit the number and future uses of copies of individual articles, and forbid manipulation of digital objects to create extracts or derivative works. Content providers are beginning to use encryption and digital rights management software to prevent duplication of content and access by users who do not purchase an item or pay to view it.

Some scholars such as Lawrence Lessig argue that copyright restrictions on digital content have become so draconian that they are counter productive to innovation and knowledge generation. The Internet was once seen as a neutral platform that encouraged the free flow of content. Legal constraints on intellectual property are rapidly eroding that nascent tradition, with considerable downside possibilities for knowledge communities. Corynne McSherry contends that the "propertization" of knowledge is transforming key knowledge communities such as universities from "gift" economies to "market" economies.

The effects that such a shift might have on high quality scholarship, academic freedom, collaboration, and creativity are unknown, but it is clear that these knowledge communities have deeply developed and productive traditions that might be damaged in this process. The information objects that circulate in academic communities are "gifts" where the donor relinquishes knowledge to the larger community as a contribution to that community's larger mission of producing science, knowledge, or truth. In return, the scholar receives recognition and enhanced reputation that enhances the value of the scholar's future work.

The scholar's personal economic welfare is tied only indirectly to this process, through promotion and improved marketability to more prestigious universities that compensate better. Only in rare circumstances does a specific contribution contribute directly to the scholar's economic welfare. This has been the fundamental social contract of university for several hundred years, and has produced universities that are the envy of the world. No for profit equivalent has ever materialized. In principle, it is possible that propertization of knowledge might produce new knowledge communities that rival universities in content and quality.

But it is more than likely that propertization of knowledge within universities will encourage petty squabbles over attribution and revenue sharing that erode content and quality. Fortunately, the Web does not require the propertization of knowledge to be effective. Alternative strategies for evaluating and distributing intellectual property on the Web are evolving along the lines of the "gift" model. An early project initiated by physicists to submit and deposit "pre-prints" of journal articles electronically has mushroomed into a much larger movement for digital deposit and open archives for scholarly communications.

The open archives movement retains many of the community oriented value added functions of a "gift economy," especially peer review and editorial oversight for quality control. It replaces the strict intellectual property rights enforcement regime of publishers with "rules of the road" and community norms for attribution and recirculation of ideas that appeared earlier in published works. Lessig and others advocate the development of "knowledge conservancies" where owners of intellectual property voluntarily place their works in the public domain either to contribute to the larger social good, or in exchange for tax incentives that partially compensate donors for foregone royalty payments.

An important example of an alternative is SPARC, an alliance of more than 200 universities, research libraries, and organizations in North America, Europe, Asia and Australia to innovate in the scholarly communications system. It provides for incubation of competitive alternatives to current high priced commercial journals and digital aggregations. It also publicly advocates fundamental changes in the system and culture of scholarly communication.

SPARC education campaigns are aimed at improving awareness of scholarly communication issues and supporting expanded institutional and scholarly community roles in and control over the scholarly communication process. It remains to be seen whether open archives, knowledge conservancies, or coalitions such as SPARC will fundamentally change the parameters of information property or create a fundamentally new means for valuing and distributing knowledge. But experiments of this kind are important to developing the complementarity between the LAM and the Web most likely to bring benefits in the future.

SOCIAL STRUCTURE OF THE INFORMATION ECONOMY

The digital divide has been described by researchers in a variety of dichotomies in both contemporary American and international settings. In contemporary American society, researchers apply econometrics to socioeconomic data to portray how particular income groups have sufficient capital to purchase computer hardware and software for Internet access, while others do not.

Researchers also look at factors such as race, ethnicity, and educational attainment to further illustrate differences in technology access. Different technological standards are identified, within contemporary American society, that can contribute to uneven access to information technologies.

In international settings, the literature on the digital divide includes many of the factors described in articles about technology and information access in America, though other factors are emphasised, for example, political ones. Many research and policy papers that examine different aspects of the digital divide identify minority ethnic groups, indigenous peoples, and specific groups of people as being disadvantaged in participating in the information economy. Factors include low incomes, few educational qualifications, low literacy levels, unemployment, age or disabled status, and single parent households.

Diverse minority groups often live in large urban centers that have complex telecommunication networks, unlike persons living in rural and frontier areas. However, both rural and urban areas may have older telecommunication infrastructures, affecting access. In the 2002 report, A.Nation.Online, the Department of Commerce noted the increasing rates of Internet usage among traditionally underserved groups:

- In every income bracket, at every level of education, in every age group, for people of every race and among people of Hispanic origin, among both men and women, many more people use computers and the Internet now than did so in the recent past. Some people are still more likely to be Internet users than others are. Individuals living in low income households or having little education, still trail the national average. However, broad measures of Internet use in the United States suggest that over time Internet use has become more equitable.

However, there still exists a significant gap in the number of computers in low income schools and communities. Prieger also did not find that language was a statistically significant factor in Internet access, though many research reports indicate that English language ability is an important factor in participation in the information economy.

Households with a record of higher educational attainment would be more inclined to use computers, have Internet access, and place a high value on literacy. An important factor influencing participation in the information economy is the acquisition of information and communication technology (ICT) skills. Individuals who are members of the various groups that have been marginalised from computers and of the Internet often lack the necessary skills to use ICT applications. Cullen argues that the interaction of factors, such as cost, restricting access to equipment, low educational achievement, and cultural, age or gender based exclusion from literacy and computing skills, counteracts against the spread of such skills in disadvantaged communities.

Efforts to improve access to computers and Programmes to improve ICT technology skills among marginalised groups have been incorporated in a variety of community outreach Programmes by both public and private agencies. Many such Programmes try to establish and create a culture that is more conducive to ICT technologies.

9

Financial, Budgeting and Accounting Management in Library

FINANCIAL MANAGEMENT

Financial management is not presently managing cash or providing funds. It is the revise of the principles and practices involved in the financial operations of an organizations, industry or state. The fund function is the task of providing funds needed for the enterprise *i.e.*, provision of funds and their effective utilization. It trades with the troubles and processes of acquiring, distributing and effectively utilizing funds, balancing of revenue and expenditure and accounting of the whole transactions for bigger manage and evaluation. In other terms, significant stages or components of financial management are:

- Financial scheduling,
- Forecasting of receipts and disbursements,
- Realization of funds and revenues,
- Allocation of funds,
- Utilization of funds,
- Financial accounting,
- Financial manage,
- Financial auditing.

The task of finding money, investing funds, managing property and receiving the sanction for the budget and all other related matters of fund are the responsibility of the central executive power of the parent organization to which the library belongs. Though, the library has a major share of responsibility in estimating its own financial necessities, preparing a budget for its functions, behaviours and programmes, managing the funds appropriated and spending within the specified era, maintaining accounts, and finally preparing a statement.

PRINCIPLES OF FINANCIAL MANAGEMENT

For effective financial management, few guiding principles are necessary. An understanding of these principles is useful.

- *Effective Manage:* Financial management can job efficiently only when it is controlled properly. The way of financial manage should be easy and simple. Manage is also necessary for the economical exploit and canalization of possessions therefore that there is small wastage and the limited financial possessions can be put to maximum exploit.

- *Simplicity:* Processes for financial management should be easy and simple to operate. Simplicity results' in efficiency and economy.
- *Regularity and Farsightedness:* Financial management programmes should have a typical timetable therefore since to acquaint everybody with what he/she is expected to do at a scrupulous point of time. For instance, in the preparation of the budget for a library, inputs should approach from the heads of parts who would in turn expect cooperation from their staff. The preparation of the budget would be time bound and the budget should be submitted to the authorities on time therefore that the budgetary sanctions can be obtained in time to operate it. Likewise subscriptions to current journals should be sent to the publishers at a scrupulous time of the year. Sticking to a timetable facilitates advance thinking and preparation. Not only present requires but future necessities should be kept in view when making provisions for fund.
- *Economy:* Economy should be affected in any action and every action, more therefore in financial matters. All precautions should be taken to avoid unnecessary expenditure and wasteful exploit of scarce finances.
- *Flexibility:* Financial management should keep in mind the virtues of elasticity therefore since to learn scope for adjustment according to conditions. Only then can it be successful in times of emergency and crisis. But this does not mean that one should take undue advantage of its flexible nature. There are provisions and practices in utilizing or diverting funds appropriated for a sure thing of expenditure to the purchase of books or any equipment. But this flexibility should be within the framework of financial rules and processes. This kind of adjustment generally is done at the fag end of the financial year when unutilized funds are accessible in other items.

While these principles are useful in operating and managing finances in libraries, there are statutory financial rules and processes laid down through the executive authorities. Libraries have no option but to follow financial rules.

The other related meadows which require to be kept in mind through library and information professionals contain cost accounting and economics, several apparatus and techniques of financial management, economics and cost accounting like funds flow analysis, ratio analysis, break even analysis, operating and financial averages. Financial forecasting, capital budgeting, economic theory,

theory of manufacture, costing, etc. have adequate scope for application in library and information centre management.

FINANCIAL MANAGEMENT IN SERVICE ORIENTED AND NOT FOR PROFIT INSTITUTIONS

Information centers are paternalistic, service oriented and not for profit institutions. Financial management in such institutions is more intricate and significant than in profit oriented institutions. Money management in service oriented and not for profit institutions involves systematic scheduling, receiving funds, judicious spending and meticulous accounting of funds.

There are sure difficulties in the financial management of service oriented and not for profit institutions. The problem becomes acute if the budgets of such organizations are not intended since section of the scheduling of the parent body and if they worry more in relation to the accounting than scheduling.

In the middle of the significant aspects of service oriented and not for profit institutions are these are normally labour rigorous compared to profit oriented organization, will not have any inventory of services, will have dominance of professionals and the quality of service cannot be inspected and considered in advance *i.e.*, before rendering the service.

Further, there seems to be lack of a profit measure in such organizations and the absence of a profit motive treasure is quite typical to service oriented and not for profit institutions. Profit oriented institutions measure their output through the amount of revenue earned based on prices charged for goods and services sold. For individual profit centers, revenue is considered through transfer prices. Service oriented and not for profit institutions either should devise same monetary measures of output or rely on no monetary measures. Through and large, the output measurement is a problem in service and NFP organizations.

Usually, there is no single criterion to measure the success of such institutions. Multiple objectives, lack of a connection flanked by costs and benefits and difficulties in measuring performance and comparing performance of dissimilar elements of the similar organization are few peculiarities of such institutions.

There seems to be no direct connection flanked by the costs and benefits in service institutions. There is a clear difficulty in measuring the performance of service oriented and not for profit institutions. Further, due to different functions, the organizational elements cannot be compared in service oriented and not for profit institutions.

Market forces play a less important role in service oriented and not for profit institutions. Due to lack of shareholders, there seem to be differences in ownership and authority. Consequently there is a tendency for service oriented and not for profit institutions to be political institutions.

Historically the cost accounting and other manage techniques were urbanized for manufacturing companies and hence they have less applicability to service oriented and not for profit institutions. Further, inadequate management controls have become a custom in such organizations. Lastly, mainly service institutions are relatively small and operate at a single location.

Information centers have not given adequate attention to output measurement. In the absence of a monetary output measure, sure non-monetary measures could be employed through service and NFP institutions. The non-monetary output measures could be classified in many ways. They can be subjective or objective, discrete or scalar, quantitative or qualitative. Significant non-monetary output measures are:

- Results measures,
- Procedure measures,
- Social indicators,
- Inputs since proxy output measures.

EXPENDITURE SCHEDULING OF FINANCIAL MANAGEMENT IN LIBRARY

You now have a thought of how a library gets finances for running its services. Expenditure is the second significant aspect of financial management. Library expenditure occupies the similar lay in the revise of financial management since consumption does in the daily life of an individual. Since consumption is the end of all economic behaviours, therefore also library expenditure is the end of all the financial behaviours of a library.

IMPORTANCE OF LIBRARY EXPENDITURE

Presently since you spend money on your books and studies, therefore do libraries spend money on books and periodicals, readers' services, references and bibliographical services, documentation and information services, etc? The objective behind all these is the supply of the right document to the right reader at the right time. The library expenditure is usually undertaken to satisfy the intellectual necessities of the readers and give those documents which the readers in their individual capability cannot and do not want to purchase. Besides, no individual can purchase all the literature which comes out of the printing presses of dissimilar countries, on dissimilar subjects, in several languages, and in diverse shapes. The only agency which can acquire procedure and create accessible all this literature to readers is the library. All this means spending money and more money.

NATURE OF LIBRARY EXPENDITURE

There are three major aspects in the nature of library expenditure:

- *Library is a spending institution:* Libraries, unlike many government departments, are not revenue fetching agencies. They are spending organizations, and they participate in nation structure behaviours. The money spent through the library is a long word investment in human capital.

- *Library is a rising organism:* The library trinity of documents, readers and staff always grows. It implies that the necessities of the library will always go on rising day through day. All this means more expenditure.
- *Library expenditure is recurring:* Libraries are not only spending and rising organizations, they are also permanent bodies. In a period of educational advancement, library services will have to maintain a continuous rhythm to cope with the academic necessities of the clientele. This means that library expenditure is recurring in nature.

PRINCIPLES OF LIBRARY EXPENDITURE

- *Principle of maximum aggregate benefit:* The library exists for the service of dissimilar kinds of readers. So since a librarian, you should be neutral, and should see that no scrupulous individual is specially benefited through your expenditure policy. You should plan your library expenditure in such a manner that the majority of readers derive maximum benefit of library exploit.
- *Principle of advance scheduling:* Library expenditure should be intended in advance and a proper estimate should be made for dissimilar items therefore that adequate and balanced revenue may be allotted to dissimilar heads. Orders should be placed in advance therefore that the needed materials are acquired in time. The librarian should avoid last minute purchases.
- *Principle of equitable allocation:* Library funds should be equitably allocated for spending on dissimilar kinds of reading material covering several subject regions. For instance, books on science and technology are costlier than language books. Costly reference books become out of date faster in few subject regions are others. Though, in special libraries their principle may be applicable since mainly document has to be spent in reference and periodical literature. Normally, 70 per cent of the publication grant is allowed for periodicals. All such factors are to be taken into consideration while spending money for library exploit.

Principle of economy: It means that you should not spend more than the necessary amount on any thing, and the expenditure should not exceed your sanctioned grant. Duplication should be avoided, because the extra amount therefore saved could be bigger spent on purchasing new alternative titles covering additional subject regions.

BASIC OF PROPER FINANCING ESTIMATION

Through now you have realized the information that the success of any institution depends upon an adequate and regular flow of finances. This is true of libraries also. The basis of proper financing depends upon correct and effective estimation. Presently like the government, organizations, individuals and families effort to create financial estimations of requires and possessions, 6L. cries also have to prepare financial estimates. How to estimate, on what foundation, and. how much fund a library needs depends upon the age, jurisdiction, quantity and excellence of reading material, number of readers, and other factors' relating to that scrupulous library. Few significant bases for financial estimation for libraries are:

- User population and its composition.
- Material to be acquired.
- Services to be provided vis à vis objectives.
- Hardware and software requirement.
- Unsatisfied service pressures, if any, are the mainly regularly used factors in determining the financial requires of a library.
- Recognized national And international standards for excellence in services often expressed since minima of materials, personnel and operational funds for a given mass of library.
- Augment in prices of reading materials and inflation.

PER CAPITA WAY

In this way, a minimum amount per head is fixed which is measured essential for providing average library services. The educational and cultural standards of a society, the expectations of its future' requires,' the per capita income of the community, the standard cost of published reading material, and the salary levels of the library staff are the general factors that go to determine the per capita library fund in public and academic libraries.

The per capita estimate can be based either on the number either of literate persons or of adults. Though, the safest way is to calculate library fund per head of population.

Tice University Grants Commission Library Committee 'recommended that a university should give ₹ 15 per student and ₹ 200 per teacher for acquiring reading material for its library. The Kothari Education Commission, though, recommended that since a norm, a university should spend each year in relation to the ₹ 25 for each student and ₹ 300 per teacher". Ranganathan suggested that per capita expenditure on university and college libraries should be ₹ 20 per student and ₹ 300 per teacher or ₹ 50 per student.

In schools, per student appropriation at the rate of ₹ 10 should be made accessible for the library. For public libraries, Ranganathan suggested a 50 paise per capita expenditure method back in 1950. Now, the per capita figure necessity is much higher and this is the inherent limitation of the way since it does not give for inflation and devaluation.

PROPORTIONAL WAY

This way presupposes that the authorities give adequate finances to the library out of their regular budget, and that a scrupulous minimum limit is fixed. A usually used measure of adequate support is the percentage of the institutional budget which is allocated for library purposes. Several standards have been recommended for deciding this limit in India. The University Education Commission had recommended that 6.5 per cent of a university's budget would be a reasonable expenditure on its library. The Commission suggested that "this expenditure could modify from 6.5 to 10 per cent, depending on the level of development of each university library". In practice, the majority of the universities in India hardly spend three per cent of their total budget on their libraries. It is usually agreed through mainly authorities that a college should allocate to the library four to five per cent of its total expenditure. Ranganathan suggested that either 10 per cent of the total budget or 6 per cent should be earmarked for public library purposes. This way is likely to lead to a high disparity in case of special libraries since the budgets of high technology and capital rigorous institutions are much larger than the budgets of pure research, social science and humanities organizations.

WAY OF DETAILS

According to this way all items of expenditure of a library are reported for while preparing the financial estimates. These are of two kinds, viz,

- Recurring or current expenditure. and
- Non-recurring or capital expenditure.

For estimating public library finances, Ranganathan suggested the circulation of recurring/ current expenditure and non-recurring/capital expenditure. The Advisory Committee for libraries, Government of India followed approximately a same way for estimating the financial necessities for establishing a countrywide public library organization.

The UGC Library Committee in its statement suggested a staff formula for finding out the quantum of library staff members of several categories required for college and university libraries. It has also laid down their respective pay levels. The total amount required for meeting the cost of the staff can be calculated through this formula. For cost of books and other reading materials, the Committee has suggested a per capita expenditure formula.

SOURCES OF LIBRARY FUNDS

Library fund comprises both the funds appropriated to a library and its expenditure. Libraries depend heavily on a continuous supply of funds for organizing their behaviours, programmes and services. In dealing with this, ensuring a continuous supply of funds not merely on a yearly foundation but in excess of an era of time, *i.e.*, dime or five years is extremely significant. Fund plays an extremely important role in the organization and management of any institution, more therefore in the case of libraries which have to acquire and build up a collection on a continuous foundation during the year and even longer.

With the rising costs of books and journal subscriptions, it would be impossible to plan a collection development programme, constant with requires of users, without an ensured supply of funds. While appropriations are made for the acquisition of books and journals, funding bodies quite often overlook or underestimate the must of funds for processing the acquired materials and making them accessible for exploit.

Therefore competent persons should invariably procedure the expenditure on books. Further, a regular flow of funds ensures the rhythm and tempo of the user services. These services have to run on a continuing foundation. Unless adequate funds are provided for all these behaviours, libraries will remain ineffective.

Dissimilar kinds of libraries receive funds from dissimilar sources; however few sources are general, such since government grants. The greatest percentage of operating funds increasingly approach from public funds raised through taxes. Funds are required on a continuing foundation and a judicial estimation of funds required has to be done well in advance. The sources of funds for libraries can be broadly grouped since follows:

- Regular grants from parent body
- Ad hoc grants from other departments/organizations
- Grants from endowments and charitable organizations
- Fees, subscriptions, sale of service and miscellaneous revenues earned through the library
- Fines and miscellaneous sources: Few libraries impose fines on the late return of books since well since for loss or misuse of books. Income from this source is extremely meagre. Since a matter of information, it cannot be measured since a source of income, because the aim of the fine is not to raise revenue but to compel the user to return the borrowed book in time and not to damage or lose it throughout his/her possession. Moreover, libraries may not have the power to expropriate amount composed since fine or overdue charges for any purpose
- Miscellaneous sources may consist of money received through the sale of library publications and waste paper, reprographic services, translation and other documentation services rendered, etc. These services are rendered through libraries generally on a non-profit foundation. Normally, such funds are added to the common finance

of the parent organization for allocation through normal budgeting.

The financial support given to libraries is of two kinds:

- Recurring and
- Non-recurring.

The recurring grants are usually given for the purchase of books and periodicals, maintenance of regular services, and for anticipated contingent expenditure. The non-recurring grants are given for specific purposes such since construction of library structure, purchase of furniture and equipment and sometimes for special collections. The third kind of grant, recognized since an ad hoc grant is given on special recommendations for special purchases.

UNIVERSITY LIBRARIES

University libraries receive their funds, in varying degrees from two sources. They get financial support from the universities out of their own Ends and since special grants from both the University Grants Commission and the state governments.

The UGC grants are most plan grants, whereas the state government grants are most non-plan grants. Though, government grants are not given to the libraries directly. Generally the government provides grants to the university and then the university allots to the library the necessary share out of be similar. Grants from the University Grants Commission are most of three kinds recurring, non-recurring, and ad hoc.

Some university libraries charge a fee from their student members for the exploit of the library. A charge or fee for library exploit is not made without protest from users. These days there is a rising feeling that the university should give library services free of charge, presently since it gives lecture rooms, laboratories, and other facilities free.

COLLEGE LIBRARIES

A question often asked is "How much does it cost each year to run a good library?" The amount will modify from college to college, depending on the nature of the curriculum, the quantity and excellence of service expected, and the excellence of the present collection. The total student strength in a college is another criterion to be taken into consideration while allotting funds for the library. The troubles of financing the library of a recognized institution are extremely dissimilar from those of a new college. Requires of the former are confined to acquiring materials to remedy weaknesses and to keep the collection up to date; the latter necessity give for a complete vital collection.

There are three largest sources of funds for college libraries. The principal source is the allocation from the current operating funds of the college. Whether the college is public or privately controlled matters less in this relationship than the amount of additional money the library may require throughout any one budgetary year. Sometimes a section of the Amalgamated Finance Collection is given to the college library for the purchase of reading materials. Occasionally few portion of the contingency grant of the college is made accessible to the library through the principal. A second source of income for college libraries is grants, individual gifts, and endowments. But this is not extremely popular in India. A large number of college libraries during our country receive grants from the University Grants Commission. Other sources of income for college libraries are subscription/membership fee charged from the students, and annual recurring and non-recurring grants from the state government concerned or the governing body of the institution.

SCHOOL LIBRARIES

Promoting a good library service in schools depends extremely much on fund. In the case of transitional schools, lower fee rates for library services can be fixed since there will be less expensive books needed for students of lower classes. At present there are no fixed norms for the provision of finances to school libraries in India.

The library finance of a school should preferably comprise a fee composed from pupils, and equal contribution from the management, a matching contribution from the government or regional body, other gift or special grants that may at any time be received specifically for the library and donations from the public.

The library fee composed from students should be spent exclusively on books and equipment. The state government or any education power administering the school should meet the initial expenditure on be setting up of the school library including cost of new library structures and the initial expenditure on fittings and books covering the vital stock needed since a nucleus for library behaviours.

PUBLIC LIBRARIES

The largest sources of public library revenues are subscriptions, a library and grants from the government and endowments. Considering the library subscription since a source of funds is widely disputed. An equally forceful opposite view is that subscription defeats the entire concept of a free public library service advocated through Ranganathan. The statement of the Advisory Committee for Libraries, Government of India, also supports the inadvisability of considering subscription since a source of revenue. The Advisory Committee describes such subscription libraries since "stagnating pools."

Of the five States of the Indian Union which have library legislation, few, *viz.*, Tamil Nadu, Andhra Pradesh and Karnataka, have provision for a library. Tamil Nadu and Andhra Pradesh Library Acts have provided in the form of a surcharge on land and property tax at the rate of six per cent. The Karnataka

Act has provided for a library cess in the form of a surcharge at the rate of three per cent not only on land and home tax but also on octroi duty, vehicle tax and professional tax. In addition to the library cess, Karnataka public libraries receive a grant from the government equivalent to three per cent of the total land revenue collection. The other two states *i.e.*, Maharashtra and West Bengal, have not proposed any library cess. In these states the respective governments have made provision for grants for public libraries. Experience illustrates that library cess/rate alone cannot be enough to meet the continuously rising requires of public libraries. Besides, the taxable capacities of several regional regions differ, thereby making average and uniform public library service during the country hard.

A public library service should be completely supported through regular budget grants of the government, presently like education, public health and therefore on. Unluckily, in many countries including India, this is not the location. Since a result finances for public libraries have become inadequate. Only library legislation at the national level can transform things for the bigger. It would be proper for the government to give for the initial expenditure, while recurring demands of the libraries should be met from the proceeds of library cess, etc. Moreover, the regional authorities should be encouraged to collect more funds through giving them matching government grants.

Endowments, charitable trusts and private benefactions could be another source of public library revenue. In countries like the USA this is a general characteristic, whereas in India it is not therefore. The financial demands of the libraries are recurring in nature. Hence endowments and benefactions, however welcome, should not be taken since a permanent or continuing and adequate source of income. Endowments can best be used for constructing library structures, acquiring furniture and fittings and therefore on.

Other sources of public library revenue are fees and fines, gifts in cash or kind. The income from these sources is usually extremely meagre and cannot be measured an important source of revenue.

SPECIAL LIBRARIES

Special libraries get their funds from appropriations made through their respective parent institutions. Whenever the parent body takes up a new project or programme, which requires library and information support, adequate finances may be provided to the library to meet the special support facilities.

The library is expected to enquire for funds for any additional or special services which are generally examined before funds are provided for such services. In addition, ad hoc grants from governmental agencies are obtained for specific purposes. Of late, special libraries have been seriously considering the ways and means of generating section of their own possessions.

CLASSIFICATION OF LIBRARY EXPENDITURE IN FINANCIAL MANAGEMENT

Usually speaking, money spent on structures, costly equipment and furniture is shown against capital expenditure, and other items which happen approximately during the year like books and periodicals, stationery and postage, binding and contingency, salaries and wages, etc. are shown against current expenditure. Though, you can classify library expenditure according to dissimilar heads, *viz.*

- Salaries and wages,
- Binding,
- Stationery,
- Postage,
- Contingency,
- Books and periodicals,
- Furniture,
- Structure,
- Equipment, and
- Publications.

BUDGETING MANAGEMENT IN LIBRARY

LIBRARY BUDGETARY METHODS

Every library, no matter how small, has to operate with a budget. In mainly libraries, the librarian and his senior staff prepare the budget, according to budgetary norms issued through the authorities. The budget is scrutinized, vetted, if necessary, and approved through the Library Executive Committee before it is sent to the higher authorities for final approval and sanction. The common practice is to follow the methods and processes of the parent organization.

If they are special service of a comparatively limited scope, few small special libraries may be exempted from the preparation of a detailed budget. There are few methods of budgeting for preparing library budgets which contain traditional ones practiced through many libraries and the more innovative ones that have, in recent years, establish their method into libraries.

Line Thing or Incremental or Historical or Substance of Expenditure Kind Budgeting

Almost certainly the mainly general kind of budget is the one that divides items of expenditure, line through line, into broad categories such since books and journals, salaries and allowances, equipment, supplies, capital expenditure, contingencies, etc. with further subdivisions for each of these broad categories. This is the usual traditional way which, through taking into explanation past expenditure on each thing, prepares the current budget, hence described historical budgeting. The budget is prepared with a small augment of say 5 or 10 per cent for each major thing of expenditure of the previous year's allocation, assuming that all current programmes are since good and necessary. The advantage of this way of budgeting is that it is relatively simple to prepare, present and understand. To little extent it ensures that the funds provided are spent for the purpose stated. It is extensively practiced. But it has sure weaknesses.

This way does not suggest any future projections. It does not necessarily involve any review since to what amount ought to be spent in words of behaviours and services. Secondly, it moves in the similar manner since in the past year, without any forward push. Thirdly, this tends to ossify and rigidify the budget. In other terms, budget funds earmarked for a scrupulous thing cannot be spent for any other purpose *i.e.*, the financial rules would not permit the shifting of expenditure from one head to another. For example, funds allotted for equipment, if unspent, cannot be shifted to acquisition of some significant titles of current journals even if fully justified. It emphasizes apparatus rather than what these apparatus have to achieve. It also has a tendency to tempt to disguise requires and enquire for more money than needed.

FORMULA BUDGETING

Based on financial norms and standards this way tries to relate few inputs like users served, academic programmes supported and ratio of book stock to total funds of parent body. The formulae are used for financial estimation since well since budget justification. This seems to be a broad and quick way and hence saves a lot of time. But it does not explanation for firer variations in respect of each library and its customers and services.

PROGRAMME BUDGETING

This way propounded originally in the Hoover Commission Statement has three steps. They are:

- Report of agency objectives,
- Full consideration of alternative ways and
- Logical selection of the best based on effectiveness and efficiency.

Extended from the line thing way, this way tries to answer the questions for "what purpose the money is being spent?" and "how have the possessions to be deployed for each programme?" and more appropriate for a contracting economy. The financial plan is presented since programmes and subprograms built upon job elements or job loads. Job elements are assumed to be measurable and the job element costs are the structure blocks of the programme budget.

The focus in this way of budgeting is on the library's behaviours and the funds are to be earmarked for programmes or services that the library plans to give. For example, if a library decides to give a Current Awareness Service, the cost of that service is calculated and the expenditure estimated. The budget is therefore prepared on the foundation of the cost of programmes and whether a programme has to continue, get customized or deleted.

A library may also group its major programmes or functions, which may correspond to the organizational building of the library like administrative services, technological services, reader services, etc, Each of these services may be organized through departments such since acquisition, classification and cataloguing, reference and bibliographical services, documentation and information services, jointly with summary descriptions of these functions or programmes and relative figures of current and proposed expenditure. In this kind of budget, provision is made for several behaviours of each department to gauge their necessities and watch their expenditures.

PERFORMANCE BUDGETING

This budgeting way is same to programme budgeting but the emphasis shifts from programmes to performance. The expenditure is based on the performance of behaviours and the stress is laid upon operational efficiency. This way needs careful accumulation of quantitative data on all the behaviours in excess of an era of time. Management techniques such since cost benefit analysis are used to measure the performance and set up norms. For instance, data on the number of books acquired, classified and catalogued, actual man hours for doing the whole processing job, etc. are composed to determine the manpower and materials needed to perform the tasks.

It emphasizes the performance and operational efficiency of the programmes. Like programme budgeting starting with a report of agency objectives, full consideration to alternate ways of achieving the objectives and a logical selection of the best is made based on effectiveness, efficiency and cost benefit analysis. The element cost for specific operations multiplied through the volume of operations anticipated would provide the budget. The advantage of the way is the emphasis on the service mission of the library. Though, it is hard to quantity service excellence and behaviours. In other terms, this way measures only quantity not excellence which is rather hard to measure in words of money. In information, the budget allocation for a service institution like a library has small direct connection to the degree of satisfaction users receive from library services. Measuring benefits of libraries in rupees, the intricate interrelationship of costs of dissimilar operations and the non-linear difference of cost for every element output are few of the troubles. It may look too humble and begging for a review of each operation through power.

SCHEDULING PROGRAMMING BUDGETING ORGANIZATION (PPBS)

This way of budgeting was first proposed through USDOD. Two key units of PPBS are budgeting and organizations analysis. Since an extension of programme budgeting, PPBS involves organizations analysis, and/or other cost effectiveness procedures to give a more systematic and comprehensive comparison of costs and benefits of alternative approaches to a policy goal or programme objective. This establishes a rational foundation to enable the decision-maker to choose flanked by alternative programmes.

This way combines the best of both programme budgeting and performance budgeting. The focus in this way is on scheduling. It begins with the establishment of goals and objectives and ends with the formulation of programmes or services. The controlling aspect of measurement, which is central to performance budgeting, is also an aspect of PPBS. This way combines the functions of scheduling behaviours, programmes and services, translating them into tangible projects and finally presents the necessities in budgetary words.

Great disparities do exist in practice and lack of standards for measuring programme effectiveness/performance are the difficulties of implementing PPBS. It also suffers from other implementation troubles and few critical gaps like:

- Focusing on what will be done rather than how to do it,
- Failing to give an operating tool,
- Lack of a mechanism to evaluate the impact of several funding levels,
- Focuses on new programmes or major increases on ongoing programmes rather than forcing continuous evaluation of existing programmes, and
- Cost calculation is based on the decisions made in the scheduling and programming steps."

ZERO BASE BUDGETING (ZBB)

This way, urbanized through Peter Pharr throughout early the 1970s, needs a thorough knowledge of the organization and a lot of time, attempt and training. Having much in general with PPBS and opposite of historical budgeting, it emphasizes current behaviours and the must to justify each section of the programme every year.

It assumes a budget of 'zero' for each programme until one convinces the appropriating power that the programme is worthwhile and deserving of support at a specified level. It does not allow for incremental growth in budget. ZBB is an operating, scheduling and budgeting procedure which needs each manager to justify his whole budget request in detail from scratch and shifts the burden of evidence to each manager to justify why he should spend at all.

This come needs that all behaviours be recognized and urbanized since "decision packages" and that there should be a systematic evaluation and ranking of these "decision packages" preferably by a computer. It does not take into explanation what happened in the past but spaces emphasis on current behaviours. Every programme and action is spelled out in detail and the financial necessities are worked out without any reference to the past. In other terms the request for financial support has to be recognized afresh every year. No action, in information, could continue basically because that action was undertaken in the previous year. In other terms, the whole budget is justified from scratch. Steps involved in preparation of ZBB are:

- Behaviours/programmes are grouped to lowest level entity.
- Objectives and behaviours of each programme examined and alternative methods evaluated.
- Programmes are then grouped into a series of "decision packages" with their report of purpose.
- Ranking of the "decision packages".
- Cut off point corresponds to the total budget allocation.

ZBB improves the plans and budgets of libraries and helps to develop good management teams. It also helps to add follow on benefits in excess of the years. Yet the serious problem of the enormous time and attempts required jointly with other administrative troubles and troubles of developing and ranking "decision packages" prevents its adoption in libraries.

Few of these budgetary methods are of recent origin and present a more readily understandable view of the budgetary necessities of behaviours and services, a more objective justification for them and are bigger instruments for purposeful spending. In practice it is necessary to understand the "politics" of the budget procedure within the parent organization and look for opportunity for personally participating in the final negotiations/ deliberations since well since by personal informal contacts effectively.

In India, approximately all libraries follow the conventional historical way of budgeting. It is only in recent years that little attention is given to other, newer, methods. One aspect that requires careful examination is that mainly library functions and services are of a continuing nature and cannot be discontinued on any explanation without reference to the past. While it is necessary to evaluate performance and effect improvements to ensure excellence of service, discontinuity of existing services would prove undesirable, particularly if circumstances do not warrant. It is, though, possible to create a more objective assessment of these methods of budgeting only if Indian libraries start making their budgets through these newer methods and gain enough experience in their operations.

LIBRARY BUDGETING AND FINANCIAL SCHEDULING

Budgeting is a scheduling procedure in which the expenditure and revenue of the organization in excess of a specific time era are reported for. The budget is a plan document and a financial report which gives details of the proposed revenues and their utilization for expenditure for a specific era, generally a year. It is a means of check and manages on what money should have been received and how money is to be spent. Budgeting require not be presently confined to money. It can be expressed both in financial and non-financial words. But it is a practice that it is expressed with a general denominator described the rupee. Hence, budgeting is the procedure of quantifying all the plans of an operation to determine whether they will achieve the desired results and to adjust accordingly where they will not achieve the desired results. The budget is a quantitative expression of a plan of action, a tool in the hands of the library or information centre manager, a management actions towards the destination, and a tracking device ay highlight variations from the plan and illustrate the require for corrective actions to put the operation back on track. In other terms, the budget aids orderly and progressive scheduling, coordination and implementation, serves since an instrument of financial a device for evaluating result.

It has already been stated that the budget is a systematically prepared report revenue and expenditure of an institution for an era of time, generally a year. The objective of this procedure is to produce a financial plan. The budget serves the dual purpose of limiting expenditure to income and assuring wisely intended spending.

Financial scheduling and budgeting have sure obvious advantages. They create goals clearer, assist in fixing responsibility, reveal weaknesses in the building of the organization force quantification of targets and attainments, lead to the waist productive exploit of possessions, pinpoint timely actions and indicate the require for corrections from deviations, if any. Therefore much therefore budgeting in common can also cause few troubles.

- It may place much emphasis on easily observable factors.
- The budget may tempt one to become routine without improving operations.
- Library services are not quantifiable in words of the rupee.
- The budget needs continues version to meet changed conditions.
- It does not job automatically.
- The budget and, budgetary manage are required to be used intelligently.

The budget is a guide on how to incur expenditure for the dissimilar behaviours and operations of an institution during the year. The common principle is that the estimated expenditure should not exceed the revenue. In other terms, income and expenditure should balance each other.

The budget should not be confused with annual financial statements. The latter is an official document to know what was achieved and what was not achieved throughout a given year. It is in information a factual record of the state of affairs of the finances of an institution throughout a scrupulous year. The budget, on the other hand, is only an estimate for the forthcoming year. In short, a budget is a preparation for the future whereas the financial statement is an analysis and evaluation of the past.

The budget is also an extremely significant instrument of manage, discourse, co-ordination, evaluation and motivation. It controls since it canalizes the expenditure according to set financial rules and processes. Budget estimates communicate to the staff and others concerned the total financial outlay of the institution and the allocation of funds for each major thing of expenditure and regulate spending; coordinate through distribution of general expenditure of dissimilar elements not only to economize on expenditure but also to maximize finance utilization; evaluate performance on the foundation of the utilization of funds within the prescribed era; motivate staff to perform well, for funds have been provided for the behaviours for which they were sought, envisaging future growths.

BUDGETARY NORMS AND STANDARDS

For the purpose of financial scheduling and budgeting, standards and norms have been set/ proposed through professional experts, committees and bodies. They are quite useful in estimating the budget, seeking and justifying funds since well since allocating the budget in the middle of several items of expenditure. Having got few thought of the methods of budgeting, let us now talk about the standards and norms that form the foundation of estimating be requirement of library funds required and also the sharing of funds to major items of expenditure within the total library budget. We have studied three methods of estimating funds, namely,

- Per capita way,
- Proportional way and
- Way of details.

The second aspect of budgetary norms and standards that requires attention in this element is the actual sharing of budgetary funds to dissimilar competing heads of expenditure. The major heads of expenditure in libraries are books and journals, and salaries and allowances, both of which are to be combined to generate services. Ranganathan has suggested that the proportion of the expenditure of a university library on these two major items be since follows:

- *Staff:* 50 per cent.
- *Books and other reading, materials:* 40 per cent.
- *Miscellaneous:* 10 per cent.

The University Grants Commission Library Committee has suggested that a university library with 5,000 students and 500 teachers and research fellows should have a budgetary provision of ₹.3,50,000 out of which ₹ 175,000 would be spent on books, journals and other kindred materials, and a same amount on staff, implying thereby that the expenditure on books and staff may be equal But common trend is that the expenditure on staff salaries trends to be higher than on books. Item into amount the recommendations of University Grants Commission, university and education commissions and library experts, the common norms seem to be since follows:

- Salaries and allowances 50 per cent.
- Books 20 per cent.
- Periodicals 13 per cent.
- Binding 75 per cent.
- Others 10 per cent.

In the case of public libraries, the sharing is more or less the similar for the major items of expenditure.

- Salaries and allowances 50 per cent.
- Books 20 per cent.
- Periodicals and Newspapers 5 per cent.
- Binding 5 per cent.
- Others 20 per cent.

Current thinking on library and information services, library budgeting and related characteristics, is on the following lines:

- Library and information services are to be completely oriented to user requires, irrespective of the kinds of libraries. User requires necessity be systematically assessed and obtained, on the foundation of which libraries should organize their services.
- Library budgets, consequently, are to be in tune with requiring based services.
- The element cost of every operation in a library has to be worked out and budgetary estimates have to be built on this data. The cost of library operations and services, particularly in India, is not attempted. Libraries mostly operate on appropriated funds through the parent institutions without any scientific foundation for allotment. Cost accounting is essential for fixing budgetary estimates.
- With the tremendous augment in the cost of books, journal subscriptions, staff salaries, library and information services, etc., the question extremely often arises whether library services should be sustained to be given without any charge. Few of these services like literature search, document supply, compilation of bibliographies, SDI, CAS etc. can be priced. Of course, in the context of Indian circumstances these services may be subsidized partially. On the entire, a more scientific foundation for library expenditure has to be evolved in view of the importance of library services. Library budgeting has to be more innovative and in tune with the new demands.

PRINCIPLES OF BUDGET MAKING IN LIBRARY

The budgets of dissimilar libraries modify substantially. Nevertheless, there are few units which are essential and general for dissimilar library budgets. They may be reduced to some guiding principles and applied to the perpetration of any library budget.

The librarian should be invited through the authorities to submit the library budget. The librarian in turn necessity consults his departmental heads in relation to the book funds, and the library staff members in relation to the personnel and other administrative costs. The final choice of what goes into the budget and how much to enquire for should rest with the librarian.

The librarian should request enough funds in each head of the budget to support a sound programme of library development. Calculating the expenditure and anticipating income, inflation rate, foreign swap rates, salary increases, insurance rate, public utility charges, etc. since well since time delay are extremely significant.

The budget should be prepared and submitted in time. This facilitates recruitment of additional staff, ordering of materials and therefore on in a proper method. The budget should symbolize library scheduling in words of educational goals and should not basically be a "crisis" operation in which urgent current requires are hastily converted into rupee estimates to meet a budget deadline. Scheduling to meet educational goals implies that the library will take into explanation proposed new curricular changes, the impact of new courses on library books and personnel, the effect of price increases in binding and the like.

The budget should be reasonably flexible in its execution; Classification of the budget categories should enable the library to check its financial records easily against the periodic balance reports. Few significant sources of fund for a library or information centre contain:

- Regular grants from parent organization and/or government,
- Ad hoc grants or subsidies,
- Fines, fees and service charges.

Significant heads of expenditure of an information centre or library are:

- Collection structure and updating,
- Binding and other maintenance costs,
- Furniture and equipment,
- Structure,
- Salaries and wages,
- Stationery, postage, etc.

Depending on the mass of the library or information centre and the nature of its parent organization the complexity of the budget and the budgetary manage organization may modify from a easy fairly fixed voted grant of the budget from the parent organization for books, journals and other reading materials to a mainly intricate situation where grants are received from the parent institution and other agencies in addition to sure revenues earned. These sources of fund may have many restrictions in their deployment. Allocation has to be done to all heads since explained through kind of material through subjects, or through departments and therefore on. "Effective budgeting can display endless diversity". The budgeting way used through a library or information centre is normally decided through the parent institution.

JUSTIFYING THE BUDGET REQUEST

The final decision in relation to the library budget is often taken through the chief executive of the parent organization. The officials who are responsible for providing library funds will quite naturally want to know why the funds are required. They will believe critically the merits of the library request in relation to those of other departments or agencies and the total financial possessions at their disposal. It is probable that funds will not be enough to meet all the necessities in full and that budget allocations may be affected accordingly. The library budget request should state apart and clearly the purposes for which funds are requested and explain why additional funds may be required in sure categories. The supportive documentation and justification for the budget has to be urbanized during the year. The justification for the library's budget will already have been made if the arguments for services have been well presented in detailed and timely statements other terms, budget preparation should not become a once a earlier. It is also necessary to understand the "politics" of the budget procedure and build up effective rapport with the key members of the team or committee.

Sometimes the librarians may think it expedient to present an inflate information that the authorities generally sanction less than what is ash" practice. Padding the budget is not only ethically questionable but because it is hard to justify amounts in excess of proven requires, of the college/university or other parent body and, since such, necessity realize that there are many demands and constraints on the limited possessions in the majority of organizations.

The librarian should neither minimize the necessities of the library, nor be unduly discouraged if the library committee or fund committee is unable to provide all that he asks for because of other pressing and urgent necessities of the parent institution. The best that can be done is to present an honest picture of the cost of running a library, in words of material needed and of services expected for the clientele. After making an honest budget, the budget request necessity be accompanied through a free, clear, and forceful argument proving require for the amount asked. Keep in mind that there is no bigger method of sowing suspicion in the minds of the generally hard headed fund authorities than presenting an unrealistically inflated budget.

While preparing the budget you should remind yourself that, regardless of any other values it may have, the budget document necessity be easily understood and therefore convincing in its arguments that the appropriating power will be persuaded to accept it and give the necessary funds. To produce such a document, you should exploit all the techniques and supporting data that are accessible with you.

APPROVAL OF THE BUDGET

The librarian presents the budget to the library committee or any other power distant discussion and approval. The library budget, with the approval and recommendations of the committee, is sent to the university institutions office or any suitable office to be included in the total university or organization budget. The whole university budget is passed through the Executive Council/ Syndicate of the university. Plan necessities of the university library are assessed through the visiting committee of the University Grants Commission. The visiting committee visits the library and discusses the library necessities with the librarian. The approved recommendations are consolidated and submitted for sanction to the University Grants Commission.

In a college, generally the principal of the college approves the library budget, after taking into explanation the necessities and opinions of the heads of dissimilar teaching departments, and the necessities in dissimilar subject regions. In public and special libraries, same processes are there to get the budget approved and sanctioned through suitable authorities.

NOTIFICATION OF THE BUDGET TO THE LIBRARY

When the budget is passed, the similar is communicated to the library. This comprises both plan and non-plan budgets. The plan budget is approved through the university authorities in consultation with the state government wherever necessary. After the budget notification, the university librarian informs the dissimilar academic departments concerning the budget allocations. These allocations, in information, are funds in the names of dissimilar departments placed at the disposal of the university librarian. Money is spent through the librarian on items recommended through the heads of the departments. The subject wise allocations for books and periodicals are done through the library committee. This is purely an internal arrangement of the library after the passing of the budget. If there are differences of opinion on allocations to dissimilar subjects, they are generally adjusted, erased and balanced through the library committee. Likewise is the case for special libraries.

BUDGET EXCESS

Bill or library commitments which exceed the sanctioned budget, if any, for the library are generally adjusted in two ways, *i.e.*:

- Through adjustment of the excess amount in next year's budget and/ or

- Through additional allocation subject to agreement through the authorities.

Though, it has been observed in practice that the second alternative is not only theoretical but also a doubtful and remote possibility. A budget excess adversely reflects on the attitudes and. awareness of the management towards the library.

PREPARATION OF LIBRARY BUDGETING

The preparation of the budget is the responsibility of the chief librarian who also has the responsibility for allocating and administering funds within the overall behaviours and services of the library. This responsibility can be delegated to the next level department or part heads but the overall coordination and accountability still rests with the chief librarian.

Adequate discussion should take lay flanked by the chief librarian and his part heads, When the information needed for making the estimates for the library budget has been assembled the next step is the preparation of the budget itself. Preparation of a budget takes substantial time and attempts. Usually throughout the transitional of a financial year, budget estimates (BE) for the next financial year and revised estimates (RE) for the current financial year are described for through the office concerned.

Estimates are prepared on the foundation of past experience, present demands and future expectations of necessities. The estimates should take into explanation the actual expenditure of the previous financial year, spillover's, if any, amount spent up to the date of preparation of the budget throughout the current financial year; foreign swap (FE) necessities, advance commitments to be made for the next financial year, capital items, etc. No set of rules can be given for preparing this report, but the librarian should bear in mind the impact of inflation on the cost of books, periodicals, binding, and other supplies. The augment in enrolment, the probable require for annual salary increases at least comparable to those of the past five years and the possible impact of new technical growths on library economy and efficiency are few of the other factors. The librarian discusses the budget proposals with the sectional and departmental heads before the final consolidation. Budget necessities are filled up in a preformed approved through the institution. The preformed commonly used for a historical budget in academic libraries is of two kinds.

- Schedule of expenditure on pay and allowances of staff and
- Schedule of expenditure on all other items.

SCHEDULE OF EXPENDITURE ON STAFF SALARIES

It is generally prepared under the following heads:

- Serial number,
- Designation of staff member,

- Pay stale,
- Vital pay. on 1st April,
- Total for twelve months,
- Date of increment,
- Rate of increment,
- Total amount of increment,
- Dearness pay rate and amount,
- Dearness allowance rate and amount,
- Home rent rate and amount,
- Contribution to GPF/CPF rate and amount ,
- Any other honorarium rate and amount,
- Interim relief rate and amount,
- Total of amounts of columns 5,8 to 14,

SCHEDULE OF EXPENDITURE ON ALL OTHER ITEMS

This contains, inter alia, the following heads:

- Establishment,
- Salaries,
- Allowances,
- Contribution to provident finance, gratuity,
- Other recurring expenditure,
- Binding,
- Stationery,
- Postage,
- Contingency,
- Books, periodicals and back sets,
- Other non-recurring expenditure,
- Construction or expansion of library structure,
- Maintenance or library structure,
- Purchase of repair of furniture,
- Equipment,
- Employing additional staff for specific time and purpose such since processing for books needed for special purposes,
- Special collections.

All the items are to be shown in four kinds, *viz.*, and actual expenditure for the last year; estimated expenditure for the current year; revised financial estimates for the current year; and estimated expenditure for the next year. Therefore the budget is a linkage flanked by three years.

FINANCIAL MANAGE AND ACCOUNTING MANAGEMENT IN LIBRARY

Mainly practitioners of librarianship are much concerned and serious in relation to the stage of actual exploit of funds, accounting, auditing and financial manage. This stage in itself involves allocation of funds since envisaged in the budget, encumbering funds under each head, finance accounting and financial audit.

ENCUMBERING FUNDS

The mainly hard task in the budgetary manages procedure in libraries or information centers are encumbering funds. Encumbering funds is an intricate procedure that allows one to set aside money to pay for ordered items. The procedure of encumbering funds is hard and complicated for several reasons. Firstly, it is general that there will be other under spending and/ or overspending in few heads.

Secondly, there are few uncertainties in relation to the supplies. Libraries create many orders for documents under many heads in a given financial year and supplies are received continuously at non-fixed intervals. Usually there is no automatic cancellation of non-supplied or unbilled orders and hence no disencumbering done automatically.

It is extremely general that prices, discounts and handling charges of documents since well since swap rates for foreign currencies keep changing regularly causing difference in the value of funds encumbered. Lastly, moving money back and forth through encumbering and disencumbering in a manual organization can lead to 'errors.

ALLOCATION OF FUNDS

Allocation of funds might have been based on past practices and performance, differential publication rate and inflation nut, level of demand, actual exploit and the total programme of the library or information centre. Actual allocation could be through departments/elements, through subjects, through kind of material, through users, through language or through format. Such an allocation of funds gives bigger manage and a more effective method to monitor funds and has the best chance to achieve fair balance in the development of programmes and services.

Though, a rigid allocation, particularly for collection development, may lead to difficulty in transferring funds from one explanation to another and consequently under spending may happen in few cases when the other heads starve for funds.

In addition to such ineffectiveness, approval, blanket and standing order plans since well since development of reference, common and special collections may not fit into any heads. Further, matching requires and money accessible becomes complicated, time consuming and it may be hard to develop models even after massive attempts. Though, it may be noted that such formal allocation of funds may not be necessary in a small library.

FINANCIAL MANAGE

It has been stated earlier that the budget is a tracking device to measure progress, highlight variations from the plan and illustrate require for corrective actions to put the operation back on track. Nobody has the luxury of working without financial restrictions. Nobody gets money without justifying why it is required. One should be prepared to face both sudden windfalls since well since severe cuts in budgets. The budgetary manage organization is an instance of an organization since well since a widely established manage function of the management.

Budgetary manage is one of the oldest and middle manage techniques used through managers. Budgetary manage is the procedure of comparing what was intended with what has been accomplished throughout the budget era. It is not a past oriented or post action manage but a future oriented manages organization. It is not a post mortem kind assessment but a continuous examination of the progress made, comparing it with the cost standards and time lapsed therefore that the manager is able to create adjustments in the operation on a day to day, week to week, or month to month foundation for the rest of the era of the budget.

Since the budget is only a futuristic plan, how distant the actual operations of the library or information centre have conformed to the budgeted programme will be recognized only after the completion of the budget era. Knowing post facto how much deviation or under spending or ineffective utilization of possessions has taken lay is like discussing the ways of avoiding accidents after the accident has occurred. Hence continuously monitoring the operations to look at how the operations are accepted out, whether there are any deviations, the causes for deviations and ways to rectify deviations within a week or a month will be of immense help. However the budget is prepared once in a year, the budgetary manage procedure is a day to day, weak to week, fortnight to fortnight, month to month and quarter to quarter action for a check of all revenues and expenditures budgeted and stated beforehand.

The three vital steps in the manage procedure are establishing standards, comparing: results with standards and taking corrective action. Preparation of the budget is nothing but establishing the cost average. This procedure begins with the top management setting goals and objectives and the lower level managers developing budgets for their elements and the similar successively reviewed and integrated at each higher level. Unlike profit oriented institutions where the budget for marketing expenses can power the amount of revenue, the service oriented and not for profit institutions should have dissimilar kind of easy matching of revenues and expenses.

Reports relating to commitments and actual expenditure should be frequently checked and continuously reviewed to manage the budget. In the actual practice of the budgetary manage organization; operating reports have to be prepared for each of the budget centers involved. These reports should form section of the management information organization (MIS) used to manage the performance of the library or information centre against the budget plan. A good budgetary manage organization should follow the theory of "management through exception" and focus its attention on matters that are adverse or that illustrate an rare difference in addition to providing full details of budget reports.

In practice, it may suffice to have monthly reporting in the beginning of the financial year and changing it to fortnightly throughout later section of the year. Though, the element heads my have data on a daily or weekly foundation during the year to facilitate operational manage and the similar require not be sent to the head of the library or information centre.

FINANCE ACCOUNTING IN LIBRARY

Accounting means a systematic maintenance of the income and expenditure flow on records. A properly mannered accounting organization is a vital prerequisite of efficient financial management. Its largest purpose is to ensure that the library funds are spent correctly, properly and within limits. It also helps in scheduling future budgets and for making special studies. In other terms, the purpose of finance or financial accounting for not for profit institutions is to assure proper exploit of monies provided and to create it possible to track expenditure. The major section of the finance in a library is the operating finance. For finance accounting purposes the operating finance can be divided into restricted finance and unrestricted finance. Unrestricted finance allows flexibility in exploit for purposes other than that specified whereas restricted finance cannot be used for other purposes.

The cardinal principle of finance accounting is that every financial transaction is charged too little explanation and a record exists of what the transaction involved. The finance accounting organization should allow for verification of all the transactions and give an accurate statement. Proper finance accounting through allowing one to know how much money is spent, how much is left and how much is encumbered or committed aids the budgetary manage procedure and enables a continuous checking and reviewing of the situation and examination of the require for reallocation or expropriation of funds. It creates clear to the spender how much amount he has spent and how much is left, therefore that there is neither under spending nor in excess of spending.

It helps the management to remain alert against misappropriations and maladjustments. Before setting up a book keeping organization, the librarian should consult the fund part to determine the process of accounting therefore since to serve best their mutual purposes.

FINANCIAL AUDIT

Lastly, the financial audit section of the procedure enables a meticulous but example scrutiny of financial transactions to have proper manages in excess of irregular, inappropriate and wasteful expenditures. Auditing is a scrutiny of the financial transactions of government and semi government bodies. It gives manage in excess of irregular, inappropriate and wasteful spending. It is deemed necessary from the power's point of view for their satisfaction.

Libraries and information centers normally have post audit through external/central/statutory auditors, who generally look into the loss of reading materials, irregularities in procurement procedures and outstanding advance payments and supplies. Even however two kinds of audit organizations are prevalent in our country, government departments and libraries usually follow post audit.

Post audit means that the drawing and disbursing officer prepares the bills, signs them and sends them to the treasury/bank/principal for payment. The drawing and disbursing officer is responsible for the correctness of the bills. The officer or the librarian necessity satisfies himself fully before signing the bill. In the post audit organization, only random audit is resorted to, after the financial year comes to a secure. Every thing is not checked, but few months are selected at random. Payment items occurring throughout these selected months are thoroughly and minutely verified. Mistakes, if any, are pointed out. The person concerned is advised and warned to be careful in future.

The pre audit organization is usually followed in autonomous bodies in which the audit is under the regional finance explanation. In case of pre audit, no thing can be passed for payment unless it has been first audited. The pre audit organization reduces the responsibility of the drawing/disbursing officer in the sense that all the necessary verifications such since checking of items, accessioning of items, charging of approved rates, correctness of calculations, debiting to proper heads of explanation, etc. have already been done through the audit part in advance.

Here instead of the drawing officer, the auditors satisfy themselves before the bills are passed for payment. Auditing is accepted out both through an internal audit team since well since an external/statutory audit team. The problem of collecting and noting of vouchers does not arise in pre audit processes. This simplifies matters somewhat and reduces the auditing responsibility of the librarian.

FINANCIAL RECORDS

All organizations which want to survive necessity meet sure standards of business organization and the library is no exception to the common rule. Its financial records, like its budget, should be set up in accordance with the largest accounting processes of the parent office. It is no longer measured a good practice to maintain a distinct library explanation, handled directly through the librarian. In mainly organizations, all library payments are made through a central office. The fund part of the organization maintains the library explanation while the library maintains the records of outstanding orders, bills forwarded, etc.

Since stated earlier, the largest purpose of library accounting is to keep expenditures within the budget. In addition, accounting helps in the preparation of the annual statement and budget, gives the factual monetary foundation for making decisions, assists the departments in making a wise and systematic exploit of funds and gives information for library statements, studies surveys.

Mainly of the libraries keep their financial records according to a single entry organization. However a sure amount of variety is establish in the maintenance of financial records in dissimilar libraries, one largest point to be kept in mind is that these records should be the simplest possible, constant with efficiency and should permit rapid and convenient checking against office ledgers.

Bibliography

Anand Ballabh: *Development of Library Management*, SBS Publication, Delhi, 2006.

Anil K. Dhiman and Yashoda Rani: *Learn : Library Management*, Ess Ess Publication, Delhi, 2005.

Ashwini Kumar: *Library Management*, SBS Publication, Delhi, 2006.

C.K. Sharma and Kiran Singh: *Library Management (2 Vols-Set)*, Atlantic Publication, Delhi, 2005.

Colin Barrow: *Business Success: Practical Financial Management*, Kogan Page, New York, 2011.

K C Dabas: *IT Applications for TQM and Library Marketing*, Ess Ess Publication, Delhi, 2008.

M.A. Khan: *Cataloguing in Library Science*, Sarup & Sons Publication, Delhi, 1997.

Mary Liu Kao: *Cataloging and Classification for Library Personnel*, Jaico Publication, Delhi, 2003.

N P Agarwal and B K Mishra: *Advanced Financial Management*, RBSA Publication, Jaipur, 2007.

N.P. Agarwal and R.K. Tailor: *Concepts of Accounting and Financial Management*, RBSA Publication, Delhi, 2010.

Pandey Bhat: *Cases in Financial Management*, Tata McGraw Hill, Delhi, 2012.

Patricia H. Fisher and Marseille M. Pride: *Blueprint for Your Library Marketing Plan : A Guide to Help You Survive and Thrive*, Ess Ess Publication, Delhi, 2009.

Paul Galloway and Garrett Adams: *Business Library Made E-Z*, Pentagon Press, New York, 2006.

Piyush Bhatnagar and Suvarna Sable: *Catering and Financial Management*, SBS Publication, Delhi, 2007.

Preeti Batra: *Cataloguing in the Library*, Mohit Publication, Delhi, 2004.

R.P. Verma: *Classification System in Library Collections* , ALP Books, Delhi, 2012.

Rabindra K. Mahapatra: *Capacity Building and Restructuring of Library and Information Centres*, Ess Ess Publication, Delhi, 2010.

Raghunath Pandey and M.N. Velayudhan Pillai: *Integrated Library Management*, Jnanada Prakashan, Delhi, 2011.

Ramesh Chandra and A.P. Shrivastava: *Information Preservation and Library Management*, Kalpaz Publication, Delhi, 2003.

Rashmi Upadhyay: *Digital Library Management*, Alfa Publication, Delhi, 2011.

S K Bajpai: *Book Selection and Acquisiton System in Library*, Shri Sai Printographers, Delhi, 2006.

S.K. Chaudhary: *Library Marketing*, A.P.H. Publication, Delhi, 2011.

S.K. Sangma: *Cataloguing Rules in Library Science*, Centrum Press, Delhi, 2013.

S.K. Singh: *Essentials of Integrated Library Management*, Authors Press, Delhi, 2002.

Shamim Ahmad: *Computer in Library Management*, APH Publication, Delhi, 2012.

Shyama Balakrishnan and P.K. Paliwal: *Library Management*, Anmol Publication, Delhi, 2001.

V.K. Jain: *Information Technology for Digital Library Management and Automation*, Atlantic Publication, Delhi, 2009.

William W. Sannwald: *Checklist of Library Building Design Considerations*, Ess Ess Publication, Delhi, 2009.

Y.L. Chopra and Mamta Chopra: *Challenges Before Library and Information Science in New Millennium*, Ess Ess Publication, Delhi, 2001.

Index